D1267209

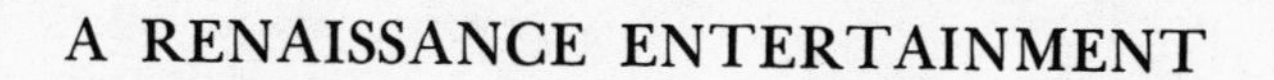

A RENAISSANCE ENTERTAINMENT

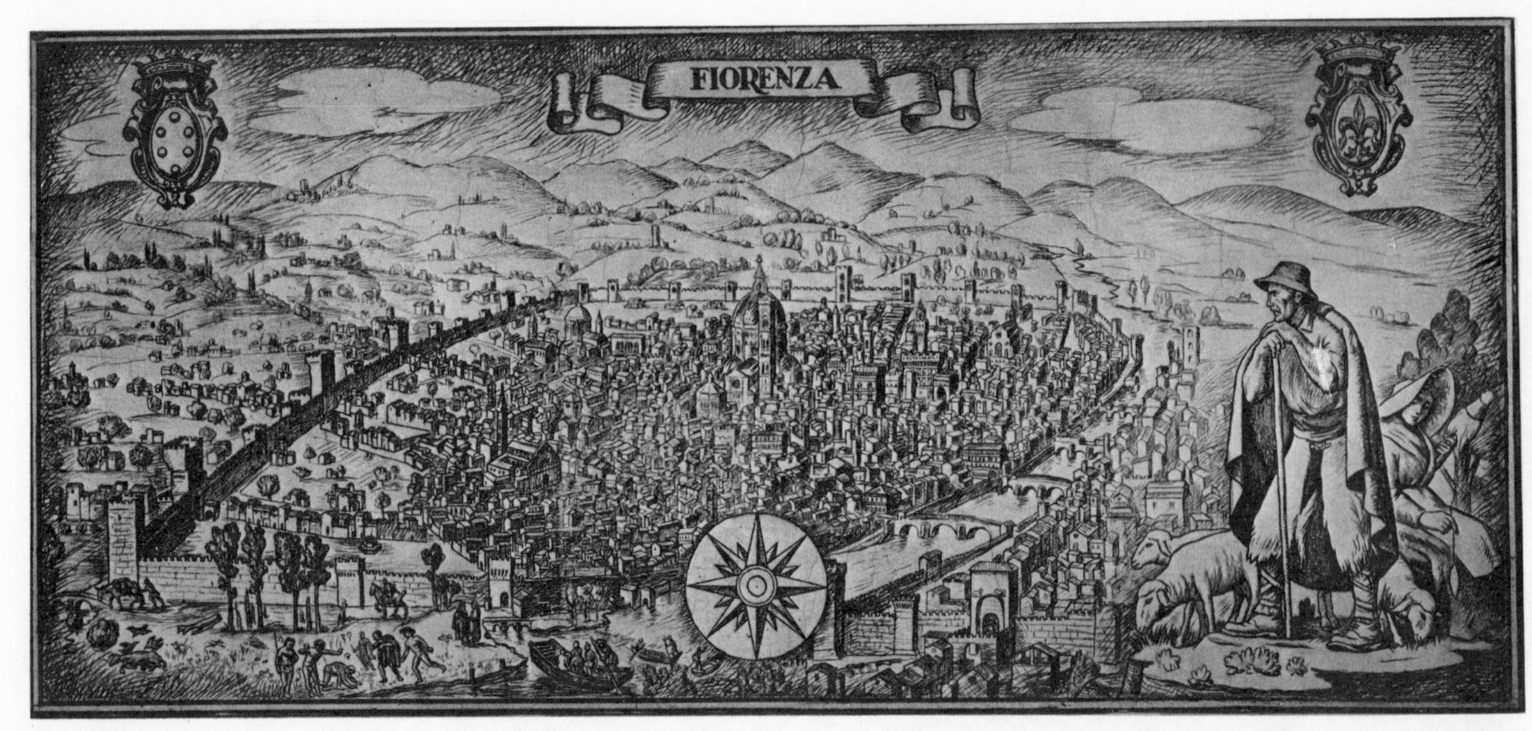

View of Florence, from a late fifteenth century woodcut
—Alinari photograph

A RENAISSANCE ENTERTAINMENT

FESTIVITIES FOR THE MARRIAGE OF COSIMO I, DUKE OF FLORENCE, IN 1539

An Edition of the Music, Poetry, Comedy, and Descriptive Account
with Commentary by

ANDREW C. MINOR AND BONNER MITCHELL

UNIVERSITY OF MISSOURI PRESS
COLUMBIA • MISSOURI

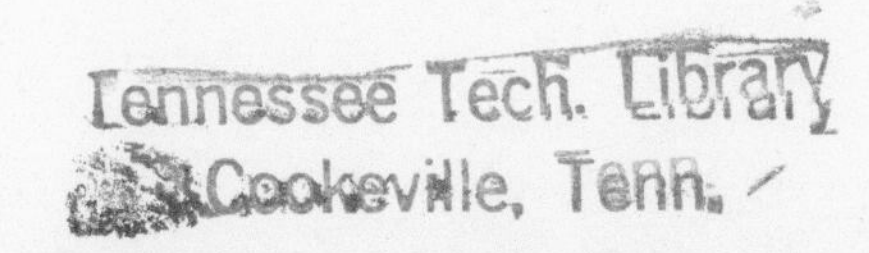

Library of Congress Catalog
Card Number 68-11348
Printed and bound in the United States of America

Preface

This edition and study originated in a concert, "Music for the Medici (1436–1539)," given by the Collegium Musicum of the University of Missouri for the meeting of the Central Renaissance Conference at Columbia in April, 1963. The latter half of that concert constituted what was probably the first complete performance since the sixteenth century of the music written for the wedding of Cosimo I. Its success convinced us that the music should be made available in modern notation for performance in the twentieth century.

In preparing the concert, we had investigated in some detail the nature and circumstances of the entire celebration in 1539. This research, fascinating and leading into related areas, made us perceive the potential value of a general study, cutting across disciplinary lines, of the whole festival. We undertook the larger project with hesitation because, while our respective trainings in musicology and literary history of the Italian Renaissance qualified us to deal with the two principal aspects of the festival, to others, of importance, we were scarcely prepared to do justice. We resolved, however, under the kind encouragement and guidance of colleagues in other disciplines, to undertake a reasonable study of several fields previously foreign to our scholarly preoccupations. This study, carried out at home and in Florence, has been a boon to our liberal educations. While it has not made of us specialists in new fields, we trust that it will have sufficed to allow us to treat with a minimum degree of competence all important aspects of the festival.

The grand princely festivals of the Renaissance and seventeenth century were long virtually neglected by scholars, but they have begun recently to receive a good deal of attention. Nearly everyone concerned with Renaissance history, literature, music, and art is now aware of the extraordinary richness of the festivals as cultural manifestations. Much credit for the development of this rewarding field of study belongs to the French Centre National de la Recherche Scientifique, which has sponsored international meetings of scholars and which has published, under the direction of Professor Jean Jacquot, a number of important studies. The most ambitious of these have been two volumes of essays, *Les Fêtes de la Renaissance*. The first, which appeared in 1956, includes papers on individual festivals and several on general topics. The second volume, 1960, is devoted to *Les Fêtes et Cérémonies au temps de Charles Quint*.

Florentine amateurs of local history, too, have maintained through the years a certain amount of interest in the festivals that took place in their city during the Republics and early Grand Duchy, and brief articles or plaquettes concerning these have appeared occasionally, even in the nineteenth century. The first general studies were done by Pietro Gori during the period between the two World Wars: *Le Feste fiorentine attraverso i secoli. Le Feste per San Giovanni* (Firenze, Bemporad, 1926) and *Firenze magnifica. Le Feste fiorentine attraverso i secoli* (Firenze, Bemporad, 1930). These books provided a needed introduction to the subject but did not aim at detailed study; they are not very useful today because of the author's omission of scholarly apparatus. In 1939 Professor Federico Ghisi published a learned and extremely valuable musicological study, *Feste musicali della Firenze Medicea (1480–1589)* (Firenze, Vallecchi). His work contains, besides much historical information, a number of examples of music, including several from the wedding of 1539.

In 1964 (after our own work was well advanced) there appeared an important general study in English: *Theatre Festivals of the Medici* (New Haven, Yale University Press) by Professor A. M. Nagler. This work, which begins with our festival of 1539 and ends with the grand "Nozze degli dei," celebrated in 1637 under the patronage of Ferdinando II, contains useful summaries of the various celebrations and reproduces handsomely a large number of drawings and designs, beginning with some done by Vasari and others for the wedding festivities of Prince Francesco in 1565–1566. Professor Nagler examined a vast amount of material in preparing his work, and it includes a great deal of helpful bibliographical information.

A detailed and profound study of one Medici wedding celebration, that for Grand Duke Ferdinando I and Cristina di Lorena in 1589, is now being carried out under the sponsorship of the Centre National de la Recherche Scientifique. As in the case of Cosimo's festival in 1539, music, literary works, and descriptions of the *apparato* are available for examination. For the event in 1589, however, a number of drawings have also survived, so that a truly comprehensive study is possible. A first volume of *Les Fêtes de Florence (1589)* appeared in 1963, with Professor D. P. Walker as editor: *Musique des intermèdes de "La Pellegrina."* This edition and study of the music is to be followed by a second volume, edited by Professor Jacquot, which will include an edition of Bastiano dei Rossi's *Descrizione dell'apparato . . .* and a general study of the festival from diverse points of view. The whole work will be of inestimable value for scholars in a number of different fields.

Though somewhat less material is available for our study of the 1539 celebrations, there is still a great deal—much more than for any similar preceding event. This is in fact the first wedding festival for which the music has survived, and the *descrizione dell'apparato,* having been done by a literary man of considerable talent, is one of the most detailed and most interesting of the entire century. The date of these celebrations, near the beginning of Cosimo's reign and of the Grand Duchy itself, makes them of particular interest in political history.

Our basic sources of information have been the following:

Pierfrancesco Giambullari, *Apparato et feste nelle nozze del Illustrissimo Signor Duca di Firenze, et della Duchessa sua consorte, con le sue Stanze, Madriali, Comedia, et Intermedii, in quelle recitati.* Firenze, Giunti, 1539.

Musiche fatte nelle nozze dello illustrissimo Duca di Firenze il signor Cosimo de' Medici et della illustrissima consorte sua mad. Leonora da Tolleto. Venezia, A. Gardane, 1539.

Giambullari's account presents itself as a letter to Giovanni Bandini, the Duke's ambassador to Emperor Charles V. Very shortly before it appeared, in August, 1539, the music had been printed in Venice on independent initiative.

Primary information has derived also from four other sixteenth-century sources. Antonio Landi's comedy *Il Commodo,* included in Giambullari's book, was reprinted in 1566 by Giunti, the original publisher, doubtless as a result of renewed interest in the 1539 celebrations occasioned by those for the marriage of Cosimo's son Francesco in 1565. In addition, there are two collections of Corteccia's madrigals published by Gardane of Venice in 1547 (fully described in our List of Works Consulted at the end of this volume). These collections contain seven of the wedding pieces. The music for Corteccia's *Ingredere,* not included there, was reproduced in a 1564 *Thesaurus musicus* (also described in our bibliography) that appeared in Nuremberg. Finally, accounts of artistic preparations for the 1539 festival are found in several of Giorgio Vasari's *Lives of the Painters, Sculptors, and Architects,* of which the first edition appeared in 1550 and a second, enlarged, in 1568.

We have translated in full Giambullari's book —the account proper, the text of the poetry, and that of the comedy—and have endeavored to provide a detailed study of it as well as a critical edition of the music. The translated account makes at times rather tedious reading, notably in the excessively detailed descriptions of costumes, but we have chosen to present the whole text— and also, in the main, to retain the author's intricate syntax—so that the full documentary value of the *Descrizione* may be preserved. Giambullari's account and the occasional poetry, written by Giovambattista Gelli, are dense with significant historical and literary allusions. We have attempted to explain these and to point out their contemporary pertinence in a large number of notes. Along with this direct commentary on the texts, we have prepared essays containing germane background information in four areas: political history, literary and theatrical history, music history, and art history. We hope, in fact, that the edition and study may be of specific value to students of the Renaissance in all these fields. It will be least so, no doubt, to students of art history, since no works of art from the festival have survived and Giambullari's description, though of intense cultural interest, permits no critical or technical evaluation.

We have chosen, in the translated edition, to insert the music at the proper chronological places in Giambullari's account. The Italian text of all the poetry and songs is, of course, preserved alongside the English translation.

It is clearly impossible to provide anything approaching a complete bibliography for the various areas of study concerned in this project. We have elected nevertheless to present a rather long List of Works Consulted in the hope of its being useful to scholars who are specialists in only one or two of the various areas. Contrary to current practice, we have furnished in nearly all cases the name of the publisher as well as the place of publication, believing that this information may be helpful in finding some rare works.

Gelli's poetry has little literary merit and is interesting, culturally, only for its prose content, but the music and the comedy do have intrinsic esthetic value and deserve, we think, not only study but performance. We should like to commend to college departments of music and drama the possibility of staging the play in entirety, with its musical prologue, *intermedii,* and finale.

We have, agreeably, to express gratitude for help received from many persons in our own fields and in others. Miss Ann McKinley, who had recently completed a doctoral dissertation on Corteccia's Latin motets, aided us in obtaining microfilms of source material for the 1963 concert. It was originally planned for her to collaborate in this study. However, later in the year she entered the community of Benedictine Sisters at Lisle, Illinois, and at that time generously turned over to us the material she had gathered on Corteccia. It was especially helpful for study of the composer's life and of musical activities at Cosimo's court.

To three other American musicologists—Professor Donald Grout of Cornell, Professor Gustave Reese of New York University, and Dr. Emmanuel Winternitz of the Metropolitan Museum—are due thanks for their help of various kinds in making possible the edition and study of the music. We wish to thank as well the members of our Collegium Musicum, who prepared and gave the original concert.

In the early stages of our research Professor John Coolidge, director of the Fogg Museum at Harvard, generously gave us a great deal of valuable advice, helping us to become oriented among the various problems that had begun to arise. He put us in contact as well with other scholars who were to give valued counsel.

We are grateful also to two eminent authorities in the field of festival studies, Professor Jean Jacquot of Paris and Professor Federico Ghisi of Florence, for having taken a benevolent interest in our project and for offering their expert advice.

We are glad to express special gratitude to two colleagues in the field of Italian literature. Professor Florindo Cerreta of the University of Iowa, a specialist in sixteenth-century comedy, gave helpful counsel in our early work on the translation and commentary of Landi's *Il Commodo*. Professor Armand De Gaetano, of Wayne State University in Detroit, the foremost authority on Giovambattista Gelli, provided us with much information on that writer's career and on literary life in Florence under Cosimo I.

Three former and present members of our own university's Department of Classical Languages, Professors Anna Benjamin, John Christopherson, and John Thibault, have at different times given indispensable help in the identification or translation of difficult Latin quotations.

Mr. Charles Sherman embossed the music and made valuable editorial suggestions.

To Signora Anna Omedeo, bibliographer at the Biblioteca Nazionale Centrale in Florence, we owe especially warm gratitude for her kind interest in our project and for her advice on matters touching an astonishing variety of fields—emblematics, costume, theatre, interior decoration, and other spheres. Signor Baglioni, director of the Sale di Consultazione Scientifica, in many instances provided guidance from his detailed knowledge of reference works and of the books in the Sala Toscana. Professor Ulrich Mitteldorf, director of the Kunsthistorischesinstitut in Florence, generously allowed us to work in the fine library of his institution. To the personnel of the French Government's Centre Universitaire International, we owe the inestimable favor of having had a commodious and pleasant place to write during several months spent in Paris.

We are indebted to the University of Illinois Library for having made available to us a microfilm copy of Giambullari's book, to the Oesterreichische Nationalbibliothek for those of the *Musiche fatte* and of the second book of Corteccia's madrigals, to the Bayerische Staatsbibliothek of Munich for that of his first book, to the New York Public Library for that of the *Thesaurus musicus,* and to E. P. Dutton & Co., Inc., of New York and J. M. Dent & Sons, Ltd., of London for permitting us to quote at length from their English edition of Vasari.

Dr. Anna Forlani-Tempesti, Director of the Biblioteca del Gabinetto Disegni e Stampe degli Uffizi, graciously gave us permission to reproduce two Vasari drawings for costumes of the 1565 wedding. We are especially grateful to her colleague Dr. Anna Maria Petrioli-Tofani for having contrived to get these drawings photographed at a time when the Uffizi's photographic service was still closed from damage in the 1966 flood.

Finally, the Research Council, a faculty committee of the University of Missouri, has generously given financial aid of various sorts during the preparation of this book.

A.M. and B.M.

Columbia, Missouri
September, 1967

Contents

List of Illustrations

Commentary

I. Political Background

The wedding was, above all, a political event. The Duke and his counselors had no doubt of this fact, and they planned most of the artistic and literary manifestations to serve political ends. Only the comedy and its *intermedii* are quite innocent of such intent. Neither the paintings and sculpture described by Giambullari nor the verses written for the banquet can be appreciated properly except in the light of Florentine history in the Middle Ages and in the early Renaissance. Because of the high level of culture of the Florentine people, this is one of the best documented of all segments of history; because of their magnificent accomplishments in art and letters, it is also one of the most assiduously studied in our own times. In political matters this period in Florence must be judged, by any standards, to be extremely complex, the complexity being due in part to a native taste for politics and in part to

Portrait of Cosimo I by Bronzino,
in the Medici Museum
–Alinari photograph

the disruptive pressure of outside events, which, in turbulent Italy, always made stability difficult to attain. The following essay provides a very elementary description of the Florentine constitution in the Middle Ages and in the Renaissance and a résumé of Florentine history in the century or so preceding 1539, during which the Medici family had been prominent in the city's affairs. Events previous to the death of Lorenzo in 1492 are given briefer consideration than those which had occurred thereafter and might still be present in the memories of people attending the wedding celebrations.[1]

❧

Twelfth-century Florence, along with some other Italian cities or communes of the time, had developed an oligarchical system of government that had some of the formal characteristics of democracy. The state's chief officers, in imitation of republican Rome, were called consuls. In 1283 was established a supreme governmental body called the Signory, composed of six priors. This institution was to endure, with short interruptions, for well over two centuries. At first the priors were elected, as Dante was in 1300; later they were chosen by lot, as some officials had been in ancient Athens. Democracy was far from absolute, of course, and, actually, little was left to chance or to popular whim in the selection of officials. The whole structure of the state depended upon the division of Florentine society into guilds, *corporazioni delle arti.* From the membership of the seven merchant guilds, *arti maggiori,* were usually chosen the priors and other important officers, though the artisan guilds, the *arti medie* and *arti minori,* attained at times a small share of power. As in fifth-century Athens, there were many formal safeguards against tyranny, either of individuals or of the masses. Constitutional procedures were extremely complicated, and terms of office were brief; Florence thus appeared in significant ways as a modern reincarnation of the ancient *polis.*

Tremendous political upheavals occurred in the fourteenth century, as in the thirteenth, but republican institutions survived, with many formal changes, and the city's independence, sym-

[1]Most of the general information about Florentine history in the following summary has been taken from Ferdinand Schevill's *A History of Florence from the Founding of the City through the Renaissance* and from Antonio Panella's *Storia di Firenze.* More specialized sources of information, especially for the years following Cosimo's accession in January, 1537, are indicated in notes.

bolized by the proud emblem of the Red Lily, was maintained. It was at the beginning of the fifteenth century that members of the Medici family first became important on the Florentine political and cultural scene. Giovanni Bicci dei Medici (1360–1429) was a *nouveau riche* who enjoyed much sympathy and confidence among the people—partly, perhaps, because of his humble origins and partly because of his supposed democratic opinions. When, in 1427, a direct, basically progressive tax was instituted, he was generally considered to have been responsible. Giovanni died in 1429, survived by his son Cosimo, who was to be even more active in politics than his father. When Florence suffered defeat in a war with Milan in 1433, Cosimo was arrested and exiled for supposedly having fomented general discontent. A year later, however, a new government recalled him, and he became *de facto* ruler of the city.

The constitution underwent little change; priors continued to be selected, though by a committee of *accoppiatori* rather than by lot. In 1454, however, in reaction against Cosimo, the lot system was revived, but his power was not effectively curbed. He survived the active opposition of important citizens, of whom the most formidable was Luca Pitti (who had begun construction of the Pitti Palace, meant to be the most elaborate residence in the city). Always, Cosimo's hand was strengthened by the support of many among the common people who considered him their ally against the wealthy classes.

Cosimo, who would later be honored by the appellation *pater patriae,* was as well a generous and intelligent patron of the arts. He lived in an extremely crucial time; the Renaissance was still new but gathering momentum, and Florence was indisputably its center. The most celebrated literary and artistic figure in the city was Leon-Battista Alberti, humanist, musician, architect, and writer. Other talented men materially encouraged by Cosimo were the humanists Bruni and Ficino, the architects Brunelleschi (author of the dome of the Cathedral) and Michelozzo (designer of the Palazzo Medici) and the sculptor Donatello. The Medici tradition of Maecenasship was founded.

When he died in 1464 Cosimo was succeeded in power, though not in any formal office, by his son Piero, who was, however, of a weak constitution and lived only till 1469. Piero was followed by his own son Lorenzo, a brilliant and forceful man who had also received an excellent humanistic education. This was Lorenzo il Magnifico; the period of his rule, 1469–1492, is often considered to have been the Golden Age of Florentine civilization. Like his grandfather, he was an effective and discriminating Maecenas, helping, among many others, the poets Pulci and Poliziano, the painters Ghirlandaio and Botticelli, the sculptor and painter Verrocchio, and the sculptor Michelangelo, who was at this time quite young. It is extremely significant that Lorenzo, besides being a highly cultivated humanist and a fine connoisseur of the plastic arts, was himself an excellent lyric poet—probably, in fact, the best of his time. High standards of both creation and appreciation were in the air. The classification of the period as a golden age of culture rests both on the number and quality of masterpieces produced and on the general refinement of taste. The Florentines of the time, Lorenzo at their head, were themselves aware that they were living in an exceptional age, far more cultivated than the immediate past and, indeed, comparable to the best epochs of Greece and Rome.

Lorenzo's term of government was not especially tranquil, though the city was not overtaken by any major disasters. At home his rule was almost ended, in 1478, by the dreadful Pazzi Conspiracy, and, as a consequence of Lorenzo's ruthless suppression of the conspiracy, serious difficulties erupted abroad. Girolamo Riario (a nephew of the reigning Pope Sixtus IV), Francesco Pazzi, and others had plotted to have Lorenzo and his brother Giuliano murdered in the Cathedral at High Mass. Giuliano was indeed killed, but Lorenzo escaped by shutting himself in a side room. In the ensuing confusion, the outraged Florentine populace helped him foil the attempt by the Pazzi family and the Archbishop of Pisa (a Salviati) to take over the government. Several leaders of the plot, including the Archbishop, were hanged from the windows of the Palazzo Vecchio, before the furious crowd. This vengeance brought excommunication upon Lorenzo, and war with the Papal States and Naples soon followed. Florence was confronted with superior forces and might have been utterly ruined if Lorenzo had not made a dramatic trip to Naples to persuade King Ferrante to dissociate himself from the Pope and to make peace on moderate terms. A treaty was signed in 1480, and reconciliation with Pope Sixtus followed. Thereafter, Lorenzo sought to promote a balance of power within Italy, relying strongly on an alliance with Louis XI of France. At home he left the Constitution in effect, making only a few changes to strengthen his *de facto* position.

On Lorenzo's death in 1492, Medici rule seemed secure, but his son Piero, who succeeded him, was weak and incompetent, incapable of dealing with crises. In 1494 King Charles VIII crossed the Alps, leading the first of a long series of French invasions of Italy in the late Renaissance. Piero had imprudently allied himself with Naples against France, but when Charles's army entered Tuscany he became fearful and made large concessions to obtain a royal pardon. The people of Florence were so shocked by this cowardly conduct that they forced him to flee the city. Medici rule was over for eighteen years. The King of France brought his troops into Florence, where he was received somewhat equivocally, both as a traditional ally and as commander of an occupying army. His demands on the city's government, made as an ally, were stoutly resisted. It is recounted that when he threatened to sound his trumpets to mobilize his forces against the city's resistance, the Florentines angrily replied: "And we shall ring our bells." Wary of street battles, the King reduced his requirements.

With the French gone, the city amended its Constitution in order to make rule by one man impossible, that is, to ensure that the city would be governed by an oligarchy. In the new republic, however, a dominant individual influence soon arose—that of the fanatical friar of San Marco, Savonarola. This extraordinary man did not, perhaps, have personal political ambitions, but his eloquent exhortations for repentance and reform were so moving that they affected public concerns as well as private lives. In 1495 his advice to reform the Constitution was heeded, and, for a time, Florence was a kind of theocracy. A number of men from old and wealthy families, called *arrabbiati* because of their furious opposition to Savonarola, plotted against him. Helped mightily by the Borgia pope's excommunication of the friar, they succeeded in discrediting him in the eyes of the people. His influence undermined, in 1498 he was tried and, subsequently, executed in the Piazza della Signoria.

During the next three decades Italy was racked by warfare between the French and the Spanish, and in Florence as elsewhere foreign policy was the dominant concern. The new King of France, Louis XII, had brought an army to Italy in 1499 and was at first very successful. He occupied Lombardy and prepared to attack Naples. One of his Italian lieutenants, the notorious Cesare Borgia, tried to take advantage of the situation to encroach upon Florentine dominions, and in 1501 the weak city government, in a placatory gesture, made him general of its forces, with a high salary. He was eventually restrained in his most extreme ambitions by the French King himself.

In 1502 the executive powers of the republican government were strengthened by a provision that the gonfalonier should serve for life. The first man to hold the office thereafter was Piero Soderini, who had as one of his most trusted aides Niccolò Machiavelli. On the latter's recommendation, Florence, having long been dependent upon mercenaries, provided itself with a citizens' militia. In 1509, with its strengthened military forces the city succeeded in resubjugating Pisa, which had been in rebellion for years. This was the apex of the Republic's fortunes in external affairs.

Between the mighty forces of King Louis and of the Holy Roman Emperor no lasting security was possible for a small state. When in 1510 Pope Julius II tried to organize a league of Italian cities to help drive out the French, Soderini, against Machiavelli's cynical but realistic advice, elected to remain loyal to the city's traditional ally. The French were driven out of the country, mainly by Spanish arms, and the Pope decided to punish Florence for its misplaced loyalty by overthrowing the Republic and re-establishing the Medici. A Spanish army was sent to subdue the city. The Florentine forces, largely made up of militia, failed their champion Machiavelli and their fellow citizens by offering little resistance. Gonfalonier Soderini resigned and fled the city; the regime of the Republic was finished.

The fortunes of art and literature under the Republic had been very uneven. At the beginning the austere Savonarola and his followers had been directly opposed to the *joie de vivre* and love of physical beauty essential to the Renaissance and so evident in the then recent years of Lorenzo's rule. In 1497, at carnival time, there had been a symbolic burning of objects identified with earthly pleasures. The monk's fall in the next year initiated a movement in the other direction. In the remaining fourteen years of the Republic, painting and sculpture flourished as gloriously as under Lorenzo. There were times, in the first decade of the century, when Leonardo da Vinci, Raphael, and Michelangelo were all working in the city at once. (Michelangelo and Leonardo did not get along at all; Raphael became a disciple of the latter.) In literature a definite change of emphasis became apparent. Lyric and narrative poetry no longer flourished, but the city had in its government one of the great prose writers of the Renaissance: Machiavelli. His main works, to be sure, were to be written later, when he was no longer in public office.

When the Republic fell in 1512 Piero dei Medici, son of Lorenzo, was no longer living. He was, however, survived by two brothers, Giuliano and Giovanni. The latter was a cardinal and, like his father Lorenzo, a man of sound humanistic culture. He made a triumphant return to the city on September 14, 1512, and took up residence in the Palazzo Medici, empty since the flight of Piero eighteen years earlier. As on similar crucial occasions in the past, a special committee, a *balìa,* was set up to reform the Constitution. Essentially, the situation of Lorenzo's day was restored; Cardinal Giovanni became untitled ruler. His vengeance on the republicans was not severe, considering the customs of the time. Machiavelli, for example, was merely kept away, for a while, from public office and from the city. (His exile permitted him to see the Cathedral from his country house.) In 1513 the Cardinal was chosen as pope, and, since he had by this time become fairly popular in Florence, his election was looked upon as a local triumph. After moving to Rome, the new pontiff, Leo X, made his nephew Lorenzo, son of Piero, regent in Florence—without, however, ceasing to take a keen interest himself in the city's affairs. In 1516 Lorenzo became Duke of Urbino, but he continued to live mainly in Florence until his premature death, at the age of twenty-seven, in 1519. With him was extinguished the legitimate male line of Medici descended from Cosimo il Vecchio. In the female line, however, his daughter Caterina later became a famous (or infamous) Queen of France. Leo X chose as regent Cardinal Giulio dei Medici, illegitimate son of Il Magnifico's murdered brother Giuliano.

A new French king, Francis I, remaining faithful to the policy of his two predecessors, invaded Italy in 1515. He concluded a truce with Spain that same year, but lasting peace became impossible when, in 1519, the Electors chose King Carlos of Spain as Holy Roman Emperor. As Charles V this remarkable man was to strive for nothing less than absolute hegemony in Europe—something that Francis I was determined at all costs he should never attain. These two giants were to keep Italy in turmoil, with some peaceful interludes, for nearly twenty years. (There flourished in western Europe during this time a third royal giant, Henry VIII of England, but he was too far away to affect directly the fortunes of Italy.)

Leo X, who had been an ally of Spain, died in 1521. The Fleming chosen to succeed him as Hadrian VI lived only until 1523, and the new pope chosen that year was, to the delight of Florence, another Medici, Cardinal Giulio, who became Clement VII. To act as his representatives he sent to the city two young Medici bastards: Ippolito, son of Il Magnifico's third son Giuliano, and Alessandro, son of the Duke of Urbino—or, some say, of Pope Clement himself. The boys were not old enough to act as regents; that charge was given to Cardinal Passerini. These three, the young Medici and the Cardinal, soon made themselves heartily disliked by the population.

In 1525 the Spanish inflicted an especially serious defeat on the French at Pavia and in the action succeeded in capturing Francis I himself. In the hope of re-establishing a balance of power, Clement VII allied himself with the French and with the Republic of Venice against the triumphant Charles V. This was a grave error; for some time France left its allies to fend for themselves in the continuing strife. In 1527 the Emperor's German and Spanish troops captured Rome and subjected the Eternal City to its worst sack since the Dark Ages and the barbarian invasions. The Pope, having become a prisoner in the Castel Sant'Angelo, surrendered abjectly. On hearing news of this tremendous event, the Florentines, far from feeling sympathy, seized the chance to expel the Cardinal and the young Medici. The republican constitution of 1494, with its Grand Council, was restored to effect. The new gonfalonier was Niccolò Capponi, a man who possessed some of the oratorical ability of Savonarola. Thus began what was to be the last and, in some ways, the most glorious of the Florentine republics.

The city was fated to be attacked by the vengeful Clement VII as soon as he gathered sufficient strength. Meanwhile, in the continuing struggle between Spain and France, the Republic, faithful to tradition, allied itself with the latter. (Machiavelli, who died in 1527, would certainly have advised the opposite course.) In 1528, the Pope and a momentarily repentant Emperor became reconciled, to the misfortune of France and of Florence. Clement obtained from Charles a promise to help bring the rebellious city under Medici control. Instead of despairing in the face of this powerful alliance, Florence began energetically to prepare its defenses. Michelangelo was put in charge of strengthening the walls and fortifications; the militia was revived, and mercenaries were hired; Gonfalonier Capponi, judged as too cautious, was replaced by Francesco Carducci. The Pope's forces, largely lent by the Emperor, laid siege to the city in the fall of 1529. The Florentines forgot their differences and comported themselves with the heroism of a great people defending its liberty.[2] They served in the militia, and—what is perhaps more remarkable for the citizens of a merchant city—they gave money to support the Republic.

The facts of the European political situation made their cause, however, a hopeless one. Clement VII, friendlier than ever with Charles, crowned him Emperor in a great ceremony at Bologna on February 24, 1530. By this time France and Venice had also made terms; Florence stood alone. It held out, enduring great privations, until the summer of 1530. By the terms of the peace, settled in August, the city submitted officially to the Emperor rather than to the Pope. The terms of the city's submission held significance for the future, but for the moment, because of the close alliance between the conquering rulers, the immediately important factor was the return of Medici rule.

The Constitution was amended to permit government by a committee of Medici partisans, and the city, already greatly impoverished by the siege, had to give additional large sums to the victorious troops to get them to leave. In the summer of 1531 the young Alessandro returned to Florence and was recognized by the Emperor as the city's lawful ruler. The next year the ancient offices of priors and gonfalonier were abolished, and, by the Emperor's decree, Alessandro received the title of Duke, hitherto unknown in Florence. To preserve a semblance of democratic structure, a Council of Two Hundred and a Senate of Forty-Eight were established. Alessandro was, surprisingly, an intelligent and, in some respects, a beneficent ruler, despite the really outrageous excesses of his private life. The death of Clement VII in 1534 did not seriously undermine the young man's authority, but on January 5, 1537, he was murdered by his cousin and best friend Lorenzino dei Medici.

It is here that the protagonist of our story, Cosimo dei Medici, comes onto the main scene of Florentine history. By his father Giovanni delle Bande Nere he was a member of the younger line of Medici, descended from a Lorenzo, brother of

[2]A sympathetic account of this heroic episode is given by Cecil Roth in *The Last Florentine Republic, 1527–1530.*

Cosimo il Vecchio. This line, only moderately prosperous, had scarcely shared political power with their more fortunate relatives. Cosimo's grandfather Giovanni (1467–1498) had been called *Il Populano* because of his support of popular elements against the ambitions of Piero, son of Il Magnifico. Il Populano became the third husband of a famous warrior lady of the fifteenth century, Caterina Sforza. He died young, leaving his widow in extremely difficult circumstances. After having lost her fief at Forlì in Romagna to Cesare Borgia and having spent some time in a Roman prison on orders of the Borgia pope Alexander VI, Caterina settled in Florence to rear her son, also named Giovanni. When she died in 1509 the boy passed into the care of Jacopo Salviati and his wife Lucrezia, who was a daughter of Lorenzo il Magnifico. In 1516 Giovanni was married to Maria, daughter of the Salviatis, thus uniting the two Medici lines. The young man had shown very early an interest and talent for martial occupations, and in 1516 he was given a command in Pope Leo's forces.

This command was the beginning of one of the most remarkable military careers of the Renaissance. Giovanni dei Medici soon became the best-known *condottiere,* or mercenary general, of the peninsula.[3] It was the period of struggle between Charles V and Francis I for the control of Italy, with the Medici popes, Leo X and Clement VII, wavering between the two sovereigns while trying to preserve and to enlarge their own dominions. Giovanni left his young wife at home in Florence or in the Tuscan countryside while he was almost constantly engaged in preparing or in waging campaigns. He fought usually on the side of Charles V but also, in two major campaigns, in the service of Francis I, as the alliances of Clement varied. Except for a minor campaign in 1524, he never fought for Florence. Very early in his career he trained bands of professional soldiers who became fiercely loyal to him. In 1521, on the death of Leo X, he made his men carry black banners and wear black shoulder belts; they were known thereafter as the Black Bands, and their leader received the name by which he is remembered: Giovanni delle Bande Nere. He had the reputation of being absolutely fair to his soldiers, in a rough, direct way, and is supposed to have neglected his own financial interests while in-

[3]Rather detailed accounts of Giovanni's career are given in Pierre Gauthiez's *L'Italie du XVIe siècle: Jean des Bandes noires, 1498–1526* and in Christopher Hare's *The Romance of a Medici Warrior. . . .*

sisting stoutly that his men be paid. There can be no doubt that he was a remarkably courageous and aggressive soldier. By any decent standards he was also disgustingly cruel. He had a curious friendship with the eminent literary man Pietro Aretino, remembered for licentiousness and for heavy satire. The peace-loving poet Ariosto, on the other hand, suffered from the ruthlessness of the Black Bands while he was governing Garfagna for the Duke of Ferrara. Giovanni's reputation rested upon his demonstrated courage and upon his fairness; despite his cruelty and his lack of firm political convictions, he became a sort of popular hero. At one moment in 1526 Machiavelli seemed, in a letter to his friend Guicciardini, to think that the young Medici *condottiere* might be the desperately needed "prince," or at least the general, who could lead a united Italy against the invading foreign armies.[4] Giovanni was in fact killed while fighting the Germans in northern Italy that same year. He was only twenty-eight years old.

On June 12, 1519, his wife Maria had given birth to a boy in Florence. Since the Duke of Urbino, last legitimate Medici male in the main line, had died recently, the mother entertained from the beginning great hopes for her son. Giovanni, then in Rome, gave news of the birth to Leo X, who decided that the boy should be called Cosimo, after the founder of the dynasty.[5] The child was brought up by his mother, mostly in Trebbio, a country house in Tuscany.

The two Medici popes were very friendly to Giovanni, who served them well, but they gave him little financial reward. Further, because of Giovanni's inattention to business matters, Maria was often short of money. Clement VII was less interested in the boy than Leo X had been; his special favor, as we have seen, went to the two bastards Ippolito and Alessandro. When Giovanni was killed in 1526 Maria sent their young son to Venice, in whose service Giovanni had most recently been fighting. After the Medici regime in Florence had fallen the next year, she also went to Venice. In 1530 she and young Cosimo were guests of Pope Clement at his coronation of the Emperor in Bologna. Later, the two went to live in Rome. There Cosimo apparently enjoyed the company of his cousin Caterina dei

[4]Letter dated March 15, 1526, in Niccolò Machiavelli, *Opere,* Mario Bonfantini, ed., 1127-31.

[5]The rather numerous biographies of Cosimo that we have consulted are noted in the List of Works Consulted at the end of this volume. The most detailed of the general lives is Luigi Carcereri's *Cosimo Primo, Granduca.*

Medici, daughter of the Duke of Urbino and later to be a most ill-reputed Queen of France. In 1533 Maria accompanied this girl to Marseilles for her marriage to Prince Henri, son of Francis I. The Pope also traveled to France to perform the ceremony. This marriage was marked by one of the most sumptuous celebrations of the Renaissance, and the tales of it that Maria brought back to her son may well have influenced his decision to make a great public affair of his own wedding.

After Alessandro became ruler of Florence Maria and Cosimo went there to live. The boy apparently became a fairly good friend of the Duke, who was only nine years his senior. He accompanied the Duke, for example, on an important mission to Naples to justify the regime to the Emperor, who had been receiving bitter complaints against Alessandro's tyranny from former supporters of the Republic. There was, however, at this time little ground for Cosimo's entertaining political ambitions. In 1536 Alessandro, who had been constituted hereditary ruler, was married to Margaret of Austria, an illegitimate daughter of Charles V. Higher, moreover, in the Duke's esteem than Cosimo was another member of the younger Medici line: Lorenzino, later to be called also Lorenzaccio. The latter young man murdered his friend Duke Alessandro on January 6, 1537. His act, a great shock to everyone, seems to have been motivated partly by jealousy and partly by a laudable desire to rid Florence of a tyrant.

Lorenzino fled the city, and the question of succession was left quite open. The manner in which seventeen-year-old Cosimo behaved in the highly dynamic situation testifies to his discretion and cleverness.[6] When the murder occurred he was off, hunting in the Mugello country near Florence. The most important governmental official in the city was Cardinal Innocenzo Cybò, a grandson of Lorenzo il Magnifico and a nephew of Leo X. Both Medici popes had entrusted him with considerable power in the city's affairs, and after Alessandro became ruler he had remained as a sort of prime minister. He chose to keep the Duke's death secret for a day or so while he sent for the absent military commander Alessandro Vitelli and gathered troops in the city. As a means of ensuring power for himself, he thought

[6]Good accounts of the confused months after Alessandro's assassination are found in Luigi Alberto Ferrai's *Cosimo dei Medici e il suo governo, 1537–1543* and in Giorgio Spini's *Cosimo I de' Medici e la indipendenza del principato mediceo.*

of having the dead Duke's son Giulio, five years old, declared Duke and himself established as regent.

On the morning of the eighth of January, when the murder had become known, the Senate of Forty-Eight (created by the Constitution of 1532) came to the Palazzo Vecchio to deliberate upon the situation. This body had not enjoyed a great deal of power under Alessandro, but it not unnaturally hoped to profit from the new circumstances. The most eminent of the senators was Francesco Guicciardini, who had been a close friend of Machiavelli. He and his colleagues had no wish to see the Cardinal as regent. They resolved, therefore, after some uncertainty, to offer succession to Cosimo, who, they probably thought, could be maneuvered or at least restrained without great difficulty. Meanwhile, the young man had discreetly returned to the city, had been acclaimed by a part of the populace, and had paid a "modest" visit to Cardinal Cybò, who, aware that his ambitions were frustrated, acquiesced with grace to Cosimo's accession. On the morning of January 9 Cosimo was elected by the Senate as "Head and First Citizen of Florence."

He was not yet Duke; moreover, his position was not at all secure. The Senate did not intend to be ruled by him, and, from outside the city, came grave threats against his government. Many republican exiles, *fuorusciti,* had been waiting for a chance to overthrow the Medici regime; Pope Paul III, a Farnese, was not at all friendly to the family; the attitude of the Emperor was a source of uncertainty and apprehension, especially after the night of January 9, when Commander Vitelli unexpectedly took over the fortress in Charles's name. A series of crises occurred, in all of which Cosimo and his advisers acted correctly.

From Venice Filippo Strozzi, leader of the exiles, went quickly to Bologna to raise an army. In Rome, three anti-Medici cardinals, Ridolfi, Gaddi, and Salviati (Cosimo's maternal uncle), also thought of raising troops, and there was a serious possibility of their joining forces with Strozzi. In a placatory gesture the Senate invited the cardinals to pay a visit to the city—without troops. An embassy was sent to Charles V, asking him to confirm Cosimo's election and applying, on the young man's behalf, for the hand of Alessandro's widow Margaret. Thus was recognized, tacitly, Florence's subordination to the Empire. The main concern of Cosimo and his government, in these first days, naturally, was to win the approval and support of the Emperor, most powerful of the external forces involved in Florentine affairs. Within the city, on the other hand, severe measures were taken to ensure order and to constitute a ready army.

The Roman cardinals arrived at Florence on January 20. They were received courteously but required to leave their armed escorts outside the city. In the meetings of the following days they obtained virtually no concessions from the new leader. On January 23 they agreed to support Cosimo, but continued to insist that the exiles be allowed to return to Florence.

The immediate crisis had been weathered. Months later, on May 11, Count Cifuentes, envoy of Charles V, arrived in the city. He had been instructed to press for a reconciliation with the exiles (who were supported by Francis I) and to make sure that the fortresses of Florence and nearby Tuscan cities remained in the hands of commanders loyal to the Empire. The fate of the widowed Margaret was not as yet to be decided. While the Count did not bring about any softening of Cosimo's attitude toward the exiles, his impressions of the young man, communicated to the Emperor, were good. On June 21 Cosimo was confirmed as "Duke of the Republic" after pledging fidelity to the Emperor.

A few weeks later a plainly decisive event made his position secure. The *fuorusciti,* aided by French subsidies, had raised an army, and they now moved against Florence. To await reinforcements they established themselves at the fort of Montemurlo, northwest of the city. Vitelli gathered Italian and Spanish forces under his command in Florence and made a surprise attack on the exiles during the night of July 31–August 1. The attack was a complete success; the *fuorusciti* were thoroughly beaten, and their leader Filippo Strozzi was taken prisoner. Less important prisoners were, many of them, dealt with summarily; Strozzi, a famous figure and one of the wealthiest men in Europe, was kept in the *fortezza da basso* while his fate was considered. Some months later, after undergoing torture to force him to confess having had a hand in the murder of Duke Alessandro, he committed suicide in his cell, leaving a letter extolling the cause of republican liberties. Through this act, he became the most famous martyr to freedom in Florentine history.

Impressed by the victory at Montemurlo, Charles V, in September, 1537, confirmed to Florentine ambassadors in more explicit terms the legitimacy of Cosimo's dukedom. The young ruler announced this news to the people and began to style himself "Duke of Florence" in public affairs. His security continued, of course, to depend upon the good will of the Emperor, to whom the Florentine fortress still owed direct allegiance. Cosimo began, nevertheless, to assume more power personally, freeing himself deliberately from the influence of Cardinal Cybò and other advisers. Guicciardini, disappointed by his own loss of influence, soon retired and started work on his history of Italy.

The question of the Duke's marriage had been posed, as we have seen, virtually from the moment of his accession. The Emperor temporized for a while in regard to the request for the hand of his daughter Margaret and then, in 1538, announced a decision to wed her instead to Ottavio Farnese, nephew of Pope Paul III. The Pope, anxious to settle his family well during his reign, offered to Cosimo his own niece Vittoria. The Duke declined politely, resisting considerable pressure from Rome. In 1538 Giovanni Bandini, Florentine Ambassador at the Spanish and Imperial Court (and to whom Giambullari's book is dedicated) set about arranging a proper match for his Duke. Among the ladies considered were the Duchess of Milan, a sister of the Spanish Duke of Alba, and a Tudor princess. In November, 1538, the Ambassador obtained the Emperor's approval for Cosimo's marriage with one of the daughters of the Spanish Viceroy of Naples, Don Pedro de Toledo. It was her father who had suggested the match. He wished to give his eldest daughter Isabella, but the Duke himself insisted on having the second, Eleonora, whom, it is thought, he had seen on the trip to Naples.[7] As was usual, some hard bargaining about the dowry took place. When these agreements were reached, Cosimo sent to Naples two representatives, Luigi Ridolfi and Jacopo dei Medici, who acted as his proxies in the marriage ceremony.

Don Pedro was a younger son of the second Duke of Alba and stood high in the favor of the Emperor. (His reputation in history is bad because of a Spanish-style inquisition he instituted in Naples during the Counter Reformation.) Eleonora had been brought up in Spain and in

---

[7]Preserved in the Archivio di Stato in Florence, *Archivio mediceo,* "Lettere e minute dall'anno 1537 al 1543," carte 122–124, is a letter from the Duke to Bandini, in which the former states his preference for Eleonora.

Naples; according to accounts she was an extraordinarily beautiful woman and also quite "haughty" —an attribute to be admired in a lady of rank.

In their planning of the wedding celebrations Cosimo and his advisers had three dominant political aims: (1) to demonstrate their loyalty to the Emperor, (2) to ingratiate themselves with the Florentine people, and (3) to win the favor of other Tuscan cities and localities. The first objective was easily the most urgent, having dictated the arrangement of the marriage itself. It is difficult to realize today the extent of Charles V's prestige. In modern European history it has probably been matched only by that of Napoleon, which was, moreover, of a less respectable kind. Charles was no ordinary sovereign; at his coronation by Clement VII in 1530 he had been consecrated "Emperor of the Romans and Lord of the Whole World." More importantly, his dominions stretched—as details in the decorations for the wedding festivities remind us—from Peru to the Black Sea. He had beaten his greatest rival Francis I more than once, and Henry VIII of England had sought an alliance. After the sack of Rome in 1527 no pope dared oppose him. Since Florence, or even Tuscany, could not count for much alone in a Europe of emerging nation-states, the government and Cosimo calculatedly cast their lot with the greatest of the powers in Europe and Italy, the man whom his courtiers called "the new Caesar." No form or phrasing of flattery, apparently, could be thought too extreme or too abject when Charles was the theme.

The strategy to win the favor of the Florentines was somewhat equivocal and perhaps all the more effective for being so. The planners of the decorations strove both to present Cosimo as the legitimate heir of Alessandro and the older line of Medici and to emphasize the identity of his father, who enjoyed a better reputation than recent members of that main line. The mercenary Giovanni delle Bande Nere, with little justification, was remembered as a patriot and even as a defender of freedom. Moreover, his father had borne the nickname "Il Populano" because of his opposition to the tyranny of Piero. Old republicans and bitter enemies of Alessandro, on being reminded of these facts, might be persuaded to accept Cosimo, a member of the more liberal branch of the family. The presence of a number of elaborate paintings that glorified the deeds of Giovanni can thus be understood. On the other hand, old Medici partisans presumably needed to be convinced of legitimacy or, more practically, of Cosimo's respectful devotion to traditions of the old regime. This need explains the respectful reminders of Cosimo il Vecchio, Lorenzo il Magnifico, the Duke of Urbino, Alessandro, and the Medici popes, while the use of two emblems —the broken laurel with a new sprout growing from its stump and the dead bush with a new sprout nearby on the ground—served to emphasize that Cosimo was giving new life to the family's ruling line.

A third motive—to win favor in the province —was served by the personification poems of Gelli. The glories and pride of Pisa, Volterra, and other places were recognized in order to suggest that they were partners of Florence rather than subjects. Cosimo's intentions in this matter were honest; he would indeed promote local autonomy or, rather, local equality within the Duchy. It was the establishment of his own sovereignty, and not that of the city, that counted.

II. Literary Background

GENERAL

It is a common opinion that the peak of the literary Renaissance in Italy was clearly past by the second quarter of the sixteenth century. By then, it is assumed, the spark of renewal had passed on to other western countries. This judgment has some foundation, but is not always helpful. It can, in fact, be quite misleading if one infers from it that the later writers were inferior imitators of examples set in the High Renaissance, that is, in the fifteenth century and in the first years of the sixteenth. In truth, the writers in this later period often cultivated new fields, trying their hands at different genres. Moreover, the claims of the *quattrocento* itself to the title of High Renaissance may, in literary matters if not in artistic ones, be questioned. If it is individual genius and accomplishment that count, the supreme moment of renascent Florentine and Italian letters had surely come instead in the *trecento* with Petrarch and Boccaccio (even assuming that Dante must be assigned to the Middle Ages). It is plainly true, however, that the breadth and general influence of literary culture were greater during the later period. The accomplishments of the Renaissance were, in some respects and up to a certain point, cumulative, even in literature, so that the writers of the 1400's benefited from the studies and stylistic essays of those who had gone before. This argument, for what it is worth, must be applied also in defense of the *cinquecento;* the process of accumulation—in erudition, sophistication, and polish—was not spent, and the spark had not been extinguished. The spirit of rebirth was still in the air.

The cultivation of vernacular letters since 1300 had not, to be sure, been so steady as the progress of scholarship. Dante, Boccaccio, and Petrarch had devoted much of their energy to the composition of works in Latin; in the next century, during the Age of Humanism, many learned and literarily gifted men wrote practically nothing in Italian. This trend was, however, less pronounced in Florence than elsewhere. The appreciation and study of Dante's *Divine Comedy* continued there almost without interruption, from the time of

Boccaccio's biography of the poet, written in the middle 1300's. Even in the middle of the *quattrocento,* in the time of Cosimo il Vecchio, one of the city's greatest humanists and "universal men," Leon-Battista Alberti, wrote often in Italian.

The most remarkable literary culture of the century and perhaps of the entire Renaissance was achieved in Florence under Lorenzo il Magnifico, who ruled from 1469 to 1492. The passion for Greek and Latin culture was now again combined with an ambition to distinguish oneself in vernacular compositions. This culture was basically poetic. Lorenzo, apart from his active patronage of letters, was himself an excellent lyric and pastoral poet. His close friend Politian, best remembered for the *Stanze* written to celebrate Giuliano dei Medici's victory in a joust, occupies a very high place in the history of light and occasional poetry. Luigi Pulci, another protégé of Lorenzo, wrote the *Morgante maggiore,* first of those mock epics in which the Italian Renaissance found perhaps its most complete literary expression. (The other two major epics of this sort were the work of poets protected by the House of Este in Ferrara. Boiardo's *Orlando innamorato* began appearing in 1486, and Ariosto's magnificent *Orlando furioso* was published in 1516.)

The genres to be cultivated with most success in the *cinquecento* were, on the other hand—if one excepts Ariosto's epic, near the beginning, and Tasso's, near the end—prose genres: history and political theory, biography, literary criticism, treatises on social ideals, and comedy (whose development we shall discuss separately). During the first decades of the century—extremely troubled times—Florence had in the midst of its highest society one of the greatest prose writers of the age: Niccolò Machiavelli. *The Prince* was published in 1513; its author died in 1527. Another major prose work, Baldassare Castiglione's *The Courtier,* appeared in 1528. The author, who had been at the court of the Duke of Urbino and then at the Papal Court in Rome, died in 1529.

Of the Italian writers living in Florence and elsewhere at the time of the wedding, the following were the most important: Francesco Guicciardini, who had been a close friend of Machiavelli and who had helped Cosimo I come to power, was working on his *Storia d'Italia.* He was to die the next year; his work was to be published in 1541. Pietro Aretino, the satiric poet and playwright who had been an intimate friend of the Duke's father Giovanni delle Bande Nere, was forty-seven years old and living in Venice, safe from the Roman court that he had enjoyed and later held up to ridicule. The philosopher and grammarian Pietro Bembo, who had published the influential *Prose della volgar lingua* in 1525, was sixty-nine years old and living in Rome. Giangiorgio Trissino, remembered for his theoretical criticism and for his efforts to endow the Italian literature with masterpieces in the three major neoclassical genres—epic, tragedy, and comedy—was sixty and in full activity. The first parts of his *Poetica* had been published in 1529; the rest would appear only in 1562, after his death. His *Sofonisba,* the first "regular" tragedy, had been written in 1515–1516. He was working on the epic *L'Italia liberata dai Goti,* which he was to finish in 1548. His comedy *I Simillimi* would also be completed that year. Benvenuto Cellini and Giorgio Vasari, two artists whose writings are among the most creditable productions of Cosimo's reign, were both living away from Florence in 1539. Cellini returned to enter the Duke's service in 1545, Vasari definitively in 1555. Two famous women poets of the century, Vittoria Colonna and Gaspara Stampa, were living in Rome and Venice, respectively. Vittoria Colonna, a close friend of Michelangelo, had already written much of her poetry. Gaspara Stampa was just sixteen, and her verses would be published in 1554, the year of her death.

It will be useful for chronological orientation to glance briefly as well at the state of literature in other major countries of Western Europe in 1539. While the scholarly business of humanism was well launched almost everywhere, the process of "renewal" in vernacular letters was in widely differing stages of advancement. The Spanish and French sovereigns, with their armies, had had ample opportunities to observe the beauties of the Italian Renaissance, and their admiration had had profound effects at home. These influences were perhaps more apparent and more highly developed in Spain. The masterpiece of the early Renaissance in that country, Fernando de Rojas' realistic and satirical novel *La Celestina,* had appeared in 1499. The year 1508 marked the printing of the medieval novel of chivalry *Amadis de Gaula,* later to be a source of Renaissance themes. Two other major genres of the novel, the picaresque and the pastoral, were soon to receive masterpieces with the publication of the anonymous *Lazarillo de Tormes* (1554) and Montemayor's *Diana* (*ca.* 1559). Lyrical verse in the Petrarchan tradition had been written in the early part of the century by Garcilaso de la Vega (1503–1536) and would be added to later by Fray Luis de Leon. The Counter Reformation, so fervent and so severe in Spain, was about to begin, as was the perhaps related literature of religious mysticism. Saint Theresa was already twenty-four years old. Yet, the Golden Age of Spain, the *siglo de oro,* culmination of the Renaissance, was still almost fifty years in the future. Cervantes was to be born in 1547, Lope de Vega in 1562.

In France the literary renascence was also well begun. There was at the court of Francis I an excellent light poet, Clément Marot (1496–1544), who represented transition in that he used native medieval poetic forms as well as those modeled on antiquity and on Petrarch. Rabelais, the most eloquent exponent of Renaissance ideals in France, was in the full vigor of his literary career. His first novel, *Pantagruel,* had appeared in 1533 and the second, *Gargantua,* in 1534. From 1534 to 1536 he had spent a good deal of time in Italy, mainly at Ferrara and at Rome, and he had probably visited Florence in 1534.[1] The *Third Book* in his series of novels would come out in 1546 and the fourth in 1552. Meanwhile, the Reformation was gaining strength in France. John Calvin, the Protestant leader, had published the Latin version of his *Christian Institutions* in 1536. The vernacular version, which was to be highly influential for the development of French prose, would come in 1541. A second, more formal phase of the literary renaissance was just around the corner; the School of The Pléiade would be born just before mid-century. Its members—Ronsard, Du Bellay, Jodelle, and others—were to endow French literature with formal criticism and with excellent lyric poetry. They would also try their hands, not very successfully, at the neoclassical genres par excellence: epic, tragedy, and comedy. France's greatest age in literature, the neoclassical *grand siècle,* was, however, still a century in the future.

German soldiers also had been to Italy, in the service of Emperor Charles V, but the literary renaissance can scarcely be said to have arrived in that country. The Reformation, on the other hand, was in full vigor. Martin Luther's translation of the Bible (1522–1534) and religious writings were to be, even more than Calvin's works in

[1]His letters written from Rome to the Bishop of Maillezais in 1535 and 1536 contain much information about Florentine politics, especially about the efforts of Filippo Strozzi and the republicans to overthrow Duke Alessandro. See the *Oeuvres complètes de Rabelais,* 973–92.

France, important for the development of vernacular prose. The dominant genres in belles-lettres were still medieval ones, no doubt partly because German literature had been especially rich in the Middle Ages. The writer who was living in 1539 and who is best remembered today is Hans Sachs (1494–1576), poet and playwright. The neoclassical genres would not be seriously cultivated in Germany until the seventeenth century. Martin Opitz' *Book of German Poesy,* a neoclassical manifesto, was to be published in 1624.

England, far from Italy, also lagged. Humanistic scholarship was highly developed, especially at Oxford. Sir Thomas More's *Utopia* (1516) was full of the new ideas, but it had been written in Latin. As in France and Germany, however, Protestantism favored the cultivation of vernacular prose, and this impulse produced translations of the Bible and, in 1549, *The Book of Common Prayer.* At the court of Henry VIII there were two minor lyric poets of Petrarchan inspiration: Sir Thomas Wyatt and Henry Howard, Earl of Surrey. Their works would be published in 1557. Little, however, foreshadowed the greatness of the Elizabethan Age, whose writers were as yet unborn. Spenser was born in 1552, Sir Philip Sidney in 1554, Shakespeare and Marlowe in 1564. Elizabeth herself was a child of six, much overshadowed by her elder sister Mary Tudor.

THE FOUR WRITERS

Pier Francesco Giambullari was born in Florence in 1495, the son of Bernardo Giambullari, prominent as a writer of light poetry, who had enjoyed official favor under Lorenzo il Magnifico and would again under Pope Leo X. The son received an excellent humanistic education that included instruction in Hebrew and Greek as well as in Latin. He was a scholar rather than a poet, and like his father he benefited from the patronage of the ruling family. At age sixteen he became the secretary of Alfonsina Orsini dei Medici, daughter-in-law of Il Magnifico and mother of Lorenzo, Duke of Urbino. While very young he took holy orders, which made it possible for him later to be given a valued ecclesiastical post at San Lorenzo, the Medici family church. By 1539, despite a lack of published literary accomplishments, he was already known in the Florentine scholarly and literary world. In 1540 he became an early member of the Umidi and thus, the next year, a founding member of the Accademia fiorentina.[2] That body published in 1547 a volume of public lectures on Dante, of which two were by Giambullari. Three years earlier, he had written a quaint little treatise on the size and location of the Inferno.[3] He was elected thirteenth consul of the learned society in 1547; in 1551 it gave him the title, "Reformer of the Language."

The Academy's admiration for Dante and its frequent lessons on his poem were in fact closely related to the championship of Tuscan, and more particularly Florentine, as a national literary language for prose. This good cause was destined to triumph. Giambullari and his close friend Gelli, author of our stanzas, led the scholarly campaign. In 1547 the former published a work called *Il Gello* after his colleague, with whom he pretends to have a conversation. Here, in defense of Tuscan, is put forth the astonishing theory that the dialect derived from Hebrew, via Etruscan! This bizarre conception—which makes us realize the primitive state of historical philology in the Renaissance—was doubtless born of a desire to draw support from Dante, who had declared in his *De vulgari eloquentia* that Hebrew was the best of languages because it had been given directly to Adam and Eve by God. In 1551, under the Academy's auspices, Giambullari published a new linguistic work, a sort of Tuscan grammar, *Della lingua che si parla e si scrive in Firenze*. Bound together with it was a treatise by Gelli called *Ragionamento sopra le difficoltà di metter in regole la nostra lingua,* in which the author proposed living Florentine, rather than a fixed language, as the literary standard of the country.

Giambullari's most enduring work was, however, in the field of history: an unfinished *Storia dell'Europa,* published in 1556, a year after his death. The account begins in A.D. 887 and extends only to 947, but the enterprise of treating the whole of Europe—even for a short period—was nevertheless ambitious in a nearly unprecedented way. Giambullari wished to portray the time in which Latin and Germanic cultures began to fuse to form medieval civilization. The expository style of this book is unusually vivid and clear.

---

[2]Most information about the early years of the Accademia fiorentina, and much also about the careers of Giambullari, Gelli, and Landi is found in two academic publications of the eighteenth century: Iacopo Rilli, ed., *Notizie letterarie ed istoriche intorno agli uomini illustri dell'Accademia fiorentina,* (1700) and Salvino Salvini, *Fasti consulari dell'Accademia fiorentina* (1717).

[3]*De'l sito, forma e misura dello Inferno di Dante.* In the *Lettioni di Accademici fiorentini sopra Dante* of 1547 Giambullari appears as a leading Dante authority.

Giambullari is considered, in fact, to have been one of the clearest writers of prose in the *cinquecento,* which was itself perhaps the period that was most important for the development of Italian prose style.

He was presumably charged by the Duke or by some other member of the ruling family to put together the account of the wedding festivities. The fact that it is addressed to Giovanni Bandini, Florentine Ambassador at the Imperial Court, shows that the bridegroom was anxious for certain obsequious details to become known to his protector Charles V. The publication of such descriptions of public celebrations was not yet common, but it became extremely so during the remaining decades of the sixteenth century and in the seventeenth. The Magliabechiana Collection of the National Library in Florence contains hundreds of examples, many dealing with later grand events in the lives of the Medici. Even on the death of Cosimo in 1574, there appeared a meticulous account of ceremonies and a reproduction of literary compositions prepared for the occasion.[4]

GIAMBATTISTA GELLI is, in character, the most remarkable and the most appealing of the four authors. He was born in Florence in 1498 of very modest parentage. Following the example of his father, he became a hosier and apparently remained in this trade throughout his literary career. As a young man he was inspired with a passion for learning, perhaps as a consequence of frequenting humanistic discussions that, in the early decades of the century, were held in the garden of a prominent citizen, Bernardo Rucellai. Finding time from his work, he took instruction in Latin and in philosophy and, by force of effort, became perhaps one of the most learned men in the city. He probably did not begin writing until his late thirties; certainly the poetry written for the wedding constitutes his first important literary venture.[5] It may very well, too,

[4]Anonymous, *Descritione della pompa funerale fatta nelle esequie del Ser.mo Sig. Cosimo de' Medici, Gran Duca di Toscana. . . .*

[5]Rather little is known about the first four decades of his life. The best studies are Aurelio Ugolini's *Le opere di Giovambattista Gelli,* Carlo Bonardi's *Giambattista Gelli e le sue opere,* and Armand De Gaetano's Columbia University dissertation, "Giambattista Gelli: A Moralist of the Renaissance," 1954. There are two modern editions of his works: the *Opere di Giambattista Gelli,* Agenore Gelli, ed. (1855) and the *Opere,* Ireneo Sanesi, ed. (1952).

have won him the favor of the Duke and have made possible his later career. Like his friend Giambullari, he was a member of the Umidi Academy in 1540 and, then, of the official Accademia fiorentina, which made him its fifteenth consul in 1548. He believed fervently in that body's educating mission. The *Lettioni d'accademici fiorentini sopra Dante,* 1547, contained one of his lectures, and he gave public lessons also on Petrarch. Along with Giambullari, as we have seen, he concerned himself with linguistic questions and defended Florentine as a literary medium.

Gelli's efforts in belles-lettres, properly speaking, are not well considered. His poetry, of which there is little, is scarcely read. Soon after the wedding, perhaps inspired by Landi's example, he turned his hand to classical comedy, but these ventures were not notably fortunate, either. *La Sporta,* having as chief character a miser, was published in 1543. Anton Francesco Grazzini, called "Il Lasca," who was also a member of the Academy and was to become a much more successful playwright, accused Gelli of stealing this play from an unpublished manuscript of Machiavelli, and there is still doubt about the matter.[6] Another comedy, *L'Errore,* produced in Florence in 1555, recalls in its plot the *Commedia in versi* of Lorenzo Strozzi.

Gelli is best remembered for his philosophical works. In 1548 appeared *I Capricci del Bottaio (The Caprices of the Cooper),* a series of ten dialogues between the author's body and his soul. Some of the ideas expounded in this book were offensive to zealots of the Counter Reformation, and the author was forced to repudiate them. Another set of dialogues, *La Circe,* was published in 1549. In this work a number of Greeks who have been turned into animals by Circe explain to Ulysses why they prefer to remain animals rather than to become men again. This was the sort of philosophical fairy tale that was to become a deadly weapon of social criticism in the Age of Enlightenment.

Gelli died in 1563.

GIOVAMBATTISTA STROZZI, born in 1504, was a member of the main branch of what was the most famous of all Florentine families after the Medici themselves.[7] His father Lorenzo (1482–1549) was

[6]See Ireneo Sanesi, *La commedia,* Storia dei generi letterari italiani, I, 339–41.

[7]A detailed study of the different branches of the family is found in Pompeo Litta's *Famiglie celebri d'Italia,* Vol. 18.

the elder brother of the celebrated republican martyr Filippo Strozzi, who killed himself while imprisoned in the Fortezza da basso in 1537. Lorenzo was a more cautious man, though he, too, had been an important leader in the last Republic. He was one of the emissaries sent in 1530 to negotiate its surrender to the armies of Clement VII, and he seems afterward to have made his peace with the Medici. He is supposed to have advised Filippo against leading the ill-fated expedition of *fuorusciti* to overthrow Cosimo. There can be no doubt, however, that he sympathized privately with his brother's cause; he wrote a book about illustrious men of the Strozzi family, unpublished during his lifetime, the main section of which is a glorification of Filippo.[8] Lorenzo was also a literary figure of some importance. He wrote light poetry, and some of his *canti carnascialeschi* are included in the grand anthology published in 1750.[9] More importantly, he was the author of one of the first learned comedies, the *Commedia in versi,* presented in Florence during the second decade of the century, and is supposed to have written also two other comedies, *La Pisana* and *La Violante,* which remained unpublished.

Like Giambullari, Giovambattista Strozzi must have been introduced to the pleasures of literature by his father. It is reported that at the performance of the *Commedia in versi* he and his brother Palla were allowed to recite verses, either in the play itself or in the *intermedii.*[10] During the siege of Florence that began in 1529 he left the city and went with his friend Antonio Landi, our playwright, to study in Padua.[11] Little is known about his actual literary career; early and recent historians have nearly always confused him with one or the other of two distant cousins who were writers: (1) Giovambattista Strozzi il Giovane or il Cieco (1551–1634), also a madrigalist, and (2) the more nearly contemporary Giovanni Strozzi

---

[8]*Le vite degli uomini illustri della casa Strozzi. Commentarii di Lorenzo di Filippo Strozzi, ora intieramente pubblicati con un ragionamento di Francesco Zeffi sopra la vita dell'autore,* Pietro Stromboli, ed.

[9]*Tutti i trionfi, carri, mascherate e canti carnascialeschi andati per Firenze dal tempo del Magnifico Lorenzo dei Medici fino all'anno 1559.*

[10]Francesco Zeffi, "La vita dell'autore di queste vite," in Lorenzo Strozzi, *Le vite degli uomini illustri della casa Strozzi* (7 *supra*), xii.

[11]See Benedetto Varchi's *Storia fiorentina,* Lelio Arbib, ed., II, 184–85. Varchi was a friend of both men, and his information about their early lives is probably reliable.

(1517–1570).[12] Both of these men were prominent members of the Accademia fiorentina. Our own poet was admitted to the Academy very early, but in 1547 he allowed his name to be stricken from the rolls as a penalty for having refused to accept the office of consul when elected.[13]

Strozzi seems to have led an unusually quiet and retired life, though not an austere one, since he dwelt in the magnificent Palazzo Strozzi and was one of the richest men in Florence. According to the historian Scipione Ammirato,[14] Duke Cosimo valued the poet's friendship and often went to visit him at his country house in Montoliveto. In 1561 Cosimo made him a senator, but he declined this honor as well, pleading age and ill health. To explain his refusal he wrote a series of ten graceful madrigals obviously intended to mollify the Duke. He was the author, in 1564, of one of the best-known poems composed for the funeral of Michelangelo. Until very recently he was thought to have written as well an earlier poem about the sculptor's statue of Night that elicited a famous poetic response from the great artist. It seems clear now that those rather vapid verses, which irritated Michelangelo, were the work of Giovanni Strozzi.[15] The poems of our author, called Giovambattista il Vecchio to distinguish him from Il Giovane, were not published during his lifetime, although, to judge from his reputation, they must have had considerable circulation in the Florentine literary world. In 1593, twenty-two years after his death, many of the madrigals were collected and printed by his sons Lorenzo and Filippo.[16] In this collection, only one poem from the *intermedii,* Silenus' lament "O begli anni di oro...," is included. Many other madrigals remain in manuscript, especially among the Carte Strozziane of the State Archives in Florence. Since Giovambattista il Giovane was also a prolific madrigalist, it is often

[12]The confusion is found notably in Michele Poccianti's *Catalogus scriptorum florentinorum omnis generis* (1589), in P. Giulio Negri's *Istoria degli scrittori fiorentini* (1722), and in Giovan Maria Crescimbeni's *Dell'istoria della volgar poesia* (1730–31). Luigi Sorrento came nearest to distinguishing the careers of the three men in the Introduction to his edition of Giovambattista il Vecchio's *Madrigali* (Strassburg: Heitz, 1909).

[13]Salvino Salvini, *Fasti consulari dell'Accademia fiorentina,* 70.

[14]*Istorie fiorentine di Scipione Ammirato,* X, 279.

[15]See Paola Barocchi, ed., *La vita di Michelangelo nelle redazioni del 1550 e del 1568,* by Giorgio Vasari, II, 188.

[16]Giovambattista Strozzi, *Madrigali* (Firenze, Sermartelli, 1593).

impossible to assign the unpublished poems definitely to one poet or the other.

There is reason to believe that our Strozzi's participation in the wedding celebrations had an obvious political significance. The Duke may have invited him to take part in them as a generous gesture of clemency toward the family, or Giovambattista may have volunteered in order to affirm his loyalty—perhaps a necessary move, since other Strozzi, in exile, continued to conspire against the regime. From a purely literary point of view, to be sure, the participation was quite natural. The poet's father had written comedies, and he was himself known as a writer of madrigals. More importantly, perhaps, the playwright Landi was a close friend from student days. Whatever the real motives, however, we may speculate that both the poet and the Duke welcomed this chance to make a public demonstration of amity.

Antonio Landi is the least remembered of the four figures, and information about his life and career is scarce even in contemporary sources. He was born in Florence in 1506 of a family that may be considered to have been noble, in the nonfeudal local sense; his ancestors had on thirteen different occasions served as priors of the Republic.[17] He was a good friend of the patrician Giovambattista Strozzi, with whom, we have seen, he studied in Padua. The production of *Il Commodo* was probably the high point of his literary career so far as creativity is concerned, but he was afterward a very important figure in the Accademia fiorentina, being elected twelfth consul in 1546 and twenty-eighth in 1555. He published no other important literary compositions, though several of his sonnets are reproduced in two works of Benedetto Varchi: *Sonetti,* 1555–1557, and *Sonetti spirituali,* 1573.

Landi was a merchant, and literature was probably not even his main private concern (as it certainly was for the hosier Gelli). A very different picture of his character and activities from that recorded in the stately *Fasti consulari* of the Academy is given us in several pages of Benvenuto Cellini's autobiography.[18] The celebrated jeweler and sculptor recounts in his usual lively and prejudiced manner an episode that turns

[17]Salvini, *Fasti consulari,* 64. Some genealogical charts of the family may be found on manuscript cards of the unpublished eighteenth-century encyclopedia called the "Poligrafo Gargagni," in the Biblioteca Nazionale Centrale of Florence.

[18]*The Memoirs of Benvenuto Cellini,* Anne MacDonell, trans., 276–77 and 283.

upon a large diamond sold to the Duke by Landi and a friend. According to Cellini, the sale was a shameless swindle; Landi had offered the stone to him for a little more than half the price paid by the Duke. Somewhat later, in a fit of ill temper—and hoping to divert attention from one of his own affairs—the artist tattled to Cosimo. As a result, Landi and his friend had to exile themselves temporarily in Venice.

We have not discovered the date of Landi's death. As late as 1562 he was a minor officer, a *consigliere,* of the Academy.

THE COMEDY

The principal literary contribution to the wedding celebrations—and the only one whose content was not determined by the occasion—was Landi's comedy. It belongs to a major literary genre whose form was then being evolved and that deserves special historical and critical commentary.[19] The origins of the vernacular *commedia erudita* were in fact fairly recent in 1539, though Landi cannot honestly be called a pioneer. During the fifteenth century a good number of comic plays in Latin had been written, some by students and some by literary men. These compositions were, basically, imitations of Plautus and Terence, but classical form was not rigidly observed in them. Among the best remembered of them today are Leon-Battista Alberti's *Philodoxus* (*ca.* 1426), Ugolino Pisani's *Philogenia* (1436–1437), and Tommaso de Mezzo's *Epirota* (1483). In the latter part of the century, too, the plays of Plautus and Terence were sometimes performed in the original Latin. Some were produced, for example, at the court of Lorenzo il Magnifico. Alongside these Latin plays, ancient and modern—but sharply distinguished from them—existed a highly popular comic theatre of Italian farces. In Siena, after 1531, there was an organized company, called the *Rozzi,* who staged farces often. There were probably also numerous performances in Florence.

The *commedia erudita* of the sixteenth century was to be distinguished (1) from the Latin and humanistic comedies by the fact of its being written in Italian, and (2) from the native farces by its rather strictly defined form and its greater attention to properly literary qualities, that is, to

[19]The fullest history of the comedy in Italy is Ireneo Sanesi's *La commedia,* in two volumes. A very good shorter study in English is Marvin T. Herrick's *Italian Comedy in the Renaissance.*

structure and to details of expression. Form was not immediately or ever quite definitely set, but it was considered to have enormous importance, and there was much serious discussion. The *cinquecento* was, in Italy, the great century of theoretical criticism and of the development of formal standards in vernacular literature. Critics of the time laid the basis for neoclassical letters not only in Italy but in France, Germany, and England as well.[20] Early "poetics" and similar treatises were based largely on Horace's *Ars poetica* and tended to be concerned with practical problems of expression and rhetoric. In the second half of the century, however, Aristotle's *Poetics* was often considered as well, and more attention was given to basic esthetic theory and to the concepts of genres, including that of the comedy. (The section of Aristotle's work dealing with the comedy has not survived, but much was inferred from his definitions of the genres and from his remarks on tragedy.)

The most important relevant work of critical theory to appear before 1539 was the *Poetica volgare* of Bernardino Daniello, 1536.[21] It is not at all sure that Landi knew any treatise firsthand, but we think it useful to reproduce below the main passage of Daniello's work dealing with the comedy, because it shows the temper of the theoretical speculation of the time:

No tone [*fiata*] is forbidden to the writer of comedy except to use the grandeur of the writer of tragedy. . . . Those [things] which should not be done [on stage] are the cruel, the impossible, and the dishonest. . . . And in comedies lascivious kisses, amorous hugs and embraces, and things like that. Let not the comedy overstep the limit of five acts and not stop short of it. Let four people not speak in it at once; but two or three at the most; and let the other stand aside silent and listening. Let no Deity be introduced there, save in those matters in which man by himself is not sufficient to overcome some evil situation without divine help and favor. . . . [Choruses] are not used in comedies any more; but in their place between one act and another, so that the stage

[20]There exist in English two excellent studies, Joel E. Spingarn's classic *Literary Criticism in the Renaissance,* now nearly seventy years old (new edition by Harcourt, Brace & World, Inc., 1963), and a much more exhaustive study by Bernard Weinberg: *A History of Literary Criticism in the Italian Renaissance* (1961), 2 vols.

[21]In 1529 Giangiorgio Trissino published the first four parts of his *Poetica,* but Parts V and VI, which deal with the comedy, did not appear until 1562, after the author's death. Francesco Robortello's Latin commentary on Aristotle, *In Librum Aristoteles de arte poetica explicationes,* came in 1548. Scaliger's immensely influential *Poetices libri septem* was published in 1561 and Castelvetro's *Poetica d'Aristotele vulgarizzata e sposta* in 1570.

won't remain empty, music [*suoni*] and songs, and morris dances [*moresche*] and buffoons are usually brought in mixed together.[22]

The earliest erudite comedy seems to have been the *Commedia di amicizia,* in verse, by Jacopo Nardi, of about 1497. A little better remembered is Publio Filippo Mantovano's *Formicone,* in prose, presented in Venice in 1503. The writer who did most to develop the genre and who gave it important standing in Italian letters was the celebrated Ludovico Ariosto, protégé of the Este family in Ferrara. Ariosto's fame rests mainly, however, on the mock epic *Orlando furioso,* which many critics consider to be the literary masterpiece of the Italian Renaissance. He wrote four comedies and left another unfinished: *La Cassaria,* 1508; *I Suppositi,* 1509; *Il Negromante,* 1520; *La Lena,* 1528; and *Gli Studenti,* incomplete. Several of the plays had both verse and prose versions, the latter seeming today rather more successful because of the greater naturalness of the language. The best of the compositions is probably *La Lena,* whose chief character is a woman of easy virtue, married to a weak, lazy man. In Urbino, at the carnival of 1513, were presented two good comedies (Landi alludes to the first of them in his Prologue). *La Calandra,* a rowdy but extremely clever story of illicit love, was written by Bernardo Dovizi da Bibbiena, who was to become a cardinal shortly after the play's production. Niccolò Grasso's *Eutychia,* probably also presented then, has as chief character the stock Roman comic type of the Parasite. At Siena in 1531 was performed a rather good learned comedy called *Gl'Ingannati,* of uncertain authorship. This is one of many Renaissance plays, including Landi's, that involve separated twins or brothers and that were inspired, nearly or remotely, by Plautus' *Menaechmi.*

The genre was cultivated quite early in Florence. Sometime between 1512 and 1519 an untitled *commedia in versi* was produced at the Palazzo Medici for Lorenzo Duke of Urbino. Its author was Lorenzo Strozzi, brother of Filippo (later to be martyred) and father of our poet Giovambattista. This play, with a plot modeled on Plautus, is remarkable from our point of view for its musical accompaniment and *intermedii,* in which the young Giovambattista and his brother Palla are said to have recited roles.[23] The writings

[22] *La Poetica di Bernardino Daniello, lucchese,* 38–39. The translation is our own.

[23] Francesco Zeffi, "La vita dell'autore di queste vite," in Lorenzo Strozzi's *Le vite degli uomini illustri della casa Strozzi...,* Pietro Stromboli, ed., xii.

of the art historian Vasari mention, but do not name, comedies produced in the city to celebrate the marriage of the Duke of Urbino and Madeleine de la Tour d'Auvergne, probably in September of 1518.[24] One of the artists who worked on the scenery and other decorations was Aristotile da San Gallo, who, twenty years later, after much experience, would provide the stage setting for *Il Commodo*.

About this time Niccolò Machiavelli, the Florentine statesman, political theorist, and historian, provided the erudite genre with its undisputed masterpiece, *La Mandragola*. The extraordinary appeal of this play, which is still one of the most popular in the Italian traditional repertory, depends both upon characterization and upon frankly farcical situations. The date of composition is uncertain but should probably be placed within the second decade of the century. Vasari's accounts mention very elaborate productions of this play and of another by Machiavelli, perhaps *La Clizia*, which took place not long before the Medici were sent away in 1527.[25] The young boys Ippolito and Alessandro dei Medici were present on one or both of the occasions and are said to have enjoyed the spectacle fully. One of the main designers of decorations and stage scenery was again San Gallo.

A most noteworthy production, which set a recent precedent for *Il Commodo*, was that, in 1536, of *L'Aridosia*. The occasion was the marriage of Duke Alessandro to Margaret of Austria, illegitimate daughter of Charles V, and the author was none other than Lorenzino dei Medici, soon to murder his cousin the Duke. The plot of the play turns, again, around two brothers, long separated, but some originality and profundity are provided in this repetition of basic plot through the circumstance that the two have received widely different educations. *L'Aridosia* was presented in a public square, with a magnificent *apparato* credited to San Gallo. (According to Vasari, he and San Gallo frustrated a scheme of Lorenzino to arrange for the decoration to collapse on the Duke's head!)[26] This play too, may well have had *intermedii*, though no text for them survives; Vasari's work mentions provisions for musicians and singers. Most of the spectators of Landi's play in 1539, including Duke Cosimo, probably remembered *L'Aridosia* quite well. It

---

[24] *The Lives of the Painters, Sculptors, and Architects*, A. B. Hinds, trans., III, 294.

[25] Vasari, III, 295.

[26] Vasari, III, 295–96.

may have been both the most recent and the most elaborate staging of a comedy they had seen.

Comedies were in fact often performed and even written for special occasions; more were to be created for later grand celebrations during Cosimo's reign. Little is known about the actors of the time. Permanent theatres with professional companies were practically unknown, and traveling companies, which became very important in the age of the *commedia dell'arte,* were also quite rare. Most actors, apparently, were amateurs or semiamateurs who earned their living in other ways. It is known, largely from Vasari, that there existed in Florence during the first half of the century a company called that of the *Cazzuola,* which often staged religious plays and sometimes comedies as well. This group was more like a society of *bons vivants* or a light-hearted academy than a professional troupe. Its most famous actor was Domenico Barlucchi, whose principal occupation was as Herald at the Signoria. This company, according to Vasari, performed in the production of Machiavelli's *La Mandragola,* mentioned above.[27] Much later, in 1548, it journeyed to Lyon to present Bibbiena's *La Calandra* before King Henry II and his Queen, Catherine des Médicis. It was active—or at least existent—in Florence in 1539 and may well have acted Landi's play. Barlucchi may, for example, have played Messer Ricciardo.

Il Commodo is in all formal and substantive respects an orthodox and typical example of the *commedia erudita,* and the virtues of the genre show in it to good effect. The three unities, first, are maintained. That of *time* is insisted upon in a particularly emphatic way by the themes of the *intermedii,* which keep one informed of the time of day in the play's action. Not twenty-four hours but roughly eight are required for the whole. *Unity of place* is observed perfectly, since, according to tradition, everything takes place at a spot in the street, probably at a corner, against a background of façades of handsome buildings designed by the artist San Gallo. Adherence to this unity requires some contriving, but it is also convenient, since intimate action, improper for the stage, occurs in the houses and is recounted rather than shown. Only the *unity of action* can be questioned, and even here the author's orthodoxy must, finally, be upheld. That the play has two

[27] Vasari says, for example (II, 295), that this company staged Machiavelli's *Mandragola.* His main account of the company is given in a digression within the biography of Giovan Francesco Rustice (IV, 34–37).

main plots, the respective love affairs of Leandro and Demetrio, may seem to violate the classical unities, but these come together in the end as the brothers become known to each other. Moreover, this kind of double plot had its origin, as we have seen, in classical literature, notably in Plautus' *Menaechmi,* the ancestor of a host of Renaissance plays built around lost brothers, twins, etc.

Only two scenes of *Il Commodo,* in our opinion, actually sin against unity of action. One is that, in Act IV, between Libano and Giorgetto, which serves no purpose except to introduce a little horseplay. The other, in Act III, between Giorgetto and Cornelia, has similar deficiencies. In addition, it has for modern readers the far greater defect of presenting as funny the tormenting of an old woman by a sixteenth-century juvenile delinquent. (To be sure, the energy with which Cornelia reacts diminishes the cruelty and evens the score.) These transgressions are not serious, however, and no one, even in the sixteenth century, could ask of comedy the same single-mindedness as was required for tragedy.

Landi was orthodox also in making his principal characters bourgeois; they are well off but lack political or social ambition. Their problems are serious but not tragic. Love is the mainspring of the plot, though it represents only one of the comic resources, and the satisfactory denouement of the love intrigue affords the requisite happy ending. The ending is brought about by a device greatly lacking in verisimilitude—the sudden discovery of unsuspected kinships—which was also thoroughly orthodox. The ancients had invented their tales against the backgrounds of wars and shipwrecks; sixteenth-century Italians were fond of blaming separations on depredations by the Turks, who had taken Constantinople in 1453 and whose pirate ships continued to be the terror of the Mediterranean. The improbability of specific circumstances mattered little in anyone's mind; Libano's remark, near the end, that things are working out just as in a comedy is meant to evoke a good-natured, indulgent laugh.

Verisimilitude was required only in the portrayal of society and of individual character, and, as Landi stated in his preface, he set great store by maintaining it there. The painting of customs and social commentary have, in fact, relatively little importance in the play. There is some satire of (1) professional matchmaking (but not of the custom of arranged marriages), (2) of gambling, and (3) of the greediness of priests and nuns. These matters are not dwelt upon; the important consideration is individual psychology, the depiction of character. Neoclassical comedy—and to a great extent neoclassical literature in general—was inclined toward the portrayal of "type" characters and of typical states of mind. The creation of highly individual, "unique" personages is an ideal that has been cherished rather in the romantic and modern traditions. Thus, Landi declared his intention of depicting "the nature of old men, of young ones, of masters, of servants, of married ladies, and of girls." The major comic character types he portrayed are the following: (1) young men in love (Leandro and Demetrio), (2) a frivolous and improvident young man (Cammillo), (3) a choleric old man (Messer Ricciardo), (4) a moralizing father (Lamberto), (5) a professional swindler (Travaglino), (6) a clever, shrewish wife (Cassandra), and (7) lazy, untrustworthy servants (Currado and Giorgetto).

The play is unusual in the genre for its lack of either wholly ridiculous or wholly admirable characters. There is, for example, something to be said even for Messer Ricciardo; he is right to resist the matchmaker's high-pressure salesmanship, right to distrust his wife Cassandra, right to resent her nagging. Cammillo the gambler cannot be blamed for reacting against his father's preaching. Even Travaglino the matchmaker is admirably correct in his assessments of character and general appreciations of human nature. On the other side of the scale, Cassandra, genuinely concerned for her daughter's welfare, is indisputably a nagging wife. Lamberto, sensible and right in nearly everything, is a pompous preacher to his son. Even Libano, clever and perfectly devoted to his master, is made a figure of fun at the end because of his fear of being blamed if things turn out badly. The only completely sensible and righteous character is Manoli, who, because of his purely mechanical role, can scarcely be considered to be a personage of the comedy at all.

In this relative balancing of good and bad traits, Landi relinquished the possibility of heavy satire and moralizing in favor of good-humored sophistication and breadth of vision. There is an underlying implication that we all know too much about life to believe in the frequency of either exaggerated faults or exaggerated virtues. Moreover, one infers, human nature presents on the whole an interesting and diverting spectacle, provided one is tolerant enough to enjoy it. This tone of "serene irony" was adduced by the celebrated critic Benedetto Croce as the distinctive and most essential quality of the mock epic *Or-*

lando furioso, which he considered to be the highest literary creation of the Renaissance.[28] The tone is found also in Ariosto's best play, *La Lena,* whose chief character is a dishonest, irascible—but very sensible—woman. Landi's work is not, of course, in the same class with those of Ariosto, but there is between them an affinity of period and intellectual climate.

The term *erudite comedy* is grossly misleading in one respect—in its suggestion of formal and scholarly language. In point of fact, the comedy, despite its observance of rules set by learned critics, contained the most natural and informal language of any genre. Today it has become the main source of information about conversational Italian of the time, just as the plays of Terence and Plautus provide the main texts of conversational Latin. From a strictly literary point of view, the most salient quality of the language in prose comedies, and in Landi's in particular, is the frequency (1) of metaphors and similes and (2) of proverbs. A majority of the images and general formulations have to do with psychological and moral phenomena and with the mechanism of thought and emotion:

"A bitch in a hurry has blind puppies";

"You can talk because your tooth doesn't hurt."

Most of these were no doubt clichés, but that does not invalidate their general effect, which is one of an intense, unpedantic interest in typical human psychology.

We have no reason to complain of this obsession with typical psychology, even if it often crowded out social commentary, local color, and lyricism. It was essential to the neoclassical comedy of Renaissance Italy, and it was to be just as evident a century later, when the genre reached its perfection amid another national culture, with the plays of Jean-Baptiste Poquelin Molière.

THE POETRY

The verses recited at the banquet and in conjunction with the comedy are not pure poetry, since, like the librettos of opera, they are dependent upon accompanying music for much of their effect. They have, however, a literary side, and the fact that they are printed separate from the music shows that a great deal of importance was attached to their meaning and to details of expression. During the Renaissance, in fact, the texts of songs and ditties were often written with-

[28]See especially his *Ariosto, Corneille e Shakespeare.*

out any particular music in mind; frequently, indeed, they failed ever to be set to music at all.

In his account Giambullari mentions three poetic forms: *stanze, canzoni,* and *canzonette,* but in the title of the work all of the poetic compositions in question are referred to as *madriali.* The meaning of the various terms was not, in his time, firmly fixed. In the fourteenth century *stanza* had been used normally to designate a strophe of eight lines, often *endecasillabi* in *ottava rima.* The *endecasillabo,* the classical line for serious poetry in Italian, had eleven syllables, of which the tenth, penultimate, was the last stressed. The *ottava rima* rhyme scheme was a, b, a, b, a, b, c, c. Later, the term *stanza* came to be used more loosely to mean simply strophes, or even just verses in general. It was most commonly applied to narrative or expository verse and particularly to that of occasional inspiration. The most famous example is found in Politian's *Stanze per la giostra,* written to celebrate the victory of Giuliano dei Medici in a grand joust staged in Florence in 1475. Gelli's *stanze* conform to all these definitions, both to the original formal ones and to those concerning substance.

The *canzone* was one of the oldest poetic forms in Italian; Dante had given it a good deal of critical attention in the *De vulgari eloquentia,* and many of the compositions of his *Vita nuova* are *canzoni.* The form normally entailed five or six strophes with a complicated rhyme scheme, followed by a brief *commiato* or *envoi.* The subject was usually amorous–virtually always, at any rate, lyrical. The name *canzonette* was given often to poems of the same general sort but with fewer strophes and shorter lines. In the sixteenth century the formal requirements of both kinds of poem were very ill defined.

The term *madrigal* is, in poetry if not in music, also loosely defined. Like those of the ballad, the *canzone,* and the sonnet, the madrigal form was of modern and more or less popular origin; that is, it had not been developed in antiquity and revived by scholarly writers of the Renaissance. It was common in the fourteenth century, especially in the second half. Petrarch composed a few madrigals, which are included in his collection of lyric poetry, the *Canzoniere.* Other madrigalists of the *trecento,* more important because of the quantity of their production, were Franco Sacchetti, Niccolò Soldanieri, and Alessio Donati. During the fourteenth and fifteenth centuries form and content became fairly well established. There were normally two or three tercets of *endecasillabi,* bound in a complicated rhyme scheme. The tone was usually idyllic and the content amorous. Before 1500, however, form and content as well began to vary greatly. Our poet Strozzi, who is perhaps, despite his relative obscurity, the best-remembered practitioner of the form in the sixteenth century, is credited with having given it new scope and flexibility. By 1539 the term was already quite loose in meaning; Giambullari, in his title, plainly used it to designate not only Strozzi's short poems written for the *intermedii* but also those of Gelli recited by the various geographical personifications at the banquet. For him, obviously, there was no clear distinction between *madriali* and *canzoni* or *canzonette.*

One must properly raise the question of the literary value of the poetic compositions, though it cannot of course be settled objectively. The inspiration is frankly occasional, but, as all students of older literature know, that fact is not in itself a bar to excellence or even to genius. Gelli's stanzas, the most purely occasional of the verses, have, however, little to recommend them as poetry. Their metaphors and conceits seem unusually contrived and arid, and the brilliant, terse epigrams that often enliven better narrative and expository poems of the same general kind are absent. What commends his lines to attention now is simply their content—their prose content. The *canzoni* and *canzonette,* put into the mouths of the geographical characters, are less pretentious and have, here and there, a pleasing lyrical quality. Strozzi's poems for the *intermedii* are still simpler and have more universal themes. They too, of course, are occasional, but only one of them, the song of the sirens seeking the Duchess, is obtrusively so. The others—the songs of Dawn and Night, the lament of Silenus, the song of the huntresses—are pretty poems on the light pastoral themes dear to poets of the High Renaissance, such as Lorenzo il Magnifico. Judged thus as small compositions in a minor and elegant genre, they may come off very well indeed.

EMBLEMS AND CLASSICAL INSCRIPTIONS

Many of the sculptures, drawings, and paintings Giambullari reports having seen at the triumphal arch and in the courtyards partake of literature as well as of the fine arts. A large number of drawings belong to the curious field of emblematics, which had its greatest development in the sixteenth and seventeenth centuries.[29] An emblem consisted, roughly speaking, of the representation of animals and objects—seldom of humans—for symbolic purposes. The pictures were often accompanied by interpretative inscriptions, normally in Latin but occasionally in the vernacular. Some of the mottoes were original, but many had been taken from classical literature or from the Bible. Emblems chosen by individuals as their personal symbols were called *imprese* or, in English, *devices*.

If emblems may seem to us closely related to medieval enigmas, they were also a manifestation of the Renaissance's renewed interest in antiquity. The mode for them derived in large part from the discovery of a book of *Hieroglyphica,* supposedly written by an ancient Egyptian called Horus Apollo and translated into Greek by a man named Philippus. (Horus Apollo is referred to by name in Giambullari's account.) A manuscript of the work was brought to Florence in 1419, and it eventually commanded great interest among scholars. Marsilio Ficino, notably, was fascinated by the work. It was thought that Egyptian hieroglyphics had been a purely ideographical form of writing—that they had not corresponded to words—and that priests in using them had captured divine ideas. The first printed edition, in Greek, of Horus Apollo's work appeared in Venice in 1505, the first Latin version in Bologna in 1516. As the mode of emblems grew during the sixteenth century, many other editions, including some in vernacular languages, were published. There appeared as well many original works dealing with the subject. Countless scholars studied emblems seriously, and nobles vied with each other in the invention of ingenious and elevating devices. In the general enthusiasm it was apparently felt that emblems not only *expressed* conceptions better than straightforward words could do but also that they *created* conceptions or so altered commonplace ideas that something quite new was born. Before modern readers lay such feelings to superstition or to prescientific naïveté, they may reflect that similar claims are admitted now for metaphor and symbol in contemporary poetry.

In emblem books of the time we have found interpretations of a number of the devices described by Giambullari. One of the most important emblem authorities of the century, Paolo

[29]Our information for this account is taken largely from Mario Praz's masterly work of history and bibliography, *Studies in Seventeenth Century Imagery,* 2 vols.

Giovio, was present at the wedding celebrations, where he saw "many [devices] made by cultured and ingenious men."[30]

Giovio's account discusses several of the Medici devices. His interpretations and others found elsewhere are summarized in our notes. Many of the emblems, some difficult and some easy, are left to the deciphering imagination of our readers.

The paintings, properly speaking, were a different sort of contribution to the festivities, but the inscriptions below and around them, often taken from classical literary sources, afford comparison with the emblems. The quotations attached to the scenes from the lives of Cosimo and other Medici were meant to dignify these men's deeds with an implication of universal import. Parallels between ancient and contemporary history were clearly prized. Charles V was a new

[30]*Dialogo delle imprese...*, 51.

Page of Giovio's *Dialogo delle imprese,* showing one of Cosimo's devices superimposed on a contemporary representation of Florence
—Courtesy British Museum

DI MONS. GIOVIO. 51

DOM. *Poiche voi hauete raccontate l'imprese di questi Illustrissimi Prencipi della Casa de' Medici già morti, siate cōtento anchora di dir qualche cosa di quelle, che porta l'Eccellentissimo Signor Duca Cosmo, delle quali tante se ne veggono in palazzo de' detti Medici.* GIO. *Certo che il giorno delle nozze sue io ne vidi molte fabricate da gentil' ingegni, ma sopra tutte vna me ne piacque per esser molto accōmodata à sua Eccellenza, laquale hauendo per horoscopo & ascendente suo il Capricorno, che hebbe anche Augusto Cesare (come dice Suetonio) e però fece batter la moneta con tale imagine, mi parue questo bizarro animale molto al proposito, massimamente che Carlo Quinto Imperatore, sotto la cui protettione fiorisce il principato del prefato Signor Duca, hebbe anch' egli il medesimo ascēdēte. E parue cosa fatale, che'l Duca Cosmo, quel medesimo dì di Calende d'Agosto, nel qual giorno Augusto conseguì la vittoria contra Marc'antonio e*

g 2

Augustus; the Sultan of Turkey was a new Xerxes. In one painting, that depicting the expulsion of the Capuan ambassadors by the Roman Senate, the ancient event was shown and its Florentine equivalent merely implied. Usually, the recent event was depicted, and ancient or mythological parallels were suggested by inscriptions.

One wonders which literary man was charged with choosing the quotations to be inscribed. Gelli, perhaps, or Giambullari himself. Whoever was responsible executed his commission rather carelessly. The original context of the quotations often has scarcely any meaningful relationship to the context of the paintings, though the isolated phrases may be narrowly pertinent. It was plainly considered better, in most instances, to take a rather inappropriate phrase from ancient literature than to devise a better one from scratch.

The classical authors quoted—Vergil, Horace, Catullus, Ovid, and Livy—are all from the golden, Augustan age of Latin literature, just as Augustus himself is often evoked as the most glorious of rulers. Florence had, in the earlier Renaissance, led Western Europe in Hellenic studies, but there are here no quotations from Greek literature and Greek civilization of classical times is scarcely referred to. Mythology is, of course, in evidence everywhere, but it is mythology that may be found in Vergil. No doubt the prestige of Greek philosophy was undiminished in 1539, though no evidence of that fact appears in the wedding productions. Well past, however, was the time, in the early *quattrocento,* when Leonardo Bruni could wish to present Florence as a city-state comparable to Athens.[31] Imperial Rome was the current political and cultural model. Cosimo did not aspire to be a Pericles but to become a favored vassal of the new Augustus, and the emblems used in his wedding festivities made this fact clear.

---

[31]In his *Laudatio Florentiae Urbis.* See Hans Baron, *The Crisis of the Early Italian Renaissance,* rev. ed., 211–24.

III. Musicological Background

GENERAL

Throughout the Middle Ages and the Renaissance, music played an important role in the state functions of royalty; it served to emphasize grandeur, pomp, and color, essential to the satisfaction of the love of display the ruling class indulged at every opportunity. In the late part of the fifteenth century, dramatic productions with music became an integral part of wedding festivities at court.

The tradition of music in dramatic productions is ancient, dating back to the Greek drama, if not to earlier use. While we know little about the details of performance, we are certain that portions of the ancient dramas were sung or were recited to music. With the decline of the Roman Empire, drama disappeared. When it was revived in the Middle Ages, its home was the Church. Instituted as a teaching device, liturgical drama[1] evolved into elaborate productions with costumes, staging, and music. The music followed the traditions of liturgical plainsong (Gregorian chant), and instruments were probably used to add color and support to the voices. The church became first the concert hall of the Middle Ages, then its theater as well.

The dramatic tradition of the liturgical drama was continued in the mystery plays, miracle plays, and moralities of the fifteenth century.[2] Although these were produced outside the precincts of the church, the bishop's approval was necessary before they could be performed. The productions were most elaborate and realistic as to staging and costumes; some required several days for performance. Sacred and secular monodic tunes, as well as vocal and instrumental polyphonic pieces, were used for music interludes.

In Italy, as early as the fourteenth century, re-

---

[1]For further information, see Gustave Reese, *Music in the Middle Ages,* 193–97; W. L. Smoldon, "Liturgical Drama," *New Oxford History of Music,* Vol. II, 175–219; Smoldon, "Liturgical Music-Drama," *Grove's Dictionary,* 5th ed., Vol. V, 317–43. The *Play of Daniel* and *Herod* have proved most successful in modern performances.

[2]See Walther Lipphardt, "Liturgische Dramen," *MGG,* 8, cols. 1012–48.

ligious plays called *sacre rappresentazioni* were performed during Lent.[3] In the fifteenth and sixteenth centuries, these developed into elaborate productions with costumes and scenery. As in the earlier plays, vocal and instrumental numbers were a part of the whole.

With this tradition of long standing, it is not surprising that, when secular drama was reintroduced in the late fifteenth century, music was an integral part of the productions. To a large extent these plays were written for performance at court and were considered part of the courtly scene. Since nearly every nobleman of means, in order to enhance religious services and as a mark of prestige, maintained his own musical establishment—including composers as well as singers and instrumentalists—it followed that music was woven into these secular events.

Formal and informal records of the second half of the fifteenth century refer frequently to music in these performances. Unfortunately, the music itself has not been recovered and may not have been preserved. The accompanying table lists the productions before 1540 in which music is known to have been used.[4] The list is undoubtedly incomplete; much basic research is necessary before a detailed study can be made of Italian dramatic music in the Renaissance.

The musical interludes in these plays were called *intermedii* or *intermezzi* and usually occurred at the end of each act.[5] The music followed the basic patterns of the popular secular forms of the time.

Italian secular music of the sixteenth century was dominated by the madrigal. It first appeared in print in 1530 and by 1539 had been established as the pre-eminent secular form. It developed from several of the more popular types of Italian vocal music of the late fifteenth and early sixteenth centuries. The most important of these was the *frottola*—a generic term covering several verse forms: *barzelletta, frottola* proper, *strambotto, oda, sonnet, capitolo, canzone, giustiniana, canto carnascialesco,* and *villotta.* All were simi-

---

[3]Gustave Reese, *Music in the Renaissance,* 171–73. For more detail see Alessandro d'Ancona, *Sacre rappresentazioni nei secoli XIV, XV, e XVI.*

[4]The table is based on the compilation in Hans Engel, *Luca Marenzio,* 40–41, with additions. Some discrepancies in dates found in secondary sources cannot be resolved in the present state of research in this area.

[5]For general information about the *intermedii,* see Nino Pirrotta, "Intermedium," *MGG,* 6, cols. 1310–26.

Date	*City*	*Title*	*Poet*	*Composer*
1471	Mantova	*Orfeo*	Poliziano	
1474	Urbino	*Amore al Tribunale della Pudicizia*		
1475	Pesaro			
1480	Roma	*Conversione di S. Paolo*		
1486	Ferrara	*Menaechmi*	Plautus	
	Mantova	*Rappresentazione di Febo e Pitone o di Dafne*		
1487	Ferrara	*Cefalo*	Niccolò da Correggio	Giampietro della Viola
1489	Firenze	*Rappresentazione di SS. Giovanni e Paolo*	Lorenzo il Magnifico	
1492	Napoli	Festival Drama	Jacopo Sannazzaro	
1493	Mantova	*La semidea*	Niccolò da Correggio	
1494	Firenze	*Amicizia*	Jacopo Nardi	
1495	Mantova	*Scene mitologiche*	Serafino Aquilano	
1499	Ferrara	*Trinumo*		
	Casale	*Beatrice*	Galeotto del Caretto	Tromboncino
	Pistoia	*Panfila*		
1501	Ferrara	*Cassina*		
1502	Mantova	*Nozze di Cupidine*	Galeotto del Caretto	Tromboncino
	Ferrara	*5 commedie,* including *Asinaria*	Plautus	Tromboncino
1506	Urbino	*Tirsi*	Baldassare Castiglione	Cesare Gonzaga
	Ferrara	*Pastorale*		
1507	Venezia	Festival Drama	Antonio Rossi	
1512–1519	Firenze	*Commedia in versi*	Lorenzo Strozzi	
1513	Urbino	*La Calandria*	Bibbiena	
1517	Treviso	*Tragedia*	Jacopo del Legname	
1518	Roma	*I Suppositi*	Ludovico Ariosto	
1519	Roma	*Commedie*		
1531	Siena	*Gli ingannati*		
1536	Venezia	*Il Sacrifizio*		
	Firenze	*L'Aridosia*	Lorenzino dei Medici	
1539	Firenze	*Il Commodo*	Antonio Landi	Francesco Corteccia

lar, in that they employed lines of regular length and rhythm and used repetitive stanza patterns. The *barzelletta, oda,* and *strambotto* were most frequently used. The musical settings were strophic, with clearly defined phrases and with occasional phrase repetitions. Melodic interest was in the soprano part. The lower voices (usually three) were conceived in chordal style and could be given an instrumental performance. All the *frottola* forms were intended for solo singing, that is, by only one singer on a part.

The transition from the simple, almost folklike *frottola* to the sophisticated madrigal is too involved and complicated a subject to be treated in detail here. Einstein,[6] Reese,[7] Rubsamen,[8] and others[9] have covered the subject in a comprehensive manner elsewhere. Briefly, the development involved attempts (1) to set poems of a higher literary quality; (2) to employ the more elaborate musical devices in current use in the Franco-Flemish style—the chanson and motet—and to abandon the treble-dominated style of the *frottola* for equal melodic importance of all voices; (3) to devise a more expressive musical setting of the text—emphasis of the mood and emotional quality of the text in the music to bring about a close relationship between the text and the music; (4) a through-composed setting of the text in place of the usual strophic settings.

Leading figures in the early development of the madrigal were the Northerners: Philippe Verdelot (d. *c.* 1552), Adrian Willaert (*c.* 1480–1562), Jacques Arcadelt (*c.* 1505–1572), and the Italian Costanzo Festa (*c.* 1480–1545), who had studied in Paris, probably with Jean Mouton (*c.* 1460–1522). Festa contributed to the music for the wedding that is the subject of this study. The chief contributor, Duke Cosimo's court composer Francesco Corteccia (1504–1571), was also one of the important Italian composers of early madrigals.

The madrigal, in its beginnings, was written for four or five voices in a mixture of imitative and chordal styles. This new form became exceedingly popular, and hundreds were published during the first decade (1530–1540) of its existence; the form remained popular until the sec-

[6]Alfred Einstein, *The Italian Madrigal,* I, 3–166.

[7]Reese, *Music in the Renaissance,* 153–83; 311–28.

[8]W. H. Rubsamen, *Literary Sources of Secular Music in Italy (c. 1500),* University of California Publications in Music, Vol. I, no. 1.

[9]An important recent study is James Haar, ed., *Chanson and Madrigal 1480–1530: Studies in Comparison and Contrast.* The essays by Rubsamen and Heartz and the subsequent discussion are especially valuable.

ond decade of the seventeenth century. In comparison with the later madrigals of Marenzio, Gesualdo, and Monteverdi, these early examples are comparatively simple and straightforward in their musical style and expression. They do, however, mark an important development of a new style, and they are beautiful and expressive works.[10]

As indicated in the table of early dramatic productions with music, various cities had seen such productions, and they became widespread throughout Italy during the sixteenth century. Probably the city of Florence was the scene of the most elaborate productions. The first festival for which the play, descriptions, and music have been preserved is the Medici wedding of 1539. Elaborate musical performances prior to this time were, of course, not rare in Florence; the city had been one of the great musical centers of the fourteenth century.[11] After this great flowering came a period of considerable decline for approximately a century and a half; the music of Florence did not regain international prominence until the end of the sixteenth century, at which time the innovations of the Florentine Camerata and the beginning of opera restored it to its earlier distinction. It is, however, a mistake to assume that the intervening years saw an abandonment of music. Although no new style evolved in Florence, music continued to occupy an important position in the city's life, and a number of major composers were active there at various times.

The dominating family in Florence, the Medici, also played a vital role in its musical development. Shortly after the Medici came to power, they initiated a policy of engaging the best available foreign musicians for their own chapel as well as for the city's Cathedral.[12] Antonio Squarcialupi (1416–1480) was organist at S. Maria del Fiore from 1436 until his death. The greatest composer of the time, Guillaume Dufay (*c.* 1400–1474)[13] was in Florence from 1435 to 1436 as a member of the Papal Choir during Pope Eugenius IV's stay in Florence. While there, Dufay wrote the motet *Nuper Rosarum Flores* for the dedication of Brunelleschi's dome

[10]For further information, see Einstein, *Italian Madrigal,* and Reese, *Music in the Renaissance.*

[11]For a survey of Florentine musical history, see August Buck and Bianca Becherini, "Florenz," *MGG,* 4, cols. 367–94; for a general survey of Italian music in the 15th century, see Nanie Bridgman, *La vie musicale au quattrocento.*

[12]Frank A. d'Accone, "The Singers of San Giovanni in Florence during the 15th Century," *JAMS,* 14 (1961), 307–58.

[13]Reese, *Music in the Renaissance,* 48–59; Heinrich Besseler, "Dufay," *MGG,* 3, cols. 889–911.

for the Cathedral. Evidently, he remained in contact with the Medici throughout his career. A letter to Dufay from Squarcialupi, dated May 1, 1467, enclosed a *canzone* by Lorenzo dei Medici with a request from Lorenzo that Dufay set it to music. If Dufay did so, the music has been lost.

Heinrich Isaac (*c.* 1450–1517), one of the greatest composers of his time, came to Florence in the fall of 1484, probably as music teacher for the sons of Lorenzo il Magnifico. Isaac sang in the chapel of the Baptistery of San Giovanni from 1485 until 1493. While closely connected with Lorenzo's court, Isaac composed *canti carnascialeschi* to Lorenzo's texts. The elaborate *carri,* which flourished under Lorenzo's encouragement and were drawn through the streets as part of the festivities, often contained singers who sang an appropriate *canto carnascialesco.* These productions may be considered a precedent for the later, elaborately staged *intermedii.*[14] In 1492 Isaac composed a setting of Poliziano's elegy on Lorenzo's death.[15] Other important musicians known to have been in Florence during this time included: Johannes Stochem (*c.* 1440–1500), Alexander Agricola (1446–1506), Guillaume Pietrequin, Johannes Ghiselin, Alexander Coppinus, and Bartholomaeus Florentinus Organista.[16] After the death of Lorenzo in 1492 and with the rise of Savonarola, Isaac entered the service of Emperor Maximilian I. Recent discoveries indicate that Isaac spent a good part of this period in Florence.[17]

Even after the overthrow of the Medici, Florence continued to attract distinguished musicians. A number of important composers resided in Florence (although probably only briefly) during the time of the Republic, as indicated by the motets written to timely political texts.[18] These composers included: Andreas de Silva, Costanzo Festa, Francesco di Layolle (*c.* 1475–*c.* 1540), Bernardo Pisano (1490–1548), Jacques Arcadelt, and Philippe Verdelot. One might wonder why Verdelot, one of the most famous of the early madrigal composers, was not asked to contribute to the wedding festival of 1539. As Lowinsky points out, he was probably excluded because he

---

[14]See Federico Ghisi, *I canti carnascialeschi,* and his *Feste musicali della Firenze Medicea (1480–1589).*

[15]Reese, *Music in the Renaissance,* 170.

[16]Frank A. d'Accone, "Heinrich Isaac in Florence: New and Unpublished Documents," *MQ,* 49 (1963), 464–83.

[17]D'Accone, "Heinrich Isaac in Florence."

[18]Edward E. Lowinsky, "A Newly Discovered Sixteenth-Century Motet Manuscript at the Biblioteca Vallicelliana in Rome," *JAMS,* 3 (1950), 173–232.

had been a strong supporter of the anti-Medici faction.[19]

With the return of the Medici to power, music evidently enjoyed princely patronage. Little is known, however, of the day-by-day activities of the musicians at court, for only a few documents have been found that describe them. One visitor to Florence was a writer of plays and *novelle* and a composer, Girolamo Parabosco (*c.* 1524–1557). He described his visit to Florence in his comedy *La Notte* (Venetia, 1546):

I am not quite willing to say *all,* but I will certainly concede it of the greatest share, for we have in this happy city—which God preserve and make happy—the most excellent Adrian Willaert, who–besides the perfection he has in the science of music, which is such that not only does he leave behind all those who have composed in past centuries but also causes one to believe that no one in the future can ever equal him—is so courteous, so genteel, and so pleasant and modest that one may set him up as an example of all these virtues. But now that I recall musicians, and in keeping with the subject, as I was passing through Florence not many months ago, I lodged with a Francesco Corteccia, musician of His Excellency, truly he, too, a man most perfect in this science and so courteous and gentle that it is a marvel. What shall I say then of Antonio da Lucca, also a player of His Excellency, a man of such perfection on the lute, as well as on the *cornetto* and many other instruments, that one would find none to equal him either in Italy or abroad? This man and all that rare company of players of the most illustrious Duke are so gentle, so wise, that, indeed, they are more beloved for their social grace than for their sweet and most suave harmony, which they do so marvelously all together that by all they are judged angels descended from heaven. So, Falsetta, every time you talk of musicians, speak cautiously, for although the majority are crazy and insolent, there are, however, many more throughout Italy as well as abroad who are wise, modest, and genteel, as are those whom I have mentioned to you.[20]

Additional information is found in the *Libro terzo* of the *Ragionamenti accademici* of Cosimo Bartoli (Venetia, Francesco de Franceschi Senese, 1567). The book relates a conversation that took place in the 1540's among Lorenzo Altinori, Piero Darica, and Pierfrancesco Giambullari, author of the general account of the wedding:

[19]Lowinsky, "A Newly Discovered Manuscript," 187–88.

[20]The translations for this and the following documents were taken from Ann Watson McKinley's "Francesco Corteccia's Music to Latin Texts." (Ph.D. dissertation, University of Michigan, 1962), 34.

Lorenzo Altinori: And of our countrymen here in Florence, you are not saying anything at all?

Piero Darica: Concerning Messer Francesco Corteccia, I will let Messer Pier Francesco speak here; for, both being canons at the same church and having continuously lived worthily together, he will be better able than I to speak of him.

Pierfrancesco Giambullari: Concerning him—lest it appear that I do it out of adulation—I will say only this, that there are by now so many of his compositions that they make him known by themselves; and besides this, his worthy and talented scholars, of whom he has produced so many in the now fifteen years that he has been *maestro di cappella* of His Excellency, show how excellent he is in this profession of his; but I shall also tell you a thing about him that you perhaps do not know since you have not associated with him as continuously as I have.

Lorenzo Altinori: Pray tell. . . .

Pierfrancesco Giambullari: Know, then, that I believe for certain that today he is perhaps as great a theorist as anyone else who is working in this profession. . . .

Piero Darica: Now tell me, don't we still have here Messer Matteo Rampollini, whose compositions—I give you my word—have earned for him a marvelous reputation, especially among the foreigners?

Pierfrancesco Giambullari: Certainly one cannot say anything of him but that he is skillful.

Lorenzo Altinori: I remember the last time I was in Rome, one day I visited again the house of Messer Bindo Altoviti. Many of the best musicians who could be found in Rome in those days were there; the discussion turned to his compositions, and they were greatly praised.

Piero Darica: One cannot deny him his competence, for surely, both in composing and in resetting, he is skillful, fast, and clever.

Lorenzo Altinori: Have we others here in Florence?

Piero Darica: We have many young men here who are continuously producing works, but since they are young, one cannot say anything about them as yet except that one sees much can be expected from them in time.

Lorenzo Altinori: Now tell me please, Messer Piero, which delights you more, to hear singing or to hear playing?

Piero Darica: It depends on whom I might be hearing.

Lorenzo Altinori: To me, playing is more pleasant, because in hearing singers I hear so often certain voices out of tune, rough, and mostly not together that they annoy me amazingly.

Piero Darica: You would not speak thus had you listened—at the time of Pope Leo X of blessed memory—to the singing of Carpentras, Consiglion, Bidon, and Biaseron, and others whom I do not remember right now; for, I give you my word, you should have stayed on for a year, so to speak, absorbed in hearing them, so gracefully did they handle their voices, and here in Florence there was a Messer Nicolo di Lore, who sang with a marvelous grace. And our Baccio Moschini—it is not possible that he could have sung with more grace.

Lorenzo Altinori: Beautifully, surely, for I, too, have heard him many times, and aside from him I have not heard anyone in Florence who pleases me more in his singing than Ser Piero and Batista, also of the Corteccia family, although one could praise very much Ser Giampiero[21] if he had had a good voice.

Piero Darica: But tell me now, since we are on these matters, where do we leave our Messer Antonio da Lucca?

Lorenzo Altinori: O, how well you speak. I am convinced that Nature has wanted to show in his case how much good she knows how to, and can, produce when she wants to; for although she has given us many of those whom we have mentioned, as most excellent in only one of these faculties, she has wanted to show afterwards in Messer Antonio her ultimate power in this age; because she has made him excellent not only in one of these faculties alone, but in many all at once; because he does not yield to anyone today in playing the lute, he is a marvel on the viola, and in playing the *cornetto,* I believe—rather, I am absolutely certain—he is far ahead not only of all players of the present time, but also of all of the past, and I believe that it will be well into the future before anyone will be found who will be a match for him. . . .

Lorenzo Altinori: You have placed Messer Antonio first among the *cornetto* players in our time; now tell me, was not a certain Mosatello in Milan skillful?

Piero Darica: Very skillful, certainly, and at the time of Leo there was a certain Giovan, a very wonderful master of the *cornetto,* but I like most Messer Antonio's playing, nor have I ever heard more beautiful caprices, nor more beautiful fantasies than his, nor more neatly made trills or flowing figuration—which are such that they stupefy me.

Lorenzo Altinori: Whom have we among the players of His Excellency who are exceptional, other than Messer Antonio?

Piero Darica: They are all skillful, but when it comes to playing a trombone, Bartolomeo has been and is still truly exceptional, old as he is. And even though there is in Bologna a certain Zachary and a

[21]Ghisi identifies Ser Giampiero as Giampiero Masacone, who wrote one of the madrigals in the wedding music. *Feste musicali,* xx, note 3.

son of his, and in Venice Geronimo, cousin of the said Bartolomeo, who play miraculously, Bartolomeo nevertheless has remained so exceptional in his time that he has acquired the family name and also the cognomen from his talent on that instrument. In addition to which, he still plays the *viola* very well, and when it comes to handling a *ribechino* he has no equal; nor has he only these parts, but he is so good, so pleasant, and so kind that, were one to depict the goodness, the pleasantness, and the kindness found in the world, one could certainly not do better than to portray him with a mountain of instruments and of friends around him. And besides this, in his old age he has two sons who are becoming exceptional. You also have here Messer Lorenzo da Lucca, not a bit inferior to any of these who have been mentioned; also, he has in his playing a certain grace and facility and such a pleasant way about him that he amazes me; in addition to which he also handles both the *viola* and the lute with a marvelous grace. And it is not necessary to discuss the other of His Excellency's musicians of this kind; yet rest assured that all are so skillful that there is no prince in Italy nor, perhaps, even outside of Italy, who has better [musicians] than he.

Lorenzo Altinori: But what do you say about Moschino's playing?

Piero Darica: Moschino plays either organs or other instruments with such grace, facility, and grandeur joined to such knowledge of music that I believe (rather, I am absolutely certain) that he has few equals; and if I were to say perhaps none, I do not know whether I would be making a mistake but I do not think so—and this in addition to his other parts, which are gifts by Heaven to few, for, as we [earlier] said, he has sung and still sings delightfully and has composed many very beautiful things. But what has left me marvelling in his playing is that I have heard him play sometimes for his own pleasure without many listeners, only for his own desire, and for an hour take up a manner of playing in counterpoint, which makes me put aside every annoyance, every displeasure, and every bitterness, however great, which I might have in my spirit; and I hold for certain that in this style there are few who might approach him.[22]

Another glimpse into Florentine musical life is found in Carlo Lenzoni's book *In difesa della lingua fiorentina, et di Dante* (Fiorenza: L. Torrentino, 1556). At the beginning of the *Giornata seconda,* Lenzoni describes how the academicians relaxed before they resumed their discussions:

And so our divine Antonio da Lucca and [Bartolomeo] Trombone began to sing and to play the lute with a sweet and true harmony, whereupon several

[22]McKinley, "Corteccia's Music," 38–42.

remained to hear and others went into the room in order (so they said) to hear the music more sweetly and more blended. And a double good resulted to them, for invited by the food, and by the hour, customary perhaps to some, and attracted by the harmony, they lightly went to sleep—if one can call sleep that sweet dozing which hears and understands what goes on. But as soon as the music ended—almost as though only the music had kept them thus bound—they got up, awakened and happy.[23]

THE COMPOSERS

Only a few biographical details are known about FRANCESCO CORTECCIA, who composed most of the pieces for the wedding of 1539. Born in Arezzo in 1504, it is thought that he studied with Francesco di Layolle, the younger (b. 1491), who was active in Florence during the second and third decades of the sixteenth century; Layolle was reputed to have been the music teacher also of Benvenuto Cellini and Andrea del Sarto.[24]

The earliest biographical reference to Corteccia is in Michele Poccianti's *Catalogus Scriptorum florentinorum* (Florentiae, 1589):

Francesco Corteccia, a venerable canon at San Lorenzo's and beloved disciple of music—for he was a noted organist as well as an eminent musician—whom His Serene Highness Cosimo, Grand Duke of Tuscany, made, as the best master, the head of the chapel, over which he presided with the highest distinction for almost thirty years. While he was still a young man he composed not a few madrigals, full of the greatest pleasantness; motets, moreover, and other pieces of that kind, which customarily are sung on solemn days. And finally when an old man, he published *responsoria* and also lessons for Holy Week. He died in Florence in 1571 in the month of May; his body rests in the church of San Lorenzo.[25]

In the late eighteenth century, Pier Nolasco Cianfogni made a study of the clergy attached to the basilica of San Lorenzo; his entry for Corteccia reads:

Francesco Corteccia, [son] of Bernardo, [was] already chaplain by March 5, 1531, then elected supernumerary canon by the chapter on January 25, 1549, afterwards absolute [that is, regular] canon from 1563 until June 7, 1571, when he died.[26] He was

[23]McKinley, "Corteccia's Music," 43.

[24]McKinley, "Corteccia's Music," 1–32, gives most detailed information on Corteccia's life to date.

[25]Michele Poccianti, *Catalogus scriptorum florentinorum,* 71, quoted in McKinley, "Corteccia's Music," 2.

[26]The discrepancy in the month of death between Poccianti and Cianfogni cannot be resolved at this time.

most excellent in counterpoint and was, in short, held esteemed not only in his native Florence, but also in all of Italy. He was selected by Cosimo I, who had a high opinion of his worth, as the master of his chapel.[27]

Cianfogni also found the following item in the Archives of the Curia:

1554. Don Francesco, son of the former Bernardo de Corteccia, canon at San Lorenzo's in Florence, and priest of the parish of Santa Maria de Micciano in the diocese of Arezzo.[28]

In 1549, the Duke had made Corteccia a canon at San Lorenzo. As was customary at this time, in order to increase the gift, the Duke gave Corteccia a prebend from another parish, which he could receive *in absentia.* A little later Corteccia was forced to petition the Duke to preserve this gift:

To the most illustrious and most excellent Lord Duke, Francesco Corteccia, servant of Your Excellency, deposes and says that some years ago, through Your Excellency's personal action, he had been given, and had conferred on him, the church of Micciano with its annexes at Anghiari, under the assumption that its priest was dead, and that Your Excellency afterward, having found that the said priest was not dead, willed, since he was exiled and a rebel, that the said Francesco in any case should again have the incomes: and thus up to today he has possessed them and possesses them: now since today he has been told that the said priest is dead, he therefore begs and supplicates Your Excellency that Your Excellency deign to cause him, just as the first time Your Excellency did in Your Excellency's kindness, to be invested again with the said church, along with its annexes, of which the people of Micciano and the Counts of Monte d'Oglio consider themselves masters and which by the one and the other, through Your Excellency's intercession, were conferred on him. And so he begs Your Excellency to deign to act so that he not be bereft of the said church, since there remains for him little or nothing else to live on, and to do honor to Your Excellency, whom our Lord God preserve and make happy.

To Messer Lelio, may he cause it to be done.[29]

Corteccia spent his mature artistic life in the service of Duke Cosimo I. He dedicated his pub-

[27]Pier Nolasco Cianfogni, *Memorie istoriche dell'Ambrosiana Regia Basilica di S. Lorenzo di Firenze,* I, 253, quoted in McKinley, "Corteccia's Music," 6.

[28]Cianfogni, *Memorie istoriche,* I, 254, as translated in McKinley, "Corteccia's Music," 7.

[29]Domenico Moreni, *Continuazione delle Memorie istoriche dell'Ambrosiana Imperial Basilica di S. Lorenzo di Firenze,* II, 167, as translated in McKinley, "Corteccia's Music," 8.

lications to his patron, and many of his works were special commissions of the Duke, the two most famous being the music for the wedding festivities of 1539 and of 1565.

Corteccia is an important name in the history of the madrigal as well as of the *intermedii*. His works first appeared in print in May of 1539—two madrigals in a collection of madrigals by Arcadelt. The wedding music of 1539 was published in August of the same year. His first book of madrigals, *Libro primo de madriali a quattro voci,* was printed in 1544 by Gerolamo Scotto in Venice. It was reprinted with additions in 1547 by Gardane in Venice, who had printed the faulty (according to Giambullari) edition of the wedding music. In that year Gardane also printed Corteccia's *Libro primo de madriali a cinque & a sei voci* and his *Libro secondo de madriali a quatro voci*. Seven of the wedding madrigals were included in these two collections; however, no mention of their use in the wedding festivities was made in these later publications. Madrigals by Corteccia appeared in a total of twenty-eight other collections. In all, a total of one hundred and eleven of his madrigals have been preserved. The opening work of the wedding music, the motet *Ingredere,* was reprinted in 1564 in the *Thesaurus musicus* (Nuremberg: Montanus and Nueber). Three volumes of his sacred music were published—*Responsoria* for Holy Week (1570) and two volumes of *Canticas* (1571). At least one other volume was planned, but no trace of it has been found.[30] His *Hinnario,*[31] a collection of thirty-two hymns for the entire church year, exists in manuscript in the Biblioteca Medicea Laurenziana in Florence. The collection is dedicated to Duke Cosimo.

❧

COSTANZO FESTA was one of the important figures in the early development of the madrigal.[32] He was born in the diocese of Turin, probably around 1480.[33] Evidently, he spent some time in Paris, for he composed several motets to texts

[30]See McKinley for detailed discussion of Corteccia's sacred music and for the transcription into modern notation of four hymns, six responses, seven motets, and the Canticle of Zachary.

[31]Glen Haydon, "The Dedication of Francesco Corteccia's *Hinnario,*" *JAMS,* 13 (1960), 112–16. Ten of the hymns, edited by Haydon, are published in *Musica Liturgica,* Vol. I, fasc. 4; Vol. II, fasc. 2.

[32]Einstein, *Italian Madrigal,* I, 157–59; Reese, *Music in the Renaissance,* 319-21.

[33]See Knud Jeppesen, "Costanzo Festa," *MGG,* 4, cols. 90–102.

dealing with French topics of the time. Perhaps he studied there with Jean Mouton, one of the great composers of the time, who was in the service of Francis I.[34] Otherwise, one is at a loss to explain his mastery of polyphony, a characteristic of the Northern composers only. During the time of the Republic, he lived in Florence and composed several political motets.[35] In 1517 he became a member of the Papal Chapel, and on November 1 of that year received a benefice from Pope Leo X (son of Lorenzo il Magnifico). Lowinsky believes that Festa wrote a madrigal for the accession of Alessandro Medici to the rule of Florence in 1532,[36] a circumstance that explains his inclusion among the composers for the 1539 wedding festival. In 1543 illness prevented Festa from accompanying the Pope to Bologna; he died early in March of 1545. His large musical output includes Masses, motets, Magnificats, and madrigals.[37]

Little is known of the other three contributors to the wedding music: Giovanni Pietro Masaconi, Baccio Moschini, and Matteo Rampollini. Evidently, Masaconi was a professional musician in Florence. His madrigal for the wedding banquet, "Ecco Signor Volterra," is the only composition of his known to exist; the only historical reference to him is in the passage of Bartoli's *Ragionamenti accademici* quoted above. Bartolomeo (Baccio) Moschini served as organist at S. Maria del Fiore from 1539 to 1552 and was a highly respected musician, as shown by the references to him by Bartoli and Doni. Moschini died April 30, 1552.[38]

Rampollini, a leading figure in Florence for some time, was highly esteemed as a composer by his contemporaries. The earliest record of his activities was made in the spring of 1520, when he was appointed as a replacement for Pisano in the Cathedral choir.[39] According to Poccianti,[40] he died in 1560, an old man. In 1545 he published a *Primo libro de la musica di alcune Canzoni Del*

---

[34]Edward Lowinsky, "The Medici Codex," *Annales Musicologiques,* 5, 89–98.

[35]Lowinsky, "A Newly Discovered Manuscript," 191.

[36]Lowinsky, "A Newly Discovered Manuscript," 194.

[37]A complete edition of his works, edited by Alexander Main, is in the process of publication by the American Institute of Musicology *(Corpus Mensurabilis Musicae,* XXV).

[38]Emilio Sanesi, "Maestri d'organo in S. Maria del Fiore (1436–1600)," *Note d'Archivio,* 14 (1937), 175.

[39]Frank A. d'Accone, "Bernardo Pisano, an Introduction to His Life and Works," *Musica Disciplina,* 17 (1963), 123.

[40]Poccianti, *Catalogus Scriptorum,* 125.

Divin Poeta M. Francesco Petrarca (Lyons: Jacques Moderne). This he dedicated to Duke Cosimo; it consists, with one exception, of *canzoni* by Petrarca in the new form of the cyclic *canzone,* with certain stanzas intended for performance by fewer voices. In addition to the two madrigals for the wedding banquet, seven of his madrigals were included in collections published in 1547, 1562, and 1582.[41] Only two of these were new. His total output numbers fifty-seven. None of the madrigals written for the wedding banquet were reprinted, nor are they known to exist in manuscript.

THE MUSIC

Although the wedding music was composed on commission and probably completed in a short time, its quality is consistently high throughout. The beauty of the music becomes truly apparent in performance. It was, of course, written for immediate appeal; in melodic, harmonic, and dissonant treatment and predominately duple rhythm, it follows the conventions of the time.[42] Aside from its intrinsic value as music, it is interesting as an early precursor of opera and as an early example of instrumental scoring.

Motet Ingredere. The opening piece, by Corteccia, written for outdoor performance, is in the style of the large ceremonial motet. In eight parts, according to the *Tavola* (opposite) in the cantus part of the 1539 edition, it was sung by twenty-four singers, accompanied by four *cornetti* and four *tromboni.* Doubling of this sort (there were no separate parts for the instruments) was a normal practice of the time that was especially appropriate for an outdoor presentation. Corteccia generally sets the text syllabically; harmony and rhythms are uncomplicated; phrases are short, with frequent points of imitation. The range of the parts indicates two soprano *cornetti,* two tenor *cornetti,* two tenor trombones, and two bass trombones.

BANQUET MUSIC

Eight madrigals were composed for the banquet

[41]See Emil Vogel, *Bibliothek der Gedruckten Weltlichen Vocalmusik Italiens.*

[42]Ten numbers are ₵; four, C; and the concluding dance-like *Bacco Bacco,* triple (C3). The extensive use of Ionian and Dorian modes tends towards a tonal—major-minor—feeling.

LA TAVOLA.

Ingredere a otto uoci di Franc. corteccia cantato ſopra l'arco del portone della porta al prato da uintiquatro uoci da una banda, et da l'altra da quatro tromboni, et quatro cornetti nella entrata della Illuſtriſſima Ducheſſa. II

Sacro et ſanto himeneo a noue uoci di Franc. corteccia cantato dalle muſe con le ſette ſeguenti canzonette il giorno del conuito. V

Piu che mai uaga a quatro uoci	Conſtantio feſta	X
Lieta per honorarte a quatro uoci	Ser Mattio rampollini	XII
Ecco Signor uolterra a cinque uoci	Io. Petrus maſaconus	XIIII
Come lieta ſi moſtra a quatro uoci	Conſtantio feſta	XVI
Non men ch'ogn'altra lieta a quatro uoci	Baccio moſchini	XVIII
Ecco la fida ancella a quatro uoci	Ser Mattio rampollini	XX
Ecco Signor il Tebro a cinque uoci	Baccio Moſchini	XXII

Muſicha della comedia di Franc. Corteccia recitata al ſecondo conuito.

Vattene almo riposo a quatro uoci cantata dall'aurora, et ſonata con uno graue cimbolo con organetti et con uarii regiſtri per principio della comedia XXIIII

Guardane almo paſtore a ſei uoci cantata a la fine del primo atto da ſei paſtori, et dipoi ricantata da detti et ſonata inſieme da ſei altri paſtori con le ſtorte. XXV

Chi ne l'a tolt'oime a ſei uoci cantata a la fine del ſecondo atto da tre ſirene, et da tre monſtri marini ſonata con tre trauerſe, et da tre Ninfe marine con tre liuti tutti inſieme XXVI

O begli anni del'oro a quatro uoci ſonata a la fine del terzo atto da Sileno con un uiolone ſonando tutte le parti, et cantando il ſoprano XXVII

Hor chi mai cantera a quatro uoci cantata a la fine dil quarto atto da otto nimphe cacciatrici XXVIII

Vientene almo riposo a cinque uoci cantata alla fine del quinto atto dalla notte, et ſonata con quatro tromboni XXIX

Bacco bacco eu oe a quatro uoci cantata et ballata da quatro Baccante et quatro ſatiri, et ſonata da altri otto ſatiri, con uary ſtrumenti tutti ad un tempo, laquale ſubito dopo la notte fu la fine della comedia. XXX

Tavola, Musiche fatte, 1539 edition
—Nationalbibliothek, Vienna

by Corteccia, Festa,[43] Masaconi, Moschini, and Rampollini. The opening work, *Sacro et santo Hymeneo,* by Corteccia, is scored for nine voices. Although arrangement in nine parts was not the usual practice in madrigal writing at this time, this work was thus conceived so as to represent the nine Muses. While there is no indication in the *Tavola* as to instrumental accompaniment for this madrigal, according to Giambullari each of the nine Muses carried an instrument: *trombone, dolzaina, violone, piffero, flauto, leuto, storta, cornetto,* or *ribechino.*[44] Possibly, all the abovementioned instruments were used to double the voices. The range of these instruments is varied enough to make this possible; as has been mentioned previously, doubling of this sort was a common practice. The description, however, states: "Then the Muses, most sweetly singing, pronounced the following *canzone* for nine: . . ." An unaccompanied performance would also have been entirely possible and satisfactory.

The remaining madrigals, each representing a city, river, etc.—possessions of Cosimo—are for four or five voices and in the style of the early madrigal. Neither in the Description nor the *Tavola* of the music is there any mention of instruments being used with these works; presumably they were sung unaccompanied.[45] Some of the madrigals are for low voices (men); others call for normal SATB arrangement. Possibly, these were sung by men also, with countertenors or boys singing the treble and alto parts. The participation of women in the performance of early madrigals is still an open question. In *Il Tebro* there is an amusing play on the word *Ecco (here* or *echo),* as the second voice imitates the first on this word, in the manner of an echo.

The first singer to appear at the banquet was Apollo, who, "holding a lyre in his left hand and a little bow in his right . . . sweetly playing, sang the following stanzas. . . ." Although the text of Apollo's song was printed with the rest of the music, unfortunately no music for the song was included. One may assume that he improvised his songs and accompaniment. It is especially unfortunate that this music was not preserved, for it

[43]Alfred Einstein was in error when he listed three madrigals for the banquet by Festa, in his revision of Vogel's *Bibliography of Italian Secular Music Printed Between the Years 1500–1700,* 630. The third madrigal in his list, "Ardendo in dolce spene," is actually the beginning of the second line of the madrigal in honor of Florence, "Piu che mai vaga et bella."

[44]See pp. 63–66 for description of these instruments.

[45]Use of instruments in modern performance is possible and, in some cases, desirable.

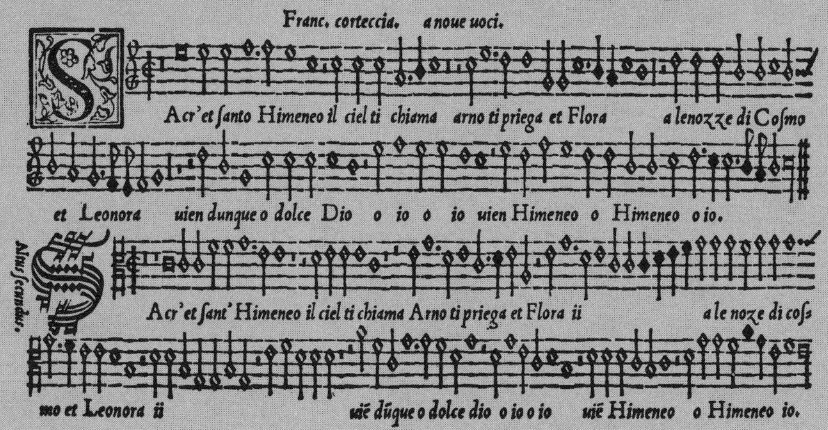

Le muse, Francesco Corteccia, 1539 edition
–Nationalbibliothek, Vienna

would have been an important early example of pre-Camerata monody.

A precedent for improvised song with string accompaniment is found in the performance of the *giustiniane* of the fifteenth century. They were named for the Venetian poet and statesman Leonardo Giustiniani (*c.* 1383–1446), who sang them to his own accompaniment on the lute, *lira da braccio,* or *viola.*[46] Soon, these songs spread throughout Italy and continued popular until the sixteenth century.

The Intermedii

The seven *intermedii* were composed in the madrigal style of the time and were, in fact, included in Corteccia's madrigal collections of 1547. It is interesting to note that in the collections no mention was made of the fact that they had previously served as *intermedii* for the wedding of 1539.[47] They are in four to six parts. While there are chordal sections, the style is essentially contrapuntal. Although the setting of the text is essentially syllabic, there are occasional melismatic passages, not necessarily always in the top part.

One of the most unusual features of the *intermedii* is the instrumental scoring. As has been stated before, there is ample evidence of a long tradition of the use of instruments to double or substitute for voices. The evidence comes from theoretical and nonmusical sources—paintings, drawings, miniatures, and literary material. Rarely does this information relate to a specific piece of music; either the work is not specified, or it seems to have perished. Here, then, is a rare incidence of specific scoring of a number of dated works. The scoring is indicated in the index of the *superius* part of the music print and is also included in the Giambullari letter. Instrumental scoring is lacking in only one—*Intermedio IV;* presumably, it was to have been sung by eight hunting nymphs, unaccompanied.

Not only are instruments indicated, but they are used in a coloristic manner. In part, the dramatic function of the *intermedii* was to indicate the passage of time in the Comedy. The choice of instruments seems to reflect the time depicted—certainly in the Prologue (Dawn) and in *Intermedio V* (Night).

---

[46]Walter H. Rubsamen, "The Justiniane or Viniziane of the 15th Century," *Acta Musicologica,* 29 (1957), 172.

[47]Probably many other madrigals in various sixteenth century prints had their origins as *intermedii.*

Prologue	Dawn—*Grave cembalo,* organ, flute, harp, violone, and voices of birds
Intermedio I	Morning Pastoral Scene—krummhorns
Intermedio II	Mid-morning—Sirens and Sea-monsters—three transverse flutes and three lutes
Intermedio III	Noon—Silenus accompanying himself on a *gamba*
Intermedio V	Night—four trombones

The use of trombones to represent darkness is the beginning of a long tradition in music, that is, the use of this instrument in dramatic productions[48] as seen in the operas of Monteverdi, Cesti, Mozart, and others. *Intermedio V* is in five parts, and, presumably, the lower four parts were played by the trombone. Although the text refers to "La Notte" as a female, the part is scored in the tenor clef and was sung by a man. The other *intermedii* employ a normal distribution of treble and bass parts. In the Renaissance period, krummhorns had a range of a ninth; it is interesting to note that none of the parts of *Intermedio II* exceed that range. In *Intermedio III,* Silenus sings his *canzone,* accompanying himself on the *gamba.* Although this piece is printed as a normal four-part madrigal, in performance Corteccia achieves monody, that is, instrumentally accompanied solo song, and thus anticipates Florentine monody by a half century.

The wedding music demonstrates that, more than fifty years before the production of the first opera, Corteccia indicated a concern for the relationship of text and music. Each *intermedio* captures the meaning and mood of the scene. The syllabic treatment of the text, combined with solo voice accompanied by instruments, evolves into a lucid presentation of the text. In many respects this was, in its period, a remarkable new use of traditional techniques. Although important historically, these works merit attention as beautiful examples of sixteenth-century music.

THE INSTRUMENTS[49]

Arpa—The Renaissance harp was a diatonic in-

[48]Robert L. Weaver, "Sixteenth-Century Instrumentation," *MQ*, 47 (1961), 363–78.

[49]For more detailed information on these instruments, see Curt Sachs, *History of Musical Instruments;* Sachs, *Real-Lexikon der Musikinstrumente;* Sibyl Marcuse, *Musical Instruments: A Comprehensive Dictionary;* Anthony Baines, *Woodwind Instruments and Their History;* Frank Harrison and Joan Rimmer, *European Musical Instruments;* Nicholas Bessaraboff, *Ancient European Musical Instruments.*

strument; the pedals of the modern harp are a nineteenth-century invention.

Cornetto—Zink, a lip-vibrated instrument. Finger holes are drilled into the side of a wooden tube of expanding bore to permit playing of all the chromatic notes within the instrument's range. A difficult instrument to master, it was the virtuoso instrument of the sixteenth and early seventeenth centuries. It was constructed in two shapes, straight *(diritto)* and curved. The *cornetto* was used as a solo instrument, in consort with trombones, and also to double choral parts in church performances. The modern cornet is not related in any way.

Dolzaina—This is a difficult instrument to identify. It is not identical to the *dulzian*—a German alternate term for the early bassoon *(curtal)*. The Italian *dolzaina* was referred to by Zacconi (1592) as being a wind-capped instrument. No further information has been found, nor have drawings or examples of the instrument been preserved.

Flauto—This was the term used for the recorder. Before 1750, the term *flauto traverso,* or simply *traversa,* designated the transverse flute (modern flute). The recorders were a family of wind instruments, blown with a "whistle" mouthpiece and fitted with six front finger holes and a rear thumb hole.

Grave cembalo a duoi registri—The Italian name for a harpsichord with two registers or stops —two sets of jacks giving different tonal characteristics—or with two sets of strings.[50]

Leuto—Italian for lute, which was one of the most popular string instruments of the Renaissance. It was fretted and had eleven to thirteen strings, which were plucked with the fingers. It was used as a melodic instrument that was intended to accompany voice or voices or to reproduce all the parts of a vocal composition.

Organo—Presumably a small organ, such as a portative.

Piffero—Probably, this refers to the treble shawm, which is a double-reed instrument with a conical bore and which was made in various sizes. The use of the word *piffero* is not consistent; in some sources it refers to a treble shawm, in others, a transverse flute.

Ribechino—Rebecchino. This is the diminutive of the rebec, a predecessor of the violin with

[50]On early Italian harpsichords, see Frank Hubbard, *Three Centuries of Harpsichord Making,* 1–42.

three strings, tuned in fifths and played as is the modern violin. According to David Boyden,[51] by the beginning of the sixteenth century *ribechino* may have referred to the violin, as it probably does in this instance.

Storta—The Italian name for the cromorne or krummhorn. It was a double-reed instrument of narrow cylindrical bore in which the reed is not placed between the player's lips, but enclosed in a wind cap. As were all Renaissance instruments, it was made in a family of various sizes: soprano, alto, tenor, bass, and great bass. Because of the use of a wind cap, the reed cannot be overblown, and the range is limited by the number of finger holes. During the Renaissance period, the range was a ninth. The word *storta* means curved or turned and refers to the curved shape of the instrument. Holes drilled on the side of the instrument permitted the playing of the chromatic intervals within its range. It flourished between 1475 and 1625.

Tamburo—Drum.

Transversa—Like the modern flute, the transverse flute of the Renaissance was entirely cylindrical, a contrast to the one-keyed baroque flute, which was practically conical. The Renaissance flute was made of boxwood, and six finger holes were bored into the tube; keys were not used. With a range of two and one-half octaves, it had a "clear positive organlike timbre." It was made in three sizes—treble (a′), tenor (d′) and bass (g). The transverse flute was widely used during the Renaissance period. Its tone was heavier and somewhat harsher than that of the baroque flute.

Tromba torta—This was a natural trumpet without valves, with about eight feet of tubing. Probably, as with the *clarino,* the tubing of this instrument, for convenience, could be bent or folded.

Trombone—This instrument evolved when the telescopic slide was added to the long trumpet, sometime around the beginning of the fifteenth century. By 1500 it had assumed its modern shape and differed from the modern instrument only in that it had a smaller bore and bell. The tone was softer, blended smoothly with the voice, and was more suitable for polyphonic music than the modern instrument.

Violone—During the early sixteenth century, the term *violone* was applied to the viol family in general. At a later date, the term was used in ref-

[51] *The History of Violin Playing,* 24.

erence to the double bass viol. In *Intermedio III,* the *violone* was undoubtedly a bass viol, as evidenced by the range of the three lower parts. According to Ganassi (1542), the tuning was D, G, c, e, a, d′. The instrument, which was fretted, was placed between the knees of the player, and the bow was held above the hand.

Voci di uccegli—Literally, this translates as "voices of birds." While no reference to this term has been found, possibly it was similar to the *serinetta* or *vogelorgel,* a small barrel organ that produced birdlike sounds.

Zufolo—Zuffolo. A whistle flute with two front finger holes and a rear thumb hole.

THE EDITION

The transcription of the wedding music is based on the 1539 print by Gardane. Later, the Corteccia pieces were reprinted, presumably under the supervision of the composer, the *intermedii* in the madrigal collection of 1547 and the *Ingredere* in a motet collection of 1564. Significant changes were incorporated in the 1547 edition and indicated in the critical notes. These changes were concerned mainly with the addition of *musica ficta.* Evidently, their omission in the 1539 edition was the basis of Giambullari's remarks concerning Gardane's poor edition of the music, which had appeared in August of 1539. Some of the added accidentals are interesting in that the chord color is changed; often these occur in spots in which *musica ficta* would not normally be added. The accidentals in the sources are placed before the note in the edition; all added by the editor are placed above the note.

Note values in the original have been reduced by one half in our edition, and sharps used to indicate cancelation of flats have been replaced by the modern natural sign. While word placement in the sources was much more specific than in the music of thirty years earlier, there are still many problematic places. Here, the editor has followed Zarlino's rules of word placement, insofar as the musical sense of the passage permits.

Sources and Critical Notes

1. *Musiche fatte nelle nozze dello illustrissimo Duca di Firenze il signor Cosimo de Medici et della illustrissima consorte sua mad. Leonora da Tolleto.* Venezia, A. Gardane, ag. 1539. 5 vol. in 8° obl. (Copy in Oesterreichische Nationalbibliothek in Vienna) (1539).

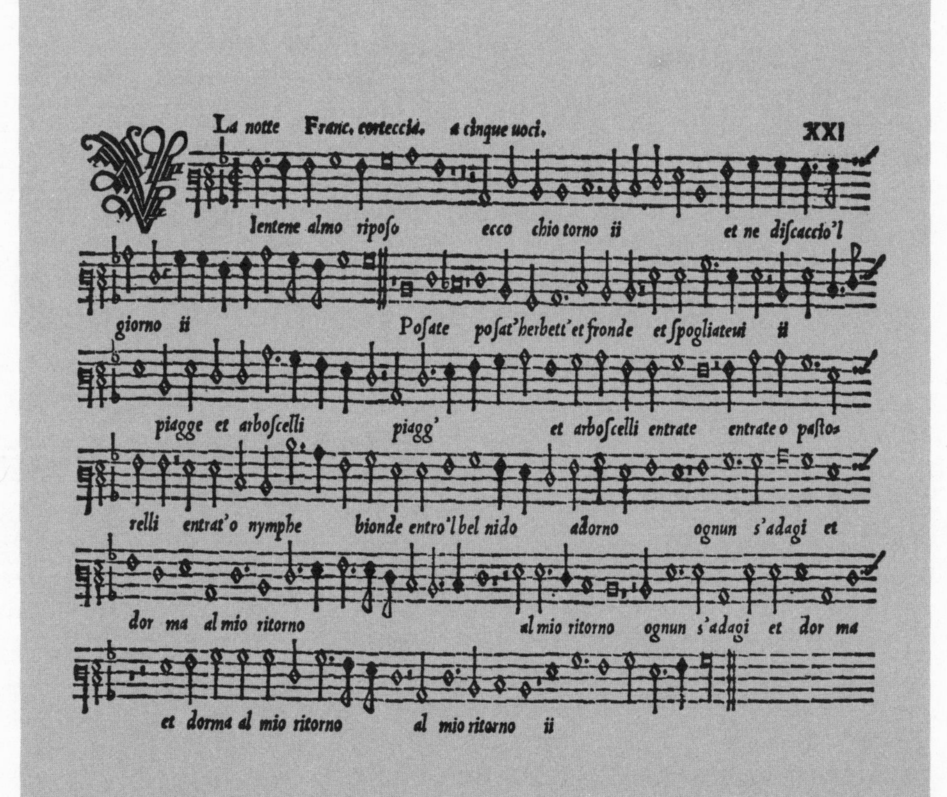

La notte, Francesco Corteccia, 1539 edition
—Nationalbibliothek, Vienna

La notte, Francesco Corteccia, 1547 corrected edition, with *musica ficta* —Staatsbibliothek, Munich

2. *Thesaurus musicus continens selectissimas octo, septem, sex, quinque et quatuor vocum Harmonias, tam a veteribus quam recentioribus symphonistis compositas, & ad omnis generis instrumenta musica accomodatas. Tomi primi continentis cantiones octo vocum.* Nürnberg, J. Montanus & U. Neuber, 1564. 8 vol. in 8° obl. (Copy in Library of Congress) (1564).

3. *Libro primo de madriali a cinque & a sei voci di Francesco Corteccia Maestro di capella dello illustrissimo & eccellentissimo duca Cosimo de Medici duca secondo di Firenze.* Venetia, A. Gardane, 1547. (Copy in Bayerische Staatsbibliothek in Munich) (1547a).

4. *Libro secondo de madriali a quatro voci di Francesco Corteccia Maestro di cappella dello illustrissimo & eccellentissimo duca Cosimo de Medici duca secondo di Firenze.* Venetia, A. Gardane, 1547. (Copy in Oesterreichische Nationalbibliothek in Vienna) (1547b).

INGREDERE

Transcription based on 1539 and 1564.

Cantus
Cantus secundus in 1564.

Discantus
Printed as second item in altus part of 1539 but not designated.

Altus
Altus secundus in 1564. 49(1–2) minor coloration in 1539.

Altus secundus
Altus in 1564.

Quinta pars
Tenor in 1564. 14(1–2) Semibreve in 1564.

Tenor
Tenor secundus in 1564. 10(3)–11(2) Breve in 1564.

Bassus secundus
Bassus in 1564.

Bassus
Bassus secundus in 1564.

SACRO ET SANTO

Transcription based on 1539 and 1547a.

Altus
Altus secundus in 1547a.

Altus secundus
Altus primus in 1547a || 31(4)–32(1) minor color 1539 || 96(4)–97 (1) minor color 1539.

Tenor
Tenor secundus in 1547a.

Quinta pars
49(1–4) no ligature 1539 || 60(1–4) no ligature 1539 || 95 (1–4) no ligature 1539.

Bassus
Bassus primus in 1547a || 30(1–4) no ligature 1539

|| 68(1–4) no ligature 1539 || 84(3) 85(2) no ligature 1539.

PIU CHE MAI

Transcription based on 1539.

LIETA PER HONORARTE

Transcription based on 1539.

ECCO SIGNOR' VOLTERRA

Transcription based on 1539.

COME LIETA SI MOSTRA

Transcription based on 1539.

NON MEN' CH'OGN'ALTRA

Transcription based on 1539.

ECCO LA FIDA

Transcription based on 1539.

ECCO SIGNORE IL TEBRO

Transcription based on 1539.

VATTEN'ALMO RIPOSO

Transcription based on 1539 and 1547b.

Cantus

8(4) dotted Semiminima f′ Fusa d′ 1539 || 9(3) double bar 1539 and 1547b in all parts.

Tenor

13(2–3) Semiminima g dotted Semiminima c′ Fusa a 1539.

GUARDAN'ALMO PASTORE

Transcription based on 1539 and 1547a.

Sexta pars

3(3)–4(2) no ligature 1539.

Bassus

47(2) Minima d in 1539.

CHI NE L'HA TOLT'OYME

Transcription based on 1539 and 1547a.

Cantus

16(1) no sharp 1539 || 26(1) no sharp 1539 || 51(1) no sharp 1539.

Quinta pars

44(1) no sharp 1539.

Sexta pars

50(1) c in 1539.

Bassus

11(3) no flat 1539.

O BEGLI ANNI DEL'ORO

Transcription based on 1539 and 1547b.

Cantus

8(1) no sharp 1539 || 49(1) no sharp 1539.

Tenor

6(1) no sharp 1539 || 7(1) no sharp 1539 || 8(4) no sharp 1539 || 11(3) no sharp 1539.

Bassus

14(1–4) no ligature 1539.

HOR CHI MAI CANTERA

Transcription based on 1539 and 1547b.

Cantus

6(4) no sharp 1539 || 11(3) no sharp 1539 || 20(2) no sharp 1539 || 35(3) no sharp 1539 || 36(1) no sharp 1539 || 41(3) no sharp 1539.

Altus

2(4) no sharp 1539 || 9(2) no sharp 1539.

Tenor

2(2) no sharp 1539 || 3 (1) no sharp 1539 || 7(4) no sharp 1539 || 9(4) no sharp 1539 || 23(4) Minima f′ 1539 || 34(4) no sharp 1539.

VIENTENE ALMO RIPOSO

Transcription based on 1539 and 1547a.

Cantus

21(4) no sharp 1539.

Altus

12(1) no sharp 1539 || 38(1) no sharp 1539 || 41(1–4) no ligature 1539 || 52(3)–53(2) no ligature 1539 || 63(1) no sharp 1539.

Tenor

40(1–4) no ligature 1539 || 53(3)–54(2) no ligature 1539.

Quintus

6(1–4) no ligature 1539 || 13(1–4) no ligature 1539 || 42(1–4) no sharp 1539 || 54(3) no sharp 1539.

BACCO BACCO

Transcription based on 1539.

PERFORMANCE

An authentic performance of the wedding music should use the historic instruments mentioned in the original sources. Only then can correct balance, tone color, and clarity of texture be achieved; this is virtually impossible with modern instruments. Modern reproductions of these historic instruments are now available, so that a performance with authentic instrumentation is possible. One should not be discouraged entirely, however, from performing the work on modern instruments. If they are used, certain precautions must be taken by the arranger and conductor to approximate tonal color and clarity of the original instruments.

The resonant and powerful sound of modern instruments is not suitable for polyphonic music, since it often overpowers the singers. For example, the modern trombone is difficult to play soft enough so as not to cover the singer. Felt cloth mutes can be used to cover the bell of the trombone; these soften the sound without altering tone quality or pitch. As indicated in the sources, a great variety of instruments were used at the festival. Other modern instruments that might be used include oboes, English horns, bassoons substituting for the krummhorns, modern flutes for the Renaissance flute, violins, violas, and cellos played both bowed and pizzicato, the pizzicato substituting for the lute sound. These instruments may be used effectively in various combinations. If recorders are available, they may be used with modern instruments.

Since music of the Renaissance was colorful, the arranger should use as varied a color scheme as is available. It was standard practice to use instrumental doubling and substitution for missing or weak voice parts. In the original sources all parts had textual underlay. However, this does not imply that it was necessary, or even desirable, to sing all the parts *a cappella.* Even in the performance of the banquet madrigals, for which there is no mention of instruments, the use of a solo voice with instruments is in accord with the practice of the time. In fact, varying the type of voice and the instrumentation and contrasting this arrangement with an occasional purely vocal performance is highly effective. Only the opening motet, which was described as being sung by twenty-four voices with four *cornetti* and four *tromboni,* would have been performed with more than one singer on a part. While not always practical, the texture of one singer on a part is preferable, since the polyphonic lines are thus more transparent.

IV. Art History Background

The contributions of the plastic arts to the festival were of several kinds: sculpture, paintings, drawings, costumes, and the stage setting for the Comedy. It is probable that nearly all these works were prepared rather quickly and without much concern for durability. The artists doubtless worked in groups—one could almost say in committees—and the whole atmosphere was probably not unlike that of decorating for Homecoming Weekend on an American college campus. (The result, it is true, must have been infinitely superior!) Nothing from these artistic productions seems to have survived. The short search we conducted in the drawings collection of the Uffizi Gallery failed, moreover, to reveal any preliminary sketches assigned to artists who are known to have participated, though there may well be some that are unattributed.

The disappearance of the works combines with our incompetence in the field of art scholarship to render critical commentary unfeasible. If, however, esthetic appreciation of the originals is now out of the question, the various creations retain, even in their secondhand and rationalized form, a great deal of cultural interest. For this reason we have judged it worth while to reproduce Giambullari's rather full descriptions and to supplement them with two accounts of the decorations included by Giorgio Vasari in his *Lives of the Painters, Sculptors, and Architects.* In 1539 this artist was not yet in the service of Duke Cosimo, and he was not present at the wedding celebrations. He was, however, already quite familiar with such occasional productions, from his employment by Duke Alessandro. Moreover, he knew personally most of the artists involved. Much of his information doubtless derived from Giambullari's description, but he also included details that cannot have come from that source. And there is, besides, the added merit of Vasari's lively style. The following passage is from the life of Niccolò, called Il Tribolo:

When Duke Cosimo and Sig. Don Pietro di Toledo, Marquis of Villafranca, then Viceroy of Naples, became united by the marriage of the Duke to Leonora, the viceroy's daughter, Tribolo was commissioned to make a triumphal arch at the Prato gate, by which the bride was to enter on her way from Poggio. Tribolo made a fine one, decorated with columns, pilasters, architraves, cornices and pediments, full of scenes and figures painted by Battista Franco of Venice, Ridolfo Ghirlandajo and Michele, his pupil, the statues being by Tribolo. The principal figure, placed in the middle upon a pedestal in relief, was a female representing Fecundity, with five children, three about her legs, one in her lap and one in her arms. It stood between two figures of the same size, a Security, who leans on a column with a slender rod in her hand, and Eternity, with a ball in her arms and an old figure at her feet, for Time, while the Sun and the Moon hang at her neck. I will not speak of the paintings, because they are described in the accounts of the preparations for the wedding. For the decoration of the palace of the Medici, of which Tribolo had special charge, he did many things relating to the wedding and those of all the illustrious members of the Medici, in the lunettes of the courtyard. In the grand court he made a sumptuous trophy, full of scenes, on the one hand, of the Greeks and Romans, and on the other of the deeds of illustrious members of the Medici house, executed by the best young painters in Florence, under Tribolo's direction: Bronzino, Pier Francesco di Sandro, Francesco Bachiacca, Domenico Conti, Antonio di Domenico and Battista Franco of Venice. On the piazza of San Marco, on a pedestal ten braccia high, over the cornice of which Bronzino had painted two fine scenes in bronze colour, Tribolo did a bronze horse twelve braccia high, rearing up and ridden by an armed figure of proportionate size, representing Sig. Giovanni de' Medici, with dead and wounded men lying beneath. The work was executed with such judgment and art that it was admired by all who saw it, and the speed with which it was produced excited astonishment, Tribolo being helped by Sandro Buglioni, the sculptor, who fell and rendered himself lame, narrowly escaping death. Under Tribolo's direction Aristotile da S. Gallo did a marvellous perspective, and Tribolo himself designed the most charming dresses that it is possible to imagine, which were made by Gio. Battista Strozzi.[1]

The other is from the life of Bastiano San Gallo:

After Lorenzo had slain Duke Alessandro, Duke Cosimo succeeded in 1539, and soon after married the incomparable lady Leonora di Toledo, who may be compared with the most famous women of antiquity, and perhaps preferred before them. For the wedding, which took place on 27 June, 1539, Aristotile surpassed himself in a scene representing Pisa, in the great court of the Medici palace containing

[1]Giorgio Vasari, *The Lives of the Painters, Sculptors, and Architects,* A. B. Hinds, trans., William Gaunt, ed., III, 176–77.

the fountain. It would be impossible to assemble a greater variety of windows, doors, façades of palaces, streets and receding distances, all in perspective. He also represented the leaning tower, the cupola and round church of S. Giovanni, with other things of the city. Of the steps and their realism I will say nothing, in order not to repeat myself. It had eight faces with square sides, very artistic in its simplicity, and imparting grace to the perspective above, so that nothing better of its kind could be desired. He next devised an ingenious wooden lantern like an arch behind the buildings, and a sun a braccia high made of a crystal ball filled with distilled water, with two lighted torches behind, illuminating the sky of the scenery and the perspective, so that it looked like a veritable sun. It was surrounded by golden rays covering the curtain, and was managed by a windlass, so as to rise to the meridian in the middle of the play, and sink in the west at its end. Antonio Landi, a Florentine noble, wrote the comedy, and Gio. Battista Strozzi, a clever youth, directed the interludes and music. But as much was written about these accessories of the comedy at the time, I will content myself by saying that, besides certain persons who did some paintings, everything was carried out by Gio. Battista Strozzi, Tribolo and Aristotile. Under the scenery of the comedy, the side walls were divided into painted squares, eight braccia by five, each surrounded by an ornamentation 1⅔ braccia broad, forming a frieze with a cornice towards the painting, making four circles in a cross with two Latin mottoes for each story, and the others containing appropriate devices. Above was a frieze of blue baize except about the proscenium, and over this a canopy covering the whole court. In the frieze above each scene were the arms of the most famous families related to the Medici. Beginning from the east, the first subject nearest the stage, by Francesco Ubertini, called Il Bacchiacca, was Cosimo's return from exile, with the device of two doves on a gold branch, and Duke Cosimo's arms in the frieze. The next, by the same hand, was Lorenzo's visit to Naples, the device a pelican, and the arms those of Duke Lorenzo, namely the Medici and Savoy. The third, painted by Pier Francesco di Jacopo di Sandro, was the visit of Leo X to Florence, the device a right arm, and the arms those of Duke Giuliano, namely the Medici and Savoy. In the fourth, by the same hand, was the taking of Biagrassa by Sig. Giovanni, the device Jove's thunderbolts, and the arms those of Duke Alessandro, namely Austria and the Medici. The fifth contained Pope Clement crowning Charles V at Bologna, the device a serpent biting its tail, the arms those of France and the Medici. This was by Domenico Conti, pupil of Andrea del Sarto, who did not display much skill, for he lacked the assistance of some youths which he hoped to have, as all artists, whether good or bad, were employed. Thus the laugh was turned against him, for he had at other times presumed to ridicule others. The sixth and last scene on that side was by Bronzino, and represented the dispute between Duke Alessandro and the Florentine exiles at Naples before the emperor, with the River Sebete and many figures, the finest picture of the series. The device was a palm, and the arms those of Spain. Opposite the return of Cosimo, was the happy birth of Duke Cosimo, the device a phoenix, and the arms the red lily of Florence. Next this was the elevation of Cosimo to be duke, the device Mercury's wand, and the arms those of the castellan of the fortress. This was designed by Francesco Salviati, but as he was obliged to leave Florence, it was excellently finished by Carlo Portelli of Loro. The third contained three rash envoys of Campana driven from the Roman senate for their insolent demands, as Livy relates in the twentieth book of his history, an allusion to the three cardinals who vainly sought to remove Duke Cosimo from the government. The device was a winged horse, and the arms those of the Salviati and Medici. The next contained the capture of Monte Murlo, the device an Egyptian horn owl on the head of Pyrrhus, and the arms those of the Sforza and Medici. This was painted by Antonio di Donnino, an artist who depicted vigorous movement, and the background contains a skirmish of cavalry that is far better than the works of some others, reputed skilled artists. The next shows Duke Alessandro invested by the emperor, the device a magpie with maple leaves in its mouth, and the frieze containing the arms of the Medici and Toledo, all by the hand of Battista Franco of Venice. The last of the series represented the marriage of Duke Alessandro at Naples, the device two crows, the ancient symbol of marriage, and the arms those of Don Pedro di Toledo, viceroy of Naples. This scene by Bronzino surpassed all the others as much as his first. Over the loggia Aristotile devised a frieze with other scenes and arms, which was much admired, and pleased the duke, who rewarded him richly. From this time Aristotile did scenery every year for the comedies played at the carnival, having become so skilled in that branch that he proposed to write upon it and to teach it. However, this proved more difficult than he had thought, and he gave it up, especially as the governor of the palace got him to employ Bronzino and Francesco Salviati to make perspectives, as will be said in the proper place.[2]

[2]Vasari, *Lives,* III, 296–99.

V. Renaissance, Anti-Renaissance, Classicism, Mannerism, and Baroque

This is very dangerous ground, since all of these terms for styles of art, whether traditional or of recent coinage, have for several years been subjected to intense examination and to repeated attempts at definition. Because we are not students of art history, the field in which most, though not all, of the debate is taking place, we cannot presume to enter the main discussion. It is, however, worth while to point out, for the attention of students of the Renaissance, some evident literary and artistic qualities[1] of the wedding celebrations that seem to fit rather neatly into one of the historical esthetic categories in question. We shall indicate first those characteristics which may be associated with "underground," "decadent," or "dissenting" tendencies and then distinguish others which seem to jibe with the august traditional conceptions of High Renaissance and Classicism. Our main theoretical guides for the discussion have been the following recent studies:

Hiram Haydn, *The Counter-Renaissance.* New York, Grove Press, 1960.

Wylie Sypher, *Four Stages of Renaissance Style.* Garden City, New York, Doubleday-Anchor, 1955.

Victor-L. Tapié, *Baroque et classicisme.* Paris, Plon, 1957.

Arnold Hauser, *The Social History of Art,* Vol. II, *Renaissance, Mannerism, Baroque.* London, Routledge and Kegan Paul, Ltd., 1962.

Eugenio Battisti, *L'Antirinascimento.* Milano, Feltrinelli, 1962.

Richard Alewyn, *L'Univers du Baroque.* Suivi de *Les Fêtes baroques,* par Karl Sälze. Danièle Bohler, trans. Genève, Editions Gonthiers, 1964.

None of the authors of these stimulating works

[1]It would not be meaningful to discuss the music of 1539 in terms of these stylistic categories, though some of them—classicism and baroque, at least—are useful for the analysis of music of the next two centuries.

should, of course, be considered responsible for our interpretations or opinions, nor is it possible in a brief discussion to do justice to many of their valuable conceptions and distinctions.

The grand, princely festival is considered by Alewyn and Sälze, and to some extent by Tapié as well, to be one of the most characteristic expressions of the baroque spirit. Its ephemeral quality—the rapid construction of flimsy, temporary decorations, even the hasty composition of literary works—attests to an insouciance for posterity and to a fancy for easy, shallow effect. Moreover, such festivals were usually given by absolute rulers and are associated with the trend toward more elaborate and stylized court life that reached its culmination during the high baroque period of the seventeenth century but had begun in some places, especially Italy, much earlier. The Florence of the Medici dukes Alessandro and Cosimo I was in fact one of the earliest heralds of this general European development.

Duke Cosimo probably did not commission work for the celebrations until he had sent his representatives to Naples in May. The arch of triumph erected at the Porta al Prato, probably of wood and plaster, must have contrasted remarkably, in its temporary quality, with the grand architectural monuments of the city, which had been slowly created from hard, resistant materials to last for centuries. Even the poetry, put together rapidly and tightly subservient to the banquet spectacle, has a frankly contrived quality that is uncommon, even for the best of occasional compositions. (Politian worked on his *Stanze per la giostra* for some time *after* the joust of 1475.) Practical political objectives are obvious in nearly all elements of the festival: The Duke must be glorified before his people and before his bride, and his devotion to Charles V must be demonstrated beyond doubt. In figuring the Duke and Duchess as brilliant lights, outshone only by the Emperor, Landi used an image that was to continue as a grand baroque metaphor.

Our Florentine festival is in fact remarkably like two much grander ones, staged over a century later for Louis XIV.[2] On August 26, 1660, Le Roi Soleil—an infinitely brighter luminary than Cosimo—entered Paris with his new bride Marie-Thérèse of Spain. The couple passed, notably, by five arches of triumph covered with allegorical representations. The third was adorned by Apollo and the Muses; the fifth bore artistic com-

[2]Tapié studies these in some detail, *Baroque et classicisme*, 166–79.

positions in which the deeds of Louis were compared to those of men of antiquity. Four years later, at the most elaborate of Louis's festivals, the *Plaisirs de l'Ile enchantée,* comedies by Molière were produced, with musical *intermedii.*

A fascination with optical illusion and with shifting scenery is considered by some, including Alewyn, to be an identifiable baroque trait. San Gallo's stage setting, which Giambullari forebears to describe, was doubtless a marvel of ingenuity and simulation, comparable perhaps to the glorious setting of Palladio's Teatro Olimpico in Vicenza (which is, however, permanent). At the banquet, a striking bit of theatrical spectacle occurred, when mermaids emerged from a painted Arno. (Some later baroque designers would have been content with nothing less than a real body of water on the stage.) Finally, the concealment of musical instruments in commonplace or bizarre objects carried by the shepherds and bacchantes of the *intermedii* was an indulgence of a lower taste for facile legerdemain.

The extravagant costumes of various actors, especially those personifying geographical localities at the banquet, may be deemed anticlassical and antirational, despite the detailed allegorical significance of all components. The headdresses in particular—for example, that of Flora with the bird's nest, red Medici eggs, and Imperial Eagle—remind one of the fantastic human heads, composed of diverse objects, designed by the highly mannerist or "anti-Renaissance" sixteenth-century painter Arcimboldi. The extreme complication in the designs for the costumes, like the great density of decoration on the arch of triumph and inside the Medici Palace, may also put one in mind of the *horror vacui* that seems to have inspired so much art of all kinds in the baroque period. They are, at any rate, far from the classical ideal of divine simplicity.

The *girandola,* or elaborate fireworks exhibition, representing a mythological battle between the Giants and the Gods, fits into a local Florentine tradition of devising ingenious and spectacular gadgets for popular enjoyment. Battisti has pointed out that such machines, or *automi,* encouraged an anticlassical taste for caprice and novelty and, also, that they contributed to the development of practical knowledge, of engineering, sometimes in conflict with Renaissance rationalism. Some *automi* came to represent naturalistic scenes from the life of the lower classes. The subject here is, however, mythological and suggests no democratic social criticism; if any message is to be extracted, it is a warning for rebels against authority.

The emblems and devices that figure so prominently in decorations for the festival have at least two aspects to their character and general cultural significance. If considered simply as extensions of literary metaphors, as poetic refinements, they are not in opposition to the ideals of classicism and the High Renaissance—except when their allegorical representations, like those of the costumes, are exceedingly intricate and far-fetched. It is, however, plain that there was about them an aura of the occult and even a suggestion of magical powers that are certainly in conflict with rationalism and with the humanistic view of man and the universe. The Duke's own device, which bears the symbol of Capricorn, betrays, further, an interest in the magical science of astrology, which was inconsistent both with rationalism and with the Christian faith. Battisti has noted, moreover, that the emblematicists' preference for animal symbolism fits into a medieval tradition of antianthropomorphism.

Horus Apollo's treatise on hieroglyphs, largely responsible for the mode of emblematics, probably harked back, as did the supposed wisdom of Hermes Trismegistus, to Hellenistic Alexandrian civilization, rather than to either Greek or Roman high classicism. Men of the Renaissance considered, however, that emblematics, like the magic of the Hermetic tradition, preserved traces of a mystical culture anterior to Plato and Aristotle. Similarly, the Cabala, evoked in the costume of one festival character, was thought to have its origin in the time of Moses. Probably no one present at the wedding was shocked by the evocations of Horus Apollo and of the Cabala; only later students of the thought of the time realize that these interests represent currents of the Counter- or Anti-Renaissance.

In the literary contributions to the festival, we can distinguish several traits attributed variously to mannerism and to baroque. The facile conceits of the poetry, especially Gelli's, are permissibly identifiable as mannerist, though the poets of the High Renaissance had sometimes indulged in similar figures. The extremely numerous references to characters and locales of mythology, often by periphrasis, work against classical clarity for all who do not have a detailed humanistic education, but such procedures are of course copied from Homer and Vergil. The unfortunate effect of their use here is due merely to tasteless excess.

No critical evaluation of the works of art is

possible on the basis of Giambullari's verbal descriptions alone. One might, however, observe that the statue of Giovanni delle Bande Nere, executed by Il Tribolo, captures a moment of violent motion and, for the man about to be crushed by Giovanni's horse, one of intense suffering. If treated with passion and with attention to torment, such a scene would be worthy of the high baroque sculptor Puget, in his work in France during the following century. The numerous paintings that represent solemn or heroic moments in the lives of the Medici may have given an effect of classical, Raphaelesque serenity and of balanced proportion, but it is likely, given the date, that in the attitudes of their personages and in their internal perspective the artists showed qualities now described as mannerist. Bronzino, with his master Pontormo, is now often cited (for his later works, it is true) as a typical mannerist.

The classical high point of the Florentine and the Roman Renaissances, fragile like all high moments of classical equilibrium, is generally thought to have passed during the third decade of the sixteenth century, well before the date of the wedding. The heroic age of humanistic scholarship was even further in the past. We may, however—not unexpectedly—find in the wedding festival traits associated with these earlier times as well as with the later mannerism and baroque. One notes first, in the many mythological allusions of the banquet poetry, in the numerous Latin quotations attached to the paintings, and in motifs of the *intermedii,* a fervent, basically uncritical reverence for classical antiquity scarcely different from that held by Petrarch and Boccaccio two centuries earlier. Roman history, whether mythological from Vergil or actual from Caesar and Livy, is the noblest and, in a strange way, the most real of histories. Contemporary events cannot attain their full solemnity and dignity until a parallel is demonstrated with ancient ones. Vergil, Ovid, Horace, and Catullus, poets of the Roman Golden Age, had expressed their thoughts more effectively than had anyone since, and their phrases might be applied with intellectual profit to all sorts of situations and occurrences. A reaction against these attitudes was, in fact, soon to set in, and Cosimo's Accademia fiorentina would be a leading force in the battle to dignify the vernacular.[3]

The classical ideals of proportion and order are most clearly seen in the "regularity" and the

[3]See chapter on Cosimo's Reign.

even, ironic tone of Landi's comedy. Observance of these unities is comparable to observance of the laws of balance in painting. (Later excessive codification of literary rules would lead, to be sure, to the "academism" that Hauser, Sypher, and others consider to be characteristic of mannerism.) The good-natured tone of the comedy, together with the emphasis upon timeless psychological traits, are consistent with a generally optimistic and satisfied view of life. No bitter social criticism appears here and no metaphysical doubts such as lend philosophical profundity to some works of Shakespeare and his contemporaries.

Finally, we must cite as at least compatible with classicism and the High Renaissance the numerous pastoral motifs of the banquet pageant and of the *intermedii*. One finds such settings and themes, of course, in the mannerist and baroque works also and even, much later, in the romantic. In Italy they were most successful, however, in the literature of the earlier Renaissance. Many of the finest Florentine works of the *quattrocento* were in the pastoral genre: Poliziano's *Stanze* and *Orfeo,* Lorenzo's lyric poetry, and Bernardo Giambullari's *Nencia da Barberino* (until recently attributed to Lorenzo). The great chivalric epics of Boiardo and Ariosto, masterpieces of Italian Renaissance literature, included long pastoral episodes. The portrayal of an unreal world in which simple but genteel men and women could devote themselves to love and light philosophy—shocking to modern sociological critics—was one of the most pleasant expressions of the classical spirit.

We see, then, in the details of the wedding festival, evidence of a number of cultural currents of the time. Grand state festivals in general, with their various distinct components, were nearly always remarkably rich cultural manifestations. For intellectual historians, accounts of them can be documents of almost incomparable value.

VI. Cosimo's Reign

The marriage was apparently a happy one; Cosimo seems even to have had no mistresses while his wife lived—certainly eloquent tribute on the part of a Renaissance ruler.[1] Ten children were born of the union. The Duchess and two of her sons died in 1562; the Duke, who in 1570 contracted a morganatic marriage with Camilla Martelli, lived until 1574.

Cosimo's reign was long and of major importance in the history of the city and of Tuscany. It inaugurated a period of political stability, and it established patterns and institutions that were to endure for a long time. Cosimo I was an autocratic ruler who frustrated completely the aspirations of Florence's old republicans. His government was, however, efficient and wise in

[1]See Giorgio Spini, *Cosimo I de' Medici e la indipendenza del principato mediceo,* 177.

Portrait of the Duchess Eleonora with her son Ferdinand I, by Bronzino, in the Uffizi Gallery —Alinari photograph

significant ways. At home, it is true, the city's commerce and industry continued to decline in importance, but this was essentially a result of general changes throughout the European economy; the Duke must be credited at least with encouraging agriculture as an antidote to losses in other areas.

In foreign policy he achieved a series of truly remarkable successes, with few failures. Here, rather like Machiavelli's Prince, he acted with calculation and could show himself humble or proud, vindictive or generous, as the situation required. In the spring of 1541, after his first son had been born, he met the Emperor at Genoa in very friendly circumstances. Two years later, in return for help against Turkish pirates, Charles turned over to him various Tuscan fortresses, including the one in Florence itself, which had been held by Imperial officers. In 1554–1555 he happily served the Emperor's cause by subduing Siena, the principal city of southern Tuscany, which, encouraged by the French, had rejected Imperial hegemony and had set up a republic. After a bitter siege reminiscent of that endured by the last Florentine Republic in 1529–1530, the Sienese defenders surrendered. For two years Siena had a Spanish governor, but in 1557 the city and its territory were added to the dominions of Cosimo, who, in order to mark a measure of autonomy left to his new subjects as well as to indicate the increase in his own importance, styled himself Duke of Florence and Siena.

Charles V had abdicated in 1555, leaving Spain, the Low Countries, and parts of Italy to his son Philip. The title of Emperor went to his brother Ferdinand, so that the former enormous concentration of power in Charles's hands was to some extent dissipated. In the new international and Italian situation Cosimo drew nearer to the Vatican. In 1559 he was influential in the election of Pius IV, a Milanese who bore the illustrious name of Medici. The new pontiff's connection with the Florentine family was extremely distant and even questionable, but he was well disposed toward Cosimo and created as cardinal one of the Duke's sons.

A later pope, Pius V, gave to Cosimo in 1569 the title of Grand Duke of Tuscany, investing him at a solemn ceremony in Rome the following year. Although the new title was not at first approved either by the Emperor or by the King of Spain, it was maintained. Of the Tuscan cities, only little Lucca escaped the Duke's dominion and kept its republic. With the solid institutions and foundations of government established by Cosimo, the Grand Duchy was to remain a stable and coherent political unit until the general European political upheavals at the time of the French Revolution and of Napoleon's campaigns. The Medici dynasty itself lasted until 1737, when Grand Duke Giangastone died without male heirs.

The character of the wedding celebrations is early evidence of the new ruler's intention of pursuing the family tradition of artistic and literary patronage established by Cosimo il Vecchio and continued brilliantly by Lorenzo il Magnifico and Leo X. The period of Florentine cultural history over which he was to preside would not be so splendid as the middle and late *quattrocento,* and his own appreciations were doubtless inferior to those of Lorenzo; nevertheless, he made a serious effort to promote excellence in the literary and artistic fields, and much was achieved —though not always, of course, as a direct result of his encouragement. If Rome, and even Venice, were in some ways more important cultural centers in this period, Florence was far from being a backwater.

Three of the four men of letters who contributed to the wedding festivities—Giambullari, Gelli, and Landi—were, as we have seen, prominent early members of an official literary establishment, the Accademia fiorentina. In 1540 this group had organized privately as the Accademia degli Umidi; in February, 1541, it accepted the Duke's patronage and assumed the grander name. Members engaged from the first in the practice of hearing and judging each other's compositions; soon they began also an ambitious program of public lectures, held in a large room of the church of Santa Maria Novella. Unlike the old Platonic Academy, founded under Cosimo il Vecchio and lasting until about 1522, the Fiorentina was strongly prejudiced in favor of the vernacular tongue and literature. The favorite subject for lectures was Dante's *Divine Comedy.* Petrarch's works also received a good deal of attention. These lectures served not only the cause of education but also that of local patriotism. The Italian *Questione della lingua,* "Question of the Language," which had been more or less settled at the end of the fourteenth century in favor of the use of Florentine for poetry, was now being debated for prose. Members of the Academy, especially Gelli, Giambullari, and Varchi, played important roles in the ultimately successful campaign to have Tuscan adopted as general literary language for the peninsula.[2]

The Academy's activities were soon looked upon as unwelcome competition by the professors of Florence's "university," the *Studio,* and there was unscholarly dispute over questions of ceremonial precedence at the funeral of the celebrated Professor Francesco Verino. In 1542 the quarrel was settled in favor of the Academy, whose consuls retained, thereafter, important privileges previously belonging to the Rector of the *Studio*. Because of its official status and because of the stability of the grand-ducal government, the Accademia fiorentina enjoyed a long life, continuing into the second half of the nineteenth century. Largely from among its members, moreover, was founded in about 1582 the rival and much better known Accademia della Crusca, which concerned itself more systematically with the definition of literary Italian and was to issue at the turn of the century a magnificent national dictionary.

Cosimo's patronage of literature was rewarded with few masterpieces, but a number of very creditable works, characteristic of an age of cultivated taste and sophistication, resulted. Writers were, perforce, cautious in the expression of philosophical ideas because of the repressive atmosphere of the Counter Reformation, initiated by sessions of the Council of Trent, 1545–1563. Lyric poetry, a safe genre, continued to be cultivated with polish by men like Strozzi, author of our *Intermedii,* but Florentine poems of the time do not rank with those of the Age of Lorenzo and few have found their way into anthologies. There was a tendency toward more elaborate and farfetched conceits, an inclination recent critics have considered a mark of mannerism. The comedy—also safe so long as religion and politics were avoided—enjoyed a great vogue. Several members of the Academy, notably Gelli, Francesco d'Ambra, Anton Francesco Grazzini (called Il Lasca), and Benedetto Varchi, tried their hands at the genre, usually in plays for special occasions.

The Duke was most interested personally in history, and his reign was enormously important for the development of Florentine and Italian

[2]See Thérèse Labande-Jeanroy's *La Question de la langue en Italie,* Robert A. Hall, Jr.'s, *The Italian Questione della Lingua: An Interpretative Essay,* and Paul Oskar Kristeller's "The Language of Italian Prose," in *Renaissance Thought II: Papers in Humanism and the Arts,* 119–41.

historiography.[3] We have already noted that Giambullari attempted a *Storia dell'Europa* for the period A.D. 887–947. This work, published in 1554, was undertaken on the author's own initiative, while he was enjoying official favor. For local history, Machiavelli's *Storie fiorentine* (1532), dealing with a large segment of the city's past preceding 1492, and Guicciardini's *Storia d'Italia* (1541), covering the short period 1494–1526, constituted high recent precedents for emulation. Guicciardini's *Storie fiorentine,* although written between 1509 and 1512, was not printed until the nineteenth century.

Cosimo made Benedetto Varchi official historian and commissioned him to work on the city's history subsequent to 1526. The product of this commission, *Storie fiorentine,* covering events up to 1538, was published, however, only in 1721. Varchi was succeeded in his official position by Giovambattista Adriani, who eventually wrote an account of the period 1536–1574, recording thus all of Cosimo's reign. It appeared under the title *Istoria dei suoi tempi* in 1583. A third official historian, Scipione Ammirato, was charged, near the end of the Duke's life, with setting down the story of Tuscany from the beginnings to the appearance of the Medici. His *Storie fiorentine,* published partly in 1600 and partly in 1640 and actually covering events through 1574, retains its position as a work of major scholarly importance.

Other Florentine historians were at work, although not under official commission. Bernardo Segni was a former republican who accepted Medici rule and, like his commissioned colleagues, had access to official records. His *Istorie fiorentine dall'anno MDXXVII al MDLV* (published in 1723) is remarkably objective, uncolored by prejudice for or against the Medici. Jacopo Nardi was, on the other hand, an unreconciled republican living in exile in Venice, and his *Istorie della città di Firenze, 1494–1530* (1582) is unyielding in its treatment of the ruling family.

Two genres related to history—biography and autobiography—gained indisputable masterpieces during Cosimo's reign. Giorgio Vasari published in Florence in 1550 the first edition of his monumental *Vite dei più illustri pittori, scultori ed architettori,* dedicating the work to the Duke as well as to Pope Julius III. A new, enlarged edition appeared in 1568. This splendid scholarly work has important literary qualities in addition

[3]See Michele Lupo Gentile's specialized *Studio sulla storiografia fiorentina alla corte di Cosimo I dei Medici.*

to its immense documentary value. The second narrative masterpiece was the autobiography of Benvenuto Cellini, dictated in Florence during the last years of the artist's life, when he had fallen from Cosimo's favor, and published in the eighteenth century. Literary and documentary values are again combined, the former, in this case, predominating strongly. In the second half of the sixteenth century Tuscan prose had become remarkably expressive and versatile.

On the whole, Cosimo was more discerning and more effective as a patron of the fine arts than as a Maecenas of letters. A large proportion of Florence's treasures of painting, sculpture, and especially of architecture, date from his reign, which coincided in large part with the period of Italian mannerism. Vasari and Cellini themselves were among the artists in the Duke's employ.

Cellini was born in Florence in 1500 and later worked for years in Rome for Pope Clement VII, a Medici. In 1545, after spending several years at the court of Francis I in Fontainebleau, he settled again in his native city and was soon high in the favor of Cosimo as jeweler and sculptor. His most famous work, commissioned by the Duke, is the bronze statue of Perseus that stands in the Loggia dei Lanzi beside the Piazza della Signoria.

Vasari, a native of the southern Tuscan town of Arezzo, had been a student of Michelangelo, for whom he retained a humble reverence. He worked for Duke Alessandro but, after that prince's assassination, left the city for a time, returning occasionally for short stays. In 1554 he settled permanently in Florence in the employ of Cosimo. During the next twenty years he was the most influential, if not always the best, artist in the city. His architecture is generally appreciated today, while his painting is held in very low regard indeed. He was largely responsible for the establishment of the Florentine Academy of Design in 1562, and he directed some of the main artistic projects of the period.

In 1540 Cosimo left the relatively modest Palazzo Medici of Via Larga and took up residence in the Palazzo Vecchio, the magnificent *trecento* edifice that for over two centuries had housed government offices and provided temporary living quarters for the priors of the Republic. (Dante may have been one of the first to reside there, in 1300.) The palace was considerably enlarged, and many changes were made in its interior, so that today it has internally more traces of Cosimo's reign than of any other period except, perhaps, that of its original construction. Vasari was in charge of most of the architectural work, including the building of the grand Sala dei Cinquecento, and the edifice contains as well a number of his historical murals, some of which depict the same solemn Medici events as were shown in the pictures for the wedding described by Giambullari. Vasari's most important architectural accomplishment is, however, the Palace of the Uffizi, next to the Palazzo Vecchio, which Cosimo commissioned for housing administrative offices and which today contains the enormous art gallery. Vasari also directed the building of the curious elevated and enclosed passageway that passes over the shops of the Ponte Vecchio to connect the Palazzo Vecchio and the Uffizi to the Palazzo Pitti on the other side of the Arno.

The Pitti Palace, most sumptuous residence in the city, dates also in large part from Cosimo's time. It had been begun in the middle of the fifteenth century by the ambitious Luca Pitti, rival of the Medici. The original architect may have been either Leon-Battista Alberti, designer of the Palazzo Rucellai, or Filippo Brunelleschi, author of the dome of the Cathedral. For many years the building lay unfinished for lack of funds. In 1549 it and the spacious grounds at its rear were purchased with funds from Duchess Eleonora's dowry, and construction was continued, mainly under the direction of the mannerist architect Bartolommeo Ammannati. Cosimo and his family moved from the Palazzo Vecchio to the Pitti about 1553. Later, the older palace was given for a while as residence to the eldest son Francesco. Ammannati is better remembered for designing the Santa Trinita Bridge, the most beautiful in Florence, which was destroyed by the Germans in 1944 but later rebuilt in its original form. Another very prominent, less felicitous creation of his is the colossal statue of Neptune that crowns the fountain in the Piazza della Signoria. The Duke might have done better to give this commission to Cellini, who desired it passionately.

Two of the principal artists who worked for the wedding celebrations, Bronzino and Il Tribolo, continued for some time in the Duke's service. Bronzino's present rather high reputation rests mainly on his portraits, including several of members of the ruling family. Il Tribolo was for a time engineer in charge of the city's roads, bridges, and waterways. Probably his most remarkable artistic achievements are a fountain and gardens at the Medici country house Villa Castello and the design for the glorious Boboli Gardens, which stretch up the hillside behind the Pitti.

The greatest of all Florentine artists, Michelangelo, lived in Rome. The Duke wanted very much to have him return to his native city, but, partly no doubt because of his republican sympathies, the old man always refused. Cosimo insisted, nevertheless, on having Vasari complete construction on the beautiful Laurentian Library, which Michelangelo had conceived and begun years earlier, while in the service of Clement VII. When the great artist died in 1564, his body was brought home for burial, amid elaborate ceremonies supervised by Vasari.[4]

Not a great deal is known about the music in Florence during Cosimo's reign. The Duke seems to have been, however, a patron of some influence in this area as well. Francesco Corteccia remained in his service, becoming Master of the Chapel in the Medici church of San Lorenzo. In 1565 the composer wrote some of the music for the wedding of Cosimo's son Francesco. Corteccia died in 1571. Rampollini was also active in Florence till his death in 1560. As we have seen, he published in 1545 a book of music for some of Petrarch's *canzoni,* dedicating the work to the Duke.

The period of Cosimo's reign included a number of solemn or joyous state occasions, some of which, like the wedding, were dignified by artistic, musical, and literary productions. We list them here, along with the principal contemporary sources of information about them, in the hope of encouraging further scholarship.

1541– The baptism of Francesco, the Duke's first son. The baptistery of San Giovanni was elaborately decorated, under the direction of Il Tribolo. There is a description in Vasari's life of that artist.

1558– The marriage of the Duke's daughter Lucrezia with Duke Alfonso d'Este. No general account of festivities in Florence for this event has been found. In the *Diario fiorentino di Agostino Lapini dal 252 al 1596* (Florence, Sansoni, 1900), 121, there is some mention of fireworks celebrations in the Piazza di Santa Croce.

---

[4]An anonymous description of the ceremonies was published: *Essequie del divino Michelangelo Buonarroti celebrate in Firenze dell'Accademia de' pittori, scultori, et architettori nella chiesa di San Lorenzo il dì 28 giugno MDLXIV.*

1563– The funerals of Duchess Eleonora and of her sons Giovanni and Garcia. See:
Collective authorship, *Poesie Toscane e Latine di diversi nella Morte di Don Giovanni Cardinale e di Don Garzia de' Medici e di Leonora di Toledo Duchessa di Firenze*. Fiorenza, 1563.

1565– The marriage of heir Francesco with Princess Johanna of Austria. See:
Domenico Mellini, *Descrizione dell'entrata della regina Giovanna d'Austria e dell'Apparato fatto in Firenze nella venuta e per le nozze di Sua Altezza con il Principe Don Francesco Medici*. Fiorenza, 1566.
Giorgio Vasari, *Descrizione dell'Apparato fatto in Firenze per le Nozze dell'Illustrissimo ed Eccellentissimo Don Francesco dei Medici, Principe di Firenze e di Siena, e della Serenissima Regina Giovanna d'Austria*. In Volume VIII of his *Opere*.
Anton Francesco Grazzini (called *Il Lasca*), *Descrizione degli intermedii rappresentati colla commedia nelle Nozze del Signor Principe di Fiorenza e di Siena*. Firenze, 1566.
Francesco d'Ambra, *La Cofanaria, commedia con gl'intermedii di Giovambattista Cini*. Firenze, 1566.
Anonymous, *Descrizione dell'Apparato della comedia et intermedii fatti nelle nozze del Principe di Fiorenza e di Siena Don Francesco dei Medici e della Regina Giovanna d'Austria*. Firenze, Giunta, 1566.

1567– Birth of Prince Francesco's first child, a daughter. See:
Giorgio Vasari, *Descrizione dell'Apparato fatto nel Tempio di San Giovanni di Firenze per il Battesimo della prima figliuola del Principe don Francesco*. Fiorenza, n.d.
Alessandro Ceccherelli, *Descrizione di tutte le feste e Mascherate fatte in Firenze per il Carnevale dell'Anno 1567 e l'ordine tenuto per il battesimo della Primagenita del Signor Principe di Fiorenza e Siena*. Firenze, 1567.

1569– An official visit of Archduke Charles of Austria. See:
Giovanni Passignani, *Descrizione degl'intermedii fatti nel Palazzo del Gran Duca Cosimo per onorare la presenza dell'Arciduca d'Austria*. Fiorenza, 1569.
Anonymous, *Raccolta di Feste fatte in Firenze per la Venuta del Archiduca Carlo d'Austria e descrizione della Mascherata delle Bufole*. Firenze, 1569.

1570– The Coronation of Cosimo as Grand Duke of Tuscany by Pope Pius V in Rome. See:
Anonymous, *Coronazione del Serenissimo Signor Cosimo dei Medici Gran Duca di Toscana, fatta dalla Santità di Nostro Signore Pio V in Roma dì 5 marzo 1569* [1570, mod-

ern style], *con il Viaggio e Regia Entratą di Sua Altezza in Roma.* Fiorenza, n.d.

1574— The funeral of Duke Cosimo. See: Anonymous, *Descrizione della pompa nelle esequie di Cosimo I dei Medici in San Lorenzo.* Firenze, Giunti, 1574.

All the above documents could be consulted at the Biblioteca Nazionale Centrale in Florence before the flood of 1966. Some are now damaged and awaiting restoration.

❧

Near the end of Cosimo's life, in 1572, a Bolognese gentleman, Mario Matasilani, wrote a little book intended to extol the superior character of the Duke and to sum up the glories of his reign. (*La Felicità del Serenissimo Cosimo Medici Granduca di Toscana.* Fiorenza, Marescotti, 1572.) In it the author draws detailed parallels between Roman and Florentine history. Duke Alessandro and his murderer Lorenzino are compared to Julius Caesar and Brutus, while Cosimo (like Charles V in the 1539 celebrations) is set alongside Augustus. Over a century later, in 1687, Charles Perrault was to compare the reign of Louis XIV to that of Augustus in *Le Siècle de Louis le Grand.* In both cases, the authors were conferring supreme praise, exalting both the political and cultural achievements of their subjects.

There are in fact probably more profound similarities between the reigns of the two modern princes than between either of these and that of the first Roman Emperor. In several important ways the rule of Cosimo in Florence was an earlier model of that of his great-great-grandson, the great Louis, in France. Both monarchs established strong central governments after periods of civil strife. In foreign affairs each was moderately successful; Cosimo accomplished at least as much, in relative terms, as the French king, though the latter was the most powerful prince in Europe. In literary and artistic matters, particularly, there is ground for very meaningful comparison. Both reigns followed extremely individualistic and creative periods—that of the High Renaissance in Italy and that of the Late Renaissance and the Age of Louis XIII in France—and both saw the development of a strong movement toward "rules" and codification. Cosimo founded the Accademia fiorentina; the Académie française, chartered in 1635, attained its full strength and prestige under Louis XIV. France received the principles for literary creation—already generally accepted—in Nicolas Boileau's *Art poétique* of

1678, as Italy in the time of Cosimo had seen the appearance of many similar, precursory treatises. The best-known Italian theorists—Trissino, Scaliger, and Castelvetro—had not, to be sure, been Florentines. Yet one can argue that the rapid development of critical theory in sixteenth-century Italy owed its early impetus largely to two members of the Accademia fiorentina, Francesco Robortello and Bernardo Segni, who published, respectively, in 1548 and 1549, Latin and Italian translations (with commentary) of Aristotle's *Poetics*.[5]

In painting, Cosimo and Louis alike favored the genre of the stiff and formal state portrait. Rigaud's celebrated portrait of Louis does not differ widely in spirit from pictures of Cosimo and his family done in the preceding century by Bronzino. The classical, simple beauty sought by a predecessor of each artist—Raphael and Poussin—gives way in these portraits to detailed artificiality. The Cosimo and Louis of Bronzino and Rigaud are noble conformists rather than either distinctive individuals or paragons of manly beauty.

Both rulers embarked on major programs of construction for official residences: the Palazzo Vecchio and the Pitti in Florence, the East End of the Louvre and Versailles in France. Despite basic differences of style, a common nature is revealed in the attention to façade, to ostentatious exterior magnificence. The Boboli Gardens on the hillside behind the Pitti may well have provided spiritual inspiration, and even some technical suggestions, for Lenôtre's design of the far grander ones at Versailles.

Returning to matters more closely related to the principal concern of our study, it may be pointed out that the reigns of both princes were punctuated by a series of grand, official fêtes of a strongly artistic and literary nature. The entrance of Louis into Paris with his new Queen, Marie-Thérèse of Austria, in 1660, was marked by productions and manifestations not at all unlike those for the arrival of Cosimo and Eleonora at Florence in 1539.[6] The scale was, of course, much grander—for example, five arches of triumph instead of one—but the motifs and themes were similar. Classical mythology and Roman history provided the allegories in each case, and in each

[5]*Francisci Robortelli Utinensis in librum Aristoteles de Arte poetica explicationes.* Florentiae: in Officina Torrentini Ducalis Typographi, 1548. And *Retorica e poetica d'Aristotele tradotte di greco in lingua volgare da Bernardo Segni.* Firenze: L. Torrentino, 1549.

[6]See Victor-L. Tapié, *Baroque et classicisme,* 166–79.

there was a strong emphasis (1) on the theme of love and (2) on that of peace. (As Cosimo had recently beaten the republican exiles, Louis had recently signed a treaty with Spain.) In the grandest show of the French king's reign, the *Plaisirs de l'Ile Enchantée* in 1664 at Versailles, there were presented, as in the marriage celebrations of 1539, a long recitation by Apollo and a comedy with musical *intermedii:* Molière's *Princesse d'Elide,* with compositions by Lulli for the entr'actes. The planners of the French fêtes had many grand examples from which to draw inspiration, and their work is not, of course, a direct imitation of what was done under Cosimo. These later festivals should be seen, rather, as the culmination of a rich tradition to which the festival of 1539 was one of the most important early contributions.

There is of course a danger of carrying such parallels too far, and a number of essential differences between Cosimo's and Louis's rules leap to mind. In political affairs contrasts between the two reigns are striking. Cosimo, unlike Louis, was not a real sovereign but was forced, especially in the early part of his rule, to cater rather meekly to the wishes of stronger foreign princes, the most important of these being Charles V. In artistic and literary matters, it must be recognized that, even though the various phases of the Renaissance come later in the North, there is between the art and letters of Florence in the sixteenth century and those of France in the seventeenth a difference in the degree of technical sophistication. A hundred years must count for something, and the French writers and artists could not approach their work in quite the same way as the precocious Italians had done a century earlier. Finally, beyond the question of sophistication, one must recall that most Frenchmen consider the literature and even the art of the Age of Louis XIV far superior to those of earlier national periods, while Florentine literature and art under Cosimo, though of high quality, are deemed by nearly everyone to be inferior to those of the High Renaissance. Nevertheless, our comparison stands on strong grounds for its significance. The sort of grand national culture created for France under Louis—official and highly formalized—had been heralded in important ways by that of Tuscany a hundred years earlier.

The Text and Music

Copy of a Letter of Mr. Pier Francesco Giambullari to the Very Magnificent Mr. Giovanni Bandini Ambassador of the Most Illustrious Lord Duke of Florence to His Caesarean Majesty

Magnificent Lord etc.:

Until now I have not written to Your Excellency about the notable and the solemn spectacles for the most happy marriage of our Lord the Duke. Because I wished to give you a full and particular account of all the festivities, I could hardly do so until they were completely finished. May Your Excellency therefore please excuse this lateness, which comes not from me but from the very matter that I describe.

The Most Illustrious Lady Eleonora of Toledo, Duchess of Florence, left Naples with seven galleys the eleventh day of June, 1539. This was a very happy day for our city, not so much for the old

APPARATO ET FESTE
NELLE NOZE DELLO ILLV/
strissimo Signor Duca di Firenze, et del/
la Duchessa sua Consorte, con le sue
Stanze, Madriali, Comedia,
& Intermedij, in
quelle reci-
tati.

M. D. XXXIX.

Title page of Giambullari's account
—Courtesy University of Illinois Library

victory of Campaldino[1] as for the birthday of our Most Excellent Lordship the Duke. And accompanied by the Lord Don García of Toledo, her brother, and by many other Spanish and Neapolitan lords and gentlemen, she arrived in happy state at Leghorn the twenty-second of the same month at dawn. There Her Excellency was visited and received in the name of the Most Illustrious Lord her Husband by the Most Reverend Archbishop of Pisa with a noble company. And to the extent that the place allowed, she was waited upon and honored.

That very day, at the same time, which was about 2 P.M., Her Ladyship the Duchess left Leghorn and His Lordship the Duke left Pisa, accompanied by many noble Florentines and by his whole court. Just about midway on that road the two Excellencies met, a most noble and beautiful couple. After marital greetings and caresses they joyfully came into Pisa, where, in order to do honor to Her Ladyship the Duchess, there had been erected triumphal arches and other sumptuous decorations. These had been made by Florentines and Pisans, who received her with the greatest joy.

She then departed from there on the twenty-fourth of the aforesaid month. I could not without difficulty recount the approval and universal happiness of the people with which she was viewed on the road. At almost every step of the way, there were varied, beautiful, and infinite decorations.

They stopped that evening in Empoli, and the next morning, which was the twenty-fifth, they came to the Poggio Caiano Castle,[2] a most divine edifice that matches the greatness of the Most Illustrious House of Medici. This castle, most superbly adorned, afforded comfortable quarters to the most holy marriage. Her Excellency stayed there happily until the following Sunday, honorably served and magnificently accompanied by very noble ladies of our city, enjoying all those

[1]On June 11, 1289, Florence, then governed by Guelfs, had defeated the Ghibellines of Arezzo at Campaldino. Dante is thought to have been a soldier in the Florentine army.

[2]The Poggio Caiano, west of Florence, was in 1539 the most luxurious of the Medici country houses. It had been erected for Lorenzo il Magnifico by the architect Giuliano da San Gallo. During the short stay at the Poggio, on June 27, Cosimo wrote letters to both of Eleonora's parents, the Viceroy and Vicereine, in Naples. A secretary's first drafts of these letters may be seen in the Florentine State Archives (*Archivio mediceo,* "Lettere e minute dall'anno 1537 al 1543, carte 138–139"). The letters are models of filial tact and thoughtfulness. The young man reassures the parents about their daughter's health and tries to comfort them in their sadness at her leaving their home.

pleasures and amusements that can be had in a delightful place.

On the aforesaid Sunday, which was the twenty-ninth, Their Excellencies left the Poggio. And from Florence came on horseback the noblest citizens, with dress so rich and varied with many kinds of cloth that they demonstrated well the ancient magnificence of their generous city. Each came according to his rank, with many servants on foot, in various fashions and liveries. Having come out of the Prato Gate for a mile, they met His Excellency, who, having lunched that morning at Peretola, three miles distant from the city, and the heat of the day being past, was joyously proceeding with his Most Illustrious Consort. There, after the due reverences and usual ceremonies, all having arranged themselves in pairs, they started toward the Gate in this order.

First came the four trumpeters of His Excellency, dressed in rich livery, and after them the lieutenant of Signor Ridolfo Baglioni,[3] with his light horses. After, the pages of His Excellency, richly dressed in livery and mounting jennet horses, which were decorated with very rich harnesses of spun gold and silver. After these came many noble young Florentines, with beautiful and fine livery, and all the rest of our nobility. Then came the Most Illustrious Lady the Duchess, with her ladies-in-waiting and with many very noble Florentine ladies. They were accompanied by a large number of gentlemen, principally from the house of His Excellency, with a number of prelates and nobles. At the entry of the gate, where His Excellency left his wife in order to go to the palace by a shorter way, they placed Her Ladyship the Duchess in their midst and kept her pleasant and courteous company as far as the residence that (as we shall tell below) had been prepared for her. Her Excellency was dressed that day in crimson satin, richly embroidered all over with beaten gold.

No sooner had Her Excellency arrived at the Gate of the City than the Fort[4] saluted her with so much artillery that I, not knowing how to describe it or to what to compare it, prefer to be silent rather than to say too little.

There was in front of the Gate a graceful and

---

[3]The Baglioni family counted a number of famous condottieri, including several named Ridolfo. This Ridolfo, who lived from 1518 to 1554, had been in the service of Duke Alessandro and had then fought for Cosimo at Montemurlo. He was to die in the war against Siena.

[4]The *Fortezza da basso,* main fortress of the city. In 1539 it was still held by troops responsible to the Emperor. See chapter on Political Background.

rich entrance way, of entirely Doric composition. It was outlined by a base of piers, pilasters, an architrave, a frieze, and a cornice. It connected the second gate to the first, each of these being contained between two columns of the same kind and style. And above the fine cornice, which went solidly around the whole, there rose up a great frontispiece, with various stories represented on it. We shall describe these in detail, beginning with that part which was first visible to a person arriving.

This part, in the shape of an Arch of Triumph, had in the highest part of its *fronton* a great figure of a lady, quite isolated, girded in ancient dress, with five beautiful nude children about her —one on her shoulders, one on her lap, and three others around her legs. She was put there to represent Fecundity, as will be clearer below from the letters of the frieze of the arch.

On her right hand, this lady had another as large as she, Security, posed on the last eave of the *fronton*. With her flank and an arm she was leaning against a column. She held a small branch in her hand, as we still see her figured in ancient medals.

Like Security, but on the left, on the other eave, was seen Eternity, with a big ball in her arms and, under her feet, a hairy old man, wearing the sun and the moon around his neck. This plainly represented Time trampled by Eternity.

In the face of the frontispiece was seen to be figured the great flood of the Adda, on whose lower bank the Most Reverend Cardinal Medici, later Pope Clement VII, with many lords and captains, seemed to be extraordinarily amazed at the ferocious animosity of Lord Giovanni, who, having gone out into the dangerous river, with his valiant company surrounding him in good order, was heading for the enemy side. Not only men seemed to be astonished at this; the vanquished river itself (which could be seen painted a little below, strangely pointing to the royal Po) was indicating almost fearfully how the ever victorious Lord Giovanni would enter Milan as conqueror.[5]

---

[5]This picture portrays one of the most celebrated exploits of Giovanni delle Bande Nere, the Duke's father. The episode occurred in the fall of 1521, when he and his bands were fighting in northern Italy for Pope Leo X and the Emperor against the armies of Francis I, who held Milan. Giovanni is said to have thrown himself into the Adda River, on horseback and in full armor, in order to lead his cavalry across. As a result of his maneuver, the French, under Odet de Foix, were driven back on Milan. The river figure below the painting suggests that this crossing of the Adda foreshadowed the taking of the Po.

To the right of this painting was seen in a smaller picture an armed Pallas, with helmet and lance in her hands, as though she were offering them. The following inscription was under her feet: IAM GALEAM PALLAS ET AEGIDA.

On the left was a Victory, in similar posture, with a laurel branch in her right hand, as the ancients showed her, and with these words: CURRUSQUE ET LAURUM PARAT VICTORIA.[6]

Under the figure of Pallas, but within the general cornice of the arch, between the column of the Gate and the pilaster of the corner, was to be seen the rescue of San Secondo.[7] Lord Giovanni, having been called to help this lady, had arrived with a small but choice troop. No sooner had he shown himself in the place than the enemy army, overcome by his formidable name, turned its disgraced banners to cowardly flight. These banners were scattering over the spacious countryside with such fury that that Lord could well say: VENIENS VICI, as the saying under this illustrated story plainly declares: IAM FULGOR ARMORUM FUGACES TERRET EQUOS.[8]

Under this, in a little tabernacle niche placed on the base, stood a Military Virtue, as shown on medals, and on the socle were these words: PALMAE PRAECIUM VICTORIBUS.[9]

On the other side of the arch, under the figure of Victory and at the same level as San Secondo, was seen the city of Milan, with the military camp of the League around it. Telling nothing of their plans to Lord Giovanni, his allies were departing suddenly, leaving the said Lord with his valiant company, when he expected to fight the next morning.[10] He was not at all frightened or dis-

---

[6]The Latin inscription is a paraphrase of lines 11–12 of the fifteenth ode of Horace's Book I, "Iam galeam Pallas et aegida currusque et rabiem parat": "Already Pallas makes ready her helmet, her aegis, her rage."

[7]Here is evoked a service rendered by Giovanni to his half sister Bianca in the summer of 1522. This lady, who was the widow of Troilo dei Rossi, Count of San Secondo, was threatened by her kinsman Bernardo dei Rossi, who wished to seize her fief. The timely arrival of Giovanni with his dreaded Black Bands ended the threat without serious fighting.

[8]"Veniens vici" is probably a paraphrase of Caesar's famous "Veni, vidi, vici." "Iam . . . equos" comes from lines 19–20 of the first ode in Horace's Book II: "Already the flash of arms terrifies the fleeing horses." The poet is encouraging his friend C. Asinus Pollius to begin writing a history of the civil war.

[9]"Palmae *pretium* victoribus" is a phrase from line 111, Book V, of the *Aeneid:* "Palm branches, prize for the victors." The passage describes the funeral games held in honor of Anchises.

[10]This painting evokes a siege of Milan in 1526 by the allied armies of Francis I and Pope Clement VII. Giovanni, fighting for the Pope, was outraged when his superior, the

Title page of 1539 edition of wedding music
—Nationalbibliothek, Vienna

mayed by this, as was shown by the spirited saying of Horace, carved under his feet: SI FRACTUS ILLABATUR ORBIS.[11]

In the tabernacle niche under this was Fame, with all the dress attributed to her by poets and on medals. On the socle could be read: HOC VIRTUTIS OPUS.[12]

Beyond the double pilasters that ended the whole construction on the outside corners, there was arranged on each side a box for musicians and singers, who, at the arrival of Her Excellency, sang as a motet these words, which could be read in carved antique letters in the main frieze of the arch, under the big picture of the Adda, between the architrave and the cornice of the big door: INGREDERE INGREDERE FOELICISS. AUSPICIIS URBEM TUAM HELIONORA AC OPTIMAE PROLIS FOECUNDA ITA DOMI SIMILEM PATRI FORIS AVO SOBOLEM PRODUCAS UT MEDICEO NOMINI EIUSQUE DEVOTISS. CIVIBUS SECURITATEM PRAESTES AETERNAM.[13]

Duke of Urbino, ordered a retreat of the besieging forces just when victory over the defending Imperials seemed to be within grasp. Refusing to withdraw at night with the rest of the army, he disdainfully led his troops away in daylight the next morning.

[11] "If the world should fall into ruins / [its debris would strike him without frightening him]." The line is taken from Horace's Ode 3, Book III. The passage is in praise of stoicism and disdain for misfortune, but, as in most cases, there is no really close parallel between the context of the Latin quotation and the recent event of the painting.

[12] "This is the work of strength." We have not found a literary source for the line.

[13] "Come in, come in, under the most favorable auspices, Eleonora, to your city. And, fruitful in excellent offspring, may you produce descendants similar in quality to your father and forebears abroad, so that you may guarantee eternal security for the Medici name and its most devoted citizenry."

CANTUS
In- gre- de- re, in- gre- de- re, in- gre- de-
DISCANTUS
In- gre- de- re, in-
ALTUS
In- gre- de- re, in- gre- de- re, in- gre-
ALTUS SECUNDUS
In- gre- de- re, in- gre- de- re, in-
QUINTA PARS
In- gre- de- re, in- gre- de- re, in- gre-de- re, in-gre-de-
TENOR
In- gre- de- re, in- gre- de- re, in-
BASSUS SECUNDUS
In- gre- de- re, in- gre-
BASSUS
In- gre- de-

6
re, in- gre- de- re fe- li- cis- si- mis au-
gre- de- re fe- li- cis- si- mis, fe- li- cis-
de- re fe- li- cis- si- mis, fe- li- cis- si-
gre- de- re fe- li- cis- si- mis, fe- li- cis- si- mis
re, in- gre- de- re fe- li- cis- si- mis,
gre- de- re fe- li- cis- si- mis au- spi- ci- is,
de- re, in- gre- de- re fe- li- cis- si- mis, fe-
re, in- gre- de- re fe- li- cis- si- mis au- spi- ci- is,

12
spi- ci- is ur- bem tu- am, ur- bem tu- am He- li- o- no- ra,
si- mis au- spi- ci- is ur- bem tu- am He- li- o- no- ra, ur-
mis au- spi- ci- is ur- bem tu- am, ur- bem tu- am,
au- spi- ci- is ur- bem tu- am, ur- bem tu- am He- li- o- no- ra,
fe- li- cis- si- mis au- spi- ci- is ur- bem tu- am, ur- bem tu- am
fe- li- cis- si- mis au- spi- ci- is ur- bem tu- am, ur- bem tu-
li- cis- si- mis au- spi- ci- is ur- bem tu- am He- li- o- no-
fe- li- cis- si- mis au- spici- is ur- bem tu- am,

18
ur- bem tu- am He- li- o- no- ra ac o- pti- me pro- lis fe- cun-
bem tu- am He- li- o- no- ra ac o- pti- me pro-
ur- bem tu- am He- li- o- no- ra ac o- pti- me, ac o- pti- me pro-
ur- bem tu- am He- li- o- no- ra ac o- pti- me pro-
He- li- o- no- ra ac o- pti- me pro- lis, ac
am Heli- o- no- ra, He- li- o- no- ra ac o- pti- me pro-
ra, ur- bem tu- am He- li- o- no- ra ac o- pti- me pro-
ur- bem tu- am He- li- o- no- ra ac o- pti- me pro- lis fe- cun-

24
da, ac o- pti- me pro-lis fe-cun- da i- ta do- mi si- mi-lem pa- tri, i-
lis fe-cun- da, ac o- pti- me pro-lis fe- cun- da i- ta do- mi si-
lis fe-cun-da, pro-lis fe-cun-da i- ta do-mi, i- ta do-
lis fe-cun- da, ac o- pti-me pro- lis fe- cun-da i- ta do- mi, i- ta do-
o- pti-me pro- lis fe-cun- da i- ta do- mi,
lis fe-cun-da, ac o- pti- me pro-lis fe- cun-da i- ta do- mi si- mi-lem pa-tri, i-
lis fe-cun- da, ac o- pti- me pro-lis fe- cun- da i- ta do- mi si-
da, ac o- pti- me pro- lis fe- cun- da i-

31
ta do- mi si- mi-lem pa- tri fo- ris a- vo, fo-
mi-lem pa- tri, si- mi-lem pa- tri fo- ris a- vo, fo- ris
mi, i- ta do- mi si- mi-lem pa- tri fo- ris a-
mi si- mi-lem pa- tri fo- ris a- vo,
i- ta do- mi si- mi-lem pa- tri fo- ris a- vo,
ta do- mi si- mi-lem pa- tri fo- ris a- vo
mi-lem pa- tri, si- mi-lem pa- tri fo- ris a-
ta do- mi si- mi-lem pa- tri fo- ris a-

37
ris a- vo so- bo- lem pro- du- cas, so- bo-lem pro- du- cas
a- vo so- bo- lem pro- du- cas ut Me-
vo, fo- ris a- vo so- bo-lem pro- du- cas, so- bo- lem pro- du- cas
fo- ris a- vo so- bo-lem pro- du- cas ut
fo- ris a- vo so- bo-lem pro- du- cas ut Me-
so- bo-lem pro- du- cas, so- bo- lem pro- du- cas ut
vo so- bo- lem pro- du- cas, so- bo- lem pro- du- cas ut Me- di- ce-
vo so- bo- lem pro- du- cas, so- bo-lem pro- du- cas

43
ut Me-di-ce- o no- mi- ni e- ius-que de-vo- tis-
di- ce- o no- mi- ni e- ius-que de- vo- tis- si- mis ci- vi- bus,
ut Me- di- ce- o no- mi- ni e- ius-
Me- di- ce- o no- mi- ni e- ius-que de- vo- tis- si- mis
di- ce- o no- mi-ni, ut Me-di-ce- o no- mi-ni e- ius-que de- vo-
Me- di- ce- o, ut Me- di- ce- o no- mi- ni e-
o no- mi- ni e- ius- que de- vo- tis-
ut, ut Me- di- ce- o no- mi- ni e- ius-que de- vo-

49
si- mis ci- vi- bus se- cu- ri- ta- tem pre- stes e- ter- nam,
e- ius-que de- vo- tis- si- mis ci- vi- bus se- cu- ri- ta- tem pre-
que de- vo- tis- si- mis ci- vi- bus se- cu- ri- ta- tem pre- stes e-
ci- vi- bus se- cu- ri- ta- tem pre- stes e- ter- nam, se- cu- ri-
tis- si- mis ci- vi- bus se- cu- ri- ta- tem pre- stes e- ter-
ius-que de- vo- tis- si- mis ci- vi- bus se- cu- ri- ta- tem pre- stes e-
si- mis ci- vi- bus se- cu- ri- ta- tem pre- stes e- ter- nam
tis- si- mis ci- vi- bus se- cu- ri- ta- tem pre- stes e- ter- nam, se-

55
se- cu- ri- ta- tem pre- stes e- ter- nam, pre- stes e- ter-
stes e- ter- nam, se- cu- ri- ta- tem pre- stes e- ter- nam,
ter- nam, se- cu- ri- ta- tem pre- stes e- ter- nam, pre- stes e- ter- nam,
ta- tem pre- stes e- ter- nam, se- cu- ri- ta- tem pre- stes e- ter- nam,
nam, se- cu- ri- ta- tem pre- stes e- ter- nam, pre- stes e- ter- nam,
ter- nam, pre- stes e- ter- nam, se- cu- ri- ta- tem pre- stes e- ter-
se- cu- ri- ta- tem pre- stes e- ter- nam, ut, ut
cu- ri- ta- tem pre- stes, se- cu- ri- ta- tem pre- stes e- ter- nam,

62
nam, ut Me- di- ce- o no- mi- ni e- ius- que
ut Me- di- ce- o no- mi- ni e- ius- que de- vo- tis- si- mis ci-
ut Me- di- ce- o no- mi- ni
ut, ut Me- di- ce- o no- mi- ni, no- mi- ni e- ius- que de- vo-
ut Me- di- ce- o no- mi- ni, ut Me- dice- o no- mi- ni e-
nam, ut Me- di- ce- o, ut Me- di- ce- o no- mi-
Me- di- ce- o no- mi- ni e- ius- que de-
ut, ut Me- di- ce- o no- mi- ni e- ius- que

68
de- vo- tis- si- mis ci- vi- bus se- cu- ri- ta- tem pre- stes e-
vi- bus, e- ius- que de- vo- tis- si- mis ci- vi- bus se- cu- ri-
e- ius- que de- vo- tis- si- mis ci- vi- bus se- cu- ri- ta- tem
si- mis ci- vi- bus se- cu- ri- ta- tem pre- stes e- ter- nam,
ius- que de- vo- tis- si- mis civ- vi- bus se- cu- ri- ta- tem pre- stes e-
ni e- ius- que de- vo- tis- si- mis ci- vi- bus se- cu- ri- ta- tem
vo- tis- si- mis ci- vi- bus se- cu- ri- ta- tem pre- stes
de- vo- tis- si- mis ci- vi- bus se- cu- ri- ta- tem pre- stes e-

74
ter- nam, se- cu- ri- ta- tem pre- stes e- ter- nam,
ta- tem pre- stes e- ter- nam, se- cu- ri- ta- tem pre- stes e-
pre- stes e- ter- nam, se- cu- ri- ta- tem pre- stes e- ter-
se- cu- ri- ta- tem pre- stes e- ter- nam, se- cu- ri- ta- tem pre- stes
ter- nam, se- cu- ri- ta- tem pre- stes e- ter- nam, pre-
pre- stes e- ter- nam, pre- stes e- ter- nam, se- cu- ri-
e- ter- nam, se- cu- ri- ta- tem pre- stes e- ter-
ter- nam, se- cu- ri- ta- tem pre- stes, se- cu- ri- ta- tem pre- stes

80
se- cu- ri- ta- tem pre- stes e- ter- nam.
ter- nam, pre- stes e- ter- nam.
nam, pre-stes e- ter- nam, se- cu- ri- ta- tem pre- stes e- ter- nam.
e- ter- nam, se- cu- ri- ta- tem pre- stes e- ter- nam, pre- stes e- ter- nam.
stes e- ter- nam.
ta- tem pre- stes e- ter- nam, se- cu- ri- ta- tem pre- stes e- ter- nam.
nam, se- cu- ri- ta- tem pre- stes e- ter-nam, e- ter- nam.
e- ter- nam, se- cu- ri- ta- tem pre- stes e- ter- nam.

This same message, though in briefer form, was enclosed by the three isolated figures in the highest part of the *fronton* already described by me. On the right flank of this arch was Slaughter, who, with her extended left hand, seemed to be offering her disheveled hair to Lord Giovanni. On the other flank was a Mars, who seemed to be offering him a sword.

Entering then into the interior of the arch, one saw on the right, between the base and that cornice on which the vault rests, the fearsome Lord Giovanni mounted and armed, on the rustic bridge between the Ticino and Biagrassa. Almost as though he were a new Horatio confronting an infinite number of enemies, he could be seen defending it against them so valiantly that they could well presume to pass into the next life but not to pass to the other side of the bridge. There was this inscription: REBUS ANGUSTIS ANIMOSUS ATQUE FORTIS.[14]

Above this cornice, between it and the top of the arch, within a great oval of porphyry, could be seen Garlasco, taken by Lord Giovanni with only a company of four squads.[15] And around a circle of trophy ornamentation that accompanied it could be read: MARTI VICTORI.

On the other side, in an oval similar to the first one, was the Bastion of Milan, taken from enemies by Lord Giovanni,[16] and with letters around a circle similar to the first, saying: MARTI PROPULSATORI.

In the middle of these two ovals, in the very top of the arch, was a coat of arms of his illustrious house, with letters above and below: IOANNES MEDICES.

Under the aforementioned oval, but within the cornice, opposite the bridge mentioned before, one saw on the left of the arch the capture of Caravaggio.[17] As the great Lord Giovanni was passing victoriously amid iron and fire, he made

[14]The biographers of Giovanni mention no such defense of a bridge. The incident is doubtless to be connected with a campaign against the French around Abbiategrasso (Biagrassa) in March and April, 1524. The Latin quotation is from line 21 of the tenth ode of Horace's Book II, and the context is, again, advice on how to face misfortune: "[Present] a strong and resolved front to difficult situations."

[15]In the spring of 1524 Giovanni and his Bands took Garlasco from the French, after effecting a very difficult crossing of moats and trenches.

[16]Giovanni took part in fighting around Milan a number of times, sometimes as attacker and sometimes as defender. This painting may evoke his decisive role in the capture of the city from the French in November, 1521. The Bastion of Milan is probably the Castello Sforzesco.

[17]On April 23, 1524, Giovanni's troops took Caravaggio from the French and then sacked the city ruthlessly.

it plain to everyone that neither iron nor fire could daunt courage. This was proclaimed broadly by the inscription: DANT TELA LOCUM FLAMMAEQUE RECEDUNT.[18]

On the lower base a river could be seen on each side, as the ancients show them, and in all the other parts, trophy ornamentations of various spoils.

I have already told you of the ornament between the two gates. I wish to add only that, in the four empty panels remaining above the base between two pilasters on each side, there were hanging tapestries, which with their rich beauty accompanied and filled up the whole. And the fringe decoration, which was continued all around, figured military spoils and weapons, some scattered and some gathered in different trophy ornamentations.

In the remaining *fronton,* which was behind people as they entered, was Lord Giovanni on horseback. Under the walls of Milan, having been challenged to single combat, he was going back and forth with his lance, past the armed knight who had come voluntarily to the dangerous joust with him.[19] And the unvanquished courage of this Lord on the ferocious horse, with his long lance broken off in his hand nearly up to the handle, seemed almost disdainfully to be uttering the motto that could be read below: SIC NUNC METUENDE IACE.[20]

Under the architrave of this arch, also behind those entering, its sides were adorned with two particular companions of the Lord in question: Liberality and Good Faith, as they were figured in medals.

In the Gate of the City, which was connected to the arch by the aforementioned ornamentation, there was, above the continued cornice, another big frontispiece. In it the Emperor was figured sitting upon a rock, crowned with laurel and with the scepter in his right hand. Under this hand, at the feet of His Majesty, lay the great river Betis leaning on a vase with two mouths, pouring out a great quantity of water. Under the left hand of Augustus was the mighty Danube, which, because it enters the Black Sea with seven

---

[18]"The weapons give way and the flames draw back." The *Aeneid,* Book II, line 633. The line comes from Aeneas' account of going into burning Troy to rescue his father.

[19]The most celebrated of Giovanni's single combats was with the French champion Charbon, outside Parma in 1521. This may be an inexact allusion to that fight.

[20]"So lie there, fearful one!" "*Istic* nunc metuende iace" is from line 585 of Book X of the *Aeneid.* Aeneas is speaking to Anxur, whom he has just felled.

mouths, was shown here by a vase seeming to pour out its water through several openings.[21]

On the right of the Emperor began a circle of three figures. The first of these was Spain, dressed as a lady, with the garments and ornaments she shows in medals.

She was followed, also on the right, by another lady, this one nude, with a simple cord around her waist, from which hung down in front a string to cover that which is always better covered. She had her right hand placed on her head, holding the knot of the headdress which, winding around the temples, pulled the hair up into a topknot according to the custom of that country. And in her other hand she held a pine cone. She showed by this costume that she was the first part of the Western Mainland submitted to the Empire.[22] After her, also in a circle, appeared the new Peru, figured as a lady draped in a sort of cloth without sleeves, tied above the shoulder, open and overlapping on the left side and held over the flesh with a belt two inches wide. She had a kind of towel on her neck, with her hair loose. She had with her, tied through the ears, a sheep with a long neck, the animal which flourishes best in that region.[23]

After her followed Neptune on a chariot in the shape of a boat, drawn by two horses, with a trident in his hand. This demonstrated that the Western Ocean[24] is dominated by His Majesty. The lively river Betis seemed to want to dip his feet into the ocean's waters.

To the left of the Emperor, behind and above the Danube, was a lady with a lance and a shield, representing Germany, as she is shown in ancient medals.

Beside her, honest and demure, appeared beautiful Italy, portrayed as by the ancients, with only this in addition—that under her left foot was figured the horrible monster Scylla, eternal terror of the Tyrrhenian Sea.[25] Next to her was Sicily, with a triangular crown of ears of grain. But the air around her was more turbid because of the excessive fumes of the burnt Mount Etna. And she had in her right hand a three-pronged scythe, such as is still seen in medals of the fa-

[21]These figurations of the Spanish river Betis (present-day Guadalquivir) and of the Danube emphasize the extent of Charles V's dominions in Europe.

[22]This figure represents Mexico, taken by Cortez in 1521.

[23]Pizzarro had conquered Peru in 1532, that is, quite recently. The long-necked sheep is, of course, a llama.

[24]The Atlantic, where Spanish sea power was yet unchallenged by England.

[25]Scylla was supposed to be a sea monster living in the Straits of Messina, that is, under the foot of Italy. It really seems, however, that the monster should be under her *right* foot.

mous Marcellus.[26] And besides standing on a triangular space, with many ears of grain under the left foot, she held her right foot on the head of the fierce old Charybdis, still crowned with the cow's head in memory of her ancient theft.[27]

In the last place was Africa, garlanded with serpents, a scorpion in her hand and a vase of fire at her feet, all this showing the nature of the country.

Under so beautiful a *fronton* could be read in antique capital letters this motto: AUGUSTUS CAESAR DIVUM GENUS AUREA CONDIT SAECULA.[28] On the sides of the arch above the door, for the true glory of His Majesty, were, on the right side, Providence, and, on the left, Peace, both copied from the ancient style.

On the top side, just at the peak of the frontispiece, appeared a very large Imperial Eagle with all the glorious insignia of His Majesty.

Behind this, but on the side facing Prato, was in an antique tablet, this saying: SPARGE ROSAS,[29] which invited Florence to all celebration and joy.

Inside the aforesaid entrance way were thirty-six young men from among the principal nobles of the city, all afoot, dressed in a livery of purple satin, crimson cloaks, red stockings, and velvet shoes and toques, with perhaps as many gildings and feathers as were never seen together at another time. As soon as the Duke had left, these young men placed the mount of the Duchess in their midst and kept her handsome, respectful company as far as the Palace, going by way of the Ognissanti quarter and then along the Arno as far as the Spini. From there, having turned back by way of Tornaquinci and Carnesecchi, by San Giovanni, they proceeded to the Cathedral in aforementioned formation, though the streets were so full of spectators that there was hardly room to pass.[30]

---

[26]Marcus Claudius Marcellus, *c.* 270–208 B.C., Roman general of the Second Punic War.

[27]Charybdis, like Scylla, was a monster living in the Straits of Messina. According to legend, she was a nymph turned into a monster by Zeus for stealing a cow from Hercules.

[28]This is a paraphrase from a famous passage of the *Aeneid* (Book VI, lines 792–793). The original words, "Augustus Ceasar divi genus, aurea condet / Saecula . . . ," are translated: "Augustus Caesar, son of a god, will found a golden age." Here the verb is put into the present and the genitive *divi* becomes *divum,* which is either a poetic genitive plural of the noun or a nominative neuter singular of the adjective *divus.* The new reading will mean either: "Augustus Caesar, the offspring of gods, founds a golden age," or: "Augustus Caesar, a divine offspring, founds a golden age."

[29]"Scatter roses." This injunction to joy is found in line 22 of Ode 19 of Horace's Book III.

[30]The streets are for the most part no longer the same, but the main landmarks and buildings, of course, remain. The party had proceeded from the Prato Gate to the Arno and

Her Excellency having arrived at the church and having dismounted from the steed, which was of course taken from her, she was received by the Archbishop and the Florentine clergy in pontifical robes with the ceremony usually given to such High Princesses. She was led to the main altar, with the usual benediction, and stayed there for a while, viewing with pleasure and delight the admirable, sumptuous pyramid and the carefully arranged distribution of altar curtains, used in our most solemn ceremonies, displayed above the choir of the pyramid, with the infinity of lights which extends over all the galleries of its great apse.

Then Her Excellency left, having remounted a new horse no less richly dressed than the first, with the same company, and in the same formation. Through the Via della Nunziata she came to the Piazza San Marco, where our ingenious Tribolo, in honor of Lord Giovanni, had made a fine horse, thirteen arms high from top to ground, figured in this way.[31]

Upon a great oval base, five arms high, rises on his hind feet a most ferocious horse, and there is mounted on him the said Lord, dressed in ancient armor, holding in his right hand a heavy club of iron, just about to strike. The other two feet of the horse, with all the rest of the figure, are suspended in the air above a man who, bent strangely by the impetuous blow, braces himself with one arm on the ground while the other is propped against the breast of the horse, as though he wished to ward off the weight that is falling onto his chest. This figure is placed so, as an ornament and as a brace of the whole creation, which, without other support, stands suspended.

In the two larger sides of the base are stories about the aforesaid Lord. On the eastern flank is shown the muddy swamp between Pavia and Binasco, where the Lord, in a terrible skirmish, is seen on horseback, bogged down in the mud, with many enemies around trying to take him prisoner. One of them, braver than the others, who presumes to grab him by the neck, seems to be knocked raging to the ground by a single blow of the heavy club. Having thus delivered himself

thence along the riverbank for a way. Then they turned back toward the center of town, toward the Baptistery of San Giovanni and the Cathedral, perhaps following a path nearly that of the present Via dei Calzaiuoli. They later continued in the same general direction, away from the river to Piazza San Marco. Then, turning about, they retraced part of the way toward the Cathedral, as far as the Palazzo Medici.

[31]Vasari's much fuller description of this statue is quoted in the chapter on Art History Background.

from this peril, the unbeaten Lord bravely escapes, with great honor.[32] In the other is seen the damage and massacre done by the same Lord in the great squadron of men-at-arms along the Biagrassa Canal.[33] In front of and behind this base is a coat of arms of his most illustrious house, with these letters: IOANNES MEDICES. Between the horse and the Palace, all down along the Via Larga,[34] gentlemen were lined up along each side to do honor to Her Excellency, who, with the prelates and lords and with the young

[32]During a campaign against the French near Milan, in the fall of 1521, Giovanni was caught in a bog on horseback and attacked by numerous enemies. He managed to hold his own until help arrived.

[33]Giovanni's fighting along the canal of Biagrassa took place in April, 1524. His enemies were the troops of Francis I.

[34]The present Via Cavour and Via dei Martelli, which run from Piazza San Marco to the Duomo. The Palazzo Medici is on the right when one is proceeding, as the Duchess was, toward the Cathedral.

The Medici Palace, Florence, scene of the wedding banquet and the play (façade extended in the seventeenth century by the Riccardi Family). Drawing from Sir Banister Fletcher, *A History of Architecture on the Comparative Method.* —Courtesy of the Athlone Press, London

men on foot, gaily proceeded to the magnificent and beautiful Palace, which was decorated in the following way:

Its superb gate was bordered by a pretty festoon, which in the highest part supported a great coat of arms of the most illustrious Houses of Medici and Toledo, joined together and embraced by the Imperial Eagle. The corridor or, in truth, lobby, between the outside door and that of the first courtyard, was, as were also all the interior loggias, hung and decorated with very rich gold-tooled leather, which, suspended from a very beautiful fringe decoration, extended almost to the floor. The leather made both an attractive ornament and a pleasant coolness. And in the empty space above the second door, the spot first seen by persons entering, there was, among many curlicues: INGREDERE ET VOTIS IAM NUNC ASSUESCE VOCARI.[35]

And opposite this, over the shoulders of a person entering: ACCIPIAT CONIUNX FOELICI FOEDERE DIVAM.[36]

This fringe, extending from bracket to bracket of the vaults, held up the pretty gold leather, leaving between the top of the vaults and itself an arch, or rather a half-moon or lunette. This lunette was divided into compartments with small, pleasant festooned borders, marking off various devices that I shall later make known to you clearly. Beginning on the right of a person entering, in the first lunette, was seen a lady pouring water from a vase in that very same pose shown us by the reverse of His Excellency's medal, with the motto: SALUS PUBLICA.

The second lunette contained a crude beehouse, bees being by their nature extremely devoted, with the motto: ET NATI NATORUM.[37]

The other lunette, which was first in the second façade, showed in the sea a cleverly constructed nest of sea gulls, around it the motto: VENTOS CUSTODIT ET ARCET AEOLUS.[38]

In the fourth was a broken laurel tree, its summit so bent toward the earth that it seemed entirely lost, but an exuberant new shoot was coming out of the old stump, completely renewing the tree, as is seen on another medal of His Excel-

[35]"Come in and accustom yourself to being called on by our petitions." Vergil's *Georgics*, Book I, line 42.

[36]"Let the bridegroom receive the goddess bound to him in this happy alliance." Line 374 of Catullus' Ode LXIV.

[37]"And the sons of his sons." From line 98 of Book III of the *Aeneid*. Apollo is prophesying that Italy will belong to Aeneas and his descendants.

[38]"Aeolus guards and keeps the winds." Ovid's *Metamorphoses*, Book XI, line 748. Aeolus' daughter Halcyone was supposed to have been changed into a sea gull.

lency. There was the motto: UNO AVULSO.[39]

In the fifth was seen the heavenly Capricorn, with the eight stars of the crown of Ariadne, and there was his motto: FIDUCIA FATI.[40]

In the sixth, a Genius of the People, as still seen in the ancient medals of Nero, with the motto: POPULO GRATIOR IT DIES.[41]

In the seventh was a cut-off branch, with a number of leaves and flowers, bound with this brief motto: ITA ET VIRTUS.[42]

In the eighth, which was the last on that façade, was seen a black dove on the branches of a dead bush. The bush had, however, a green shoot at its feet. Written around it was: ILLE MEOS.[43]

In the ninth, a Fortune, with a world, having a rudder on it in the ancient style, copied from medals, with the motto: SALUTIS MONSTRAT ITER.[44]

In the tenth could be seen the ancient yoke of the Magnificent Lorenzo and of the most happy memory of Leo the Tenth, with the "N" written above, and with his usual motto: SUAVE.[45]

---

[39]This device was discussed by Paolo Giovio in his *Dialogo delle imprese militari et amorose* . . . , 52–53. As we note in the section on Emblems and Classical Inscriptions, Giovio had been present at the wedding celebrations. The inscription is from line 143, Book VI, of the *Aeneid:* "Primo avulso, non deficet alter": "If the first has been taken away, there will be no lack of another." According to Giovio, the device alludes to the assassination of Duke Alessandro and to the consequent succession of Cosimo and the younger branch of Medici.

[40]This device was also discussed by Giovio (p. 51). He cited the inscription a little differently, as "Fidem fati virtute sequimur," to be translated: "Through my own value I shall fulfill what is promised by Fate." We have been unable to find a literary source, and perhaps there is none in this case. Giovio wrote that, in mentioning a promise of Fate, Cosimo was alluding to the fact that, like Augustus and Charles V, he had been born under Capricorn. Moreover, he had defeated the *fuorusciti* at Montemurlo on the very same day of the year as Augustus had beaten Mark Antony and Cleopatra. The implications of such coincidence could be only cheering.

[41]This inscription is a crippled excerpt from lines 5–8 of Ode 5, Book IV, of Horace. The poet is addressing Augustus, absent from Rome: "Give back the light to your homeland, O good leader! Because, since your face, another spring, has shone *before the people, the day is more joyful* and the suns are more brilliant."

[42]We have not found a literary source for this phrase, and out of context its meaning is not clear.

[43]The source for this phrase has not been found either, and its meaning is also obscure.

[44]"[Fortune] shows the way of salvation." The *Aeneid,* III, 388, an excerpt from a passage that describes how some Trojans escaping from their fallen city have discovered by chance the stratagem of disguising themselves as Greeks.

[45]According to Giovio (pp. 39–40), this inscription is taken from the biblical verse, "Iugum meu *suave* est . . ." (Matthew 11:30), which reads, in the King James version: "My yoke is easy [and my burden is light]." After Florence had been regained for his family by foreign troops in 1512, Leo X (then still a cardinal) wished to assure the populace that he would not be vengeful or tyrannical.

There followed after this the door of the second *cortile,* on the frontispiece of which were Caesar's two columns in relief, his motto written across transversely: PLUS ULTRA, and an Imperial Eagle between and behind these columns.[46] This balanced worthily with the first and principal door, which leads us in.

In the eleventh was the pure and sincere device of our Clement VII, that is, the crystal glass full of water, which, exposed to the direct rays of the sun, ignites a horrible flame in green and live wood. Around it was his motto: CANDOR ILLESUS.[47]

In the last of this façade was an eagle, with its eyes turned toward Jove, and having under it this motto: OMNE MILITABITUR BELLUM.[48]

In the other that followed it in order was the ancient device of this House, that is, a group of three diamonds, with the motto: SEMPER.[49]

In the fourteenth, a beautiful lady, rich with many children, representing (as was stated on the arch) Fecundity. The motto around her said: VENTUROS TOLLEMUS IN ASTRA NEPOTES.[50]

In the fifteenth, the Genius of the Senate, taken from the medal of Antoninus Pius, with the motto: SOLES MELIUS NITENT.[51]

In the sixteenth another old device of the House, that is, a falcon with a diamond in his foot, and the motto: SEMPER.

There were in the other, two lions with a laurel between them, formerly the device of Duke Lorenzo, with the same words: ITA ET VIRTUS.[52]

---

[46]Giovio has again furnished an explanation (pp. 16–17). The columns represent the Pillars of Hercules in the Straits of Gibraltar. The seamen and soldiers of Spain had pushed beyond (*plus ultra*) in order to reach and conquer the New World.

[47]Giovio says (pp. 45–46) that Clement VII wished by this device to show the power of the "unimpaired candor" of his soul. The soul is not represented by the water or crystal but by a white object that, unlike the green wood, reflects the rays and is not ignited by them. Giovio considers that the device was meant as a warning to anti-Medici elements in Florence.

[48]"Every war will be fought," or, more freely: "I shall take part in every campaign." Horace's first epode, lines 23–24.

[49]Diamonds were considered to be the most durable of substances. Giovio says (pp. 42–43) that this device, with its simple motto, was first used by Piero di Cosimo, father of Lorenzo il Magnifico.

[50]"We shall bear your descendants up to the stars." The *Aeneid,* III, 158. A promise to Aeneas from the gods of Troy.

[51]Antoninus Pius was Emperor, A.D. 138–161. The inscription, "The suns are more brilliant," is from line 8, Ode V, Book IV, of Horace. See note 41 above.

[52]Lorenzo, Duke of Urbino, 1492–1519, was a grandson of Il Magnifico and the father of Catherine des Médicis, Queen of France. The source of "Ita et virtus," which occurred in the seventh lunette also, has not been found.

Above the principal stairway, the last available space of this façade, was a Hercules in his usual dress, with the motto: PARATUS OMNE CAESARIS PERICULUM SUBIRE.[53]

In the first of the next side was a very white goose with just these words: SEMPER VIGIL.[54]

In the next, between this and the first corridor, the twentieth of all, was seen a Peace, seated, who was burning a great heap of arms, with the following words written under her: TENENTE CAESARE TERRAS.[55]

In the well-adorned *cortile* and loggias, Her Excellency dismounted and was received with the appropriate ceremonies by the Lady her mother-in-law and by the Most Illustrious Lord the Duke. She was accompanied to her sumptuous rooms, where she contentedly rested until the solemn banquet of her wedding, which was the following Sunday morning, the sixth day of July, 1539.

The decoration for this dinner was in the second *cortile,* which, being dressed with new, superb ornament, pretty and marvelous, smiled in the eyes of its viewers. It was made in this manner:

Under a tightly drawn ceiling of blue canopies was an adorned frieze, around three sides of the *cortile,* leaving only the northern side undressed, in order not to block sight of the marvelous stage setting, prepared there for the comedy to come.

In the southern side, above the middle of three arches of the loggia, in the already mentioned frieze, were the imperial arms of His Majesty. Under these, in a well-arranged architrave, was seen an Equity, as shown to us in the ancient medals. It was placed in a circle accompanied by two mottoes, of which the right one read: AEQUITAS, and the other CAR. V. CAES. AUG.[56] On her right side was a Victory holding with her outstretched arms a laurel, and on the left side, a Jupiter Conservator, as in the medal of Alexander Severus.[57] These seals were very ap-

[53]"Ready to undergo all the perils of Caesar." Horace's first epode, lines 3–4. A particularly pointed declaration of devotion to Charles V.

[54]Geese were supposed to have saved Rome in legendary times by warning of the approach of invaders.

[55]"While Caesar holds the land." Horace, Book III, Ode 15, lines 15–16. This must have seemed ironic to reflective spectators, for Italy had scarcely ever suffered such widespread and continuous warfare as since Charles V had taken an interest in the peninsula's affairs. Professing a love for peace was, however, a sure way to the people's hearts. Moreover, the reign of Cosimo would indeed be more peaceful for Florence than the preceding half century.

[56]Carolus Quintus Caesar Augustus.

[57]Roman Emperor A.D. 222–235.

First *cortile* in the Medici Palace
—Alinari photograph

propriate to the immense sincerity of His Majesty.

Over the eastern arch, in the rich frieze, were the arms of the Most Reverend Cibò and, under these, in the little circle, an anvil, with his usual motto: DURABO.[58] And there was on his right side a Hilarity and on the left a Faith who, posed over a little vase, was stretching upward her right hand, veiled in thin cloth.

Between this Faith and the Victory already mentioned was to be seen, in an octangle, one of the true honors of his Imperial Majesty, the taking of Goletta of Tunis, very well illustrated.[59]

The other arch, toward the west, showed in its frieze the arms of the Most Reverend Ippolito dei Medici, with his usual device below it, that is: a star having a long tail, with the motto, INTER OMNES.[60] And on the left side of this was a Liberality, dressed as a lady, with her feet over a basin and an open purse in her hand. On the right was Military Constancy, taken from the medal of Emperor Claudius II.[61]

Between the above-mentioned Constancy and the Jupiter Conservator, inside the octangle, appeared one of the holy enterprises of the Emperor, the defense of Vienna of Austria from the innumerable army of the new Xerxes.[62]

The length remaining between this loggia and the stage was on each side divided into six large squares of beautiful paintings made by various but all good masters, with so many and such diverse ornaments that I could not describe them, nor others understand them without seeing. Moreover, telling about the whole would be a

---

[58]Cardinal Innocenzo Cibò, 1491–1550, was a grandson, through his mother, of Lorenzo il Magnifico. He had been very powerful in the Florentine government, first in the service of Pope Clement VII and then under Duke Alessandro. The motto "Durabo" ("I shall endure") would, however, have seemed ironic if guests had realized that Cosimo was already depriving the Cardinal of his influence.

[59]In 1535 the Emperor had led personally a successful naval attack on forces of the pirate Barbarossa in Goletta, the port of Tunis. The Turks and pirates were for a while allied with Francis I against the Empire.

[60]Ippolito, 1511–1535, was the natural son of Giuliano dei Medici and thus a grandson of Lorenzo il Magnifico. He and Alessandro had been sent to "reign" over Florence for Clement VII in 1524. The inscription is taken from the phrase ". . . micat inter omnes / Iulium sides . . ." of Horace's *Odes,* Book I, Ode 12, lines 46-47: "The Julian star shines out among all." Giovio says (p. 47) that the Cardinal wished to express in guarded fashion his devotion to Giulia di Gonzaga.

[61]A.D. 214–270.

[62]The Turkish Sultan Suleiman the Magnificent, here compared to the Persian Xerxes, besieged Vienna unsuccessfully from September 25 to October 14, 1529. His defeat by Imperial forces ended, for the time being, the main Turkish threat to Central Europe, as the naval victory of Salamis and the land victory of Plataea had ended the Persian threat to Greece in 480–479 B.C. The comparison is justified.

very long bother. Therefore, briefly pointing out the stories with their seals and mottoes, I shall let the rest be surmised by the elevated minds, who will be able to imagine it.

I want to say only this, that each painting had four circles in the ornament that framed it, one above with the hieroglyph of the story,[63] one below with the two anchors, new seal of His Excellency, and one on each side with letters written in them, as we shall relate in the proper place later. Now let me simply point out the other coats of arms of the big frieze I had already started to describe, and which are these:

The first, on the right side near the mentioned loggia, were the royal arms of Spain, then France and Medici, then Medici and Austria, Medici and Savoy, Medici and Bologna, and, finally, the arms of His Excellency. On the left, opposite those of Spain, the arms of the Viceroy of Naples, Medici and Toledo, Medici and Sforza, Medici and Salviati, the arms of the Commander of the Fortress, and, finally, the Lily of the City.[64]

Among the stories of the east side, the right of the courtyard, first was the happy return of the Great Cosimo to his beloved homeland. In the round of the architrave, there were two doves upon a branch of gold, with these letters: SEDIBUS OPTATIS. Below: SALVE FATIS

[63]That is, the emblem.

[64]The juxtapositions of family arms recall illustrious marriages contracted by the Medici. Lorenzo, Duke of Urbino, 1492–1519, had married Madeleine de la Tour d'Auvergne, related to the ruling house of *France.* Catherine des Médicis, 1519–1589, had married Francis I's son Henry, later himself to be king of *France.* Duke Alessandro, 1510–1537, had obtained as wife Margherita d'*Austria,* illegitimate daughter of Charles V. Giuliano, Duke of Nemours, 1478–1516, had married Filiberta di *Savoia.* We have not discovered any alliance with a family of Bologna, and Giambullari's reporting may be in error for this detail. Cosimo himself was marrying into the house of *Toledo;* his grandfather Giovanni il Populano, 1467–1498, had been married to Caterina *Sforza,* and his father Giovanni delle Bande Nere, 1498–1526, to Maria *Salviati.* This last lady had no noble pretensions, but her family was much respected in Florence, and the fact that she was the Duke's mother probably worked more effectively in his favor than all the foreign and noble alliances.

The commander of the fortress was still responsible directly to the Emperor and therefore worthy of respectful attention. The glorious Red Lily evokes the defunct Republic.

[65]Cosimo il Vecchio had been exiled from Florence in 1433 by political enemies but was recalled the next year by a favorable government. His return marked the beginning of effective Medici rule. The quotations are from three different sources: "Sedibus optatis" is from line 203 of Book VI of the *Aeneid;* two doves have led Aeneas to the "desired place" in a forest where there is a tree with a branch of gold. "Salve . . . tellus" is from line 130 of Book VII: "Greetings, land owed to me by my destiny!"—Aeneas has discovered the future site of Rome. "Insigne . . . praesidium" is from Horace's *Odes,* Book II, Ode 1, line 13: "Illustrious defender of the sad (or oppressed)."

MIHI DEBITA TELLUS. On the side toward the loggia: INSIGNE MOESTIS PRAESIDIUM.[65]

There followed in the next painting the going of the Magnificent Lorenzo to Naples for the salvation of his homeland, well shown by the Pelican, set in the round of the architrave with these mottoes: DII ME TUENTUR, and the other, DIIS PIETAS MEA. Below and at the feet of Lorenzo: QUAECUMQUE MIHI FORTUNA FIDESQUE EST, IN VESTRIS PONO GREMIIS. On the right side: VICIT AMOR PATRIAE.[66]

In the third painting was shown the honored arrival in Florence of the glorious Leo X. There was in the architrave an upright basin, a very clear sign of his liberality, and one read there this motto: SEMPER HONOS NOMENQUE TUUM LAUDESQUE MANEBUNT. And below, this other one, as an answer: SEMPER HONORE MEO SEMPER CELEBRABERE DONIS. On the right side, DIES QUAE MAXIMA SEMPER.[67]

Lord Giovanni, coming triumphantly out of conquered Biagrassa, could be seen in the following painting. In the round of its architrave was a winged thunderbolt with these words around it: FIT VIA VI. NEC CLAUSTRA NEC IPSI. Below: HOC OPUS HIC LABOR EST. On the right side: REVOLANT EX AEQUORE MERGI.[68]

---

[66]After defeating the Pazzi Conspiracy in 1478, Lorenzo was excommunicated by Pope Sixtus IV for allowing the execution of the Archbishop of Pisa, who was implicated in the plot. At this juncture Florence found itself at war with the superior armies of the Papal States and of Naples. Lorenzo made a dramatic personal trip to Naples in order to see King Ferrante, from whom he obtained much better terms than the Pope would have given. "Dii me tuentur, diis pietas mea [et . . . cordi est]" is from Horace's *Odes,* Book I, Ode 17, lines 13–14: "The gods protect me, and my piety is dear to them"; "Quaecumque . . . gremiis" is from a speech of Ascanius in the *Aeneid,* Book IX, lines 260–261: "All chance and confidence have I placed in you." Thus, the fate of Florence depended upon the success of Lorenzo's mission. "Vicit amor patriae" is probably a paraphrase in the past tense of line 823, Book VI, of the *Aeneid:* "The love for his homeland will conquer."

[67]Cardinal Giovanni dei Medici, soon to become Pope Leo X, entered Florence in triumph on September 14, 1512, after his family had been in exile for eighteen years. The painting probably portrayed, however, his more pompous entry as Pope on November 30, 1515. "Semper . . . manebunt" is from a speech of Aeneas to Dido, in the *Aeneid,* Book I, line 609: "Your glory, your name, and your praises will live always"; "Semper . . . donis" is line 76 of Book VIII: "I shall always honor you and always praise you with presents." We have not found the source of "Dies quae maxima semper."

[68]Biagrassa was taken from the French in the spring of 1524. "Fit via vi" is part of line 494, Book II, of the *Aeneid,* from a passage describing the eruption of the furious Greeks into Troy: "Violence makes a way"; "Nec claustra nec ipsi":

The fifth large painting contained the most solemn coronation of the Most Serene Charles V by Clement VII. There was in its architrave a serpent that, holding its tail in its mouth, formed a circle. In this circle was painted a palace, such as was already used by the Egyptians as a figure for a monarch of the universe, and in it was this motto: IMPERIUM SINE FINE. Below: DIGNA TUIS INGENTIBUS OMNIA COEPTIS. On the right side: O FAMA INGENS INGENTIOR ARMIS.[69]

The last on this side was the painting showing us the many difficulties of Duke Alessandro in Naples, with the firm opposition of his powerful adversaries. In the round of the architrave was a palm tree, which, according to writers, rebounds against weight, with these words: VIRTUS REPULSAE NESCIA SORDIDAE. INTAMINATIS FULGET HONORIBUS. Below, and at the feet of the said Lord: NON INDEBITA POSCO REGNA MEIS FATIS. On the right side, by his adversaries: INCERTI QUO FATA FERANT. On the other side: VIM TEMPERATAM DII QUOQUE.[70]

"Neither bars of iron nor guards [can withstand the attack]" is from line 491 of the same passage. "Hoc opus hic labor est": "This is the work, this the task" is from Book VI of the *Aeneid,* line 129; the Sybil is telling Aeneas that it will be easy to go down into the underworld but very difficult to return. "Revolant . . . mergi": "The gulls fly back from the sea" is from line 361, Book I, of Vergil's *Georgics*. The return of the gulls is a sign of approaching bad weather.

[69]The coronation took place in Bologna on February 22, 1530, less than three years after Charles's troops had sacked Rome and made the Pope a prisoner. Cosimo and his mother were present at the ceremony as guests of Clement. "Imperium sine fine": "Empire without bounds" is from Book I of the *Aeneid,* line 279, part of Jupiter's prophecy of the future greatness of Rome. "Digna . . . coeptis": "All [will be] worthy of your grand plans" is from Book IX, line 296. Ascanius is assuring a young man who has volunteered for a dangerous mission that his mother will be cared for in his absence. "O fama . . . armis" is from Book XI, line 124: "O [hero] great by reputation and greater by deeds." The phrase is in laud of Aeneas. The emblem, showing a palace for a universal monarch, is taken from Horus Apollo, who is mentioned by name a little later in Giambullari's text. See section on Emblems and Classical Inscriptions.

[70]After Alessandro had become Duke, the former republicans in Florence complained so bitterly to the Emperor of their treatment under his rule that the young man was summoned to Naples, in 1535, to explain his actions. He apparently did so satisfactorily. Young Cosimo had accompanied his cousin on the mission. "Virtus . . . honoribus" is from Horace, Book III, Ode 2, lines 17–18: "Virtue, unshamed by failure, shines forth with untarnished honors"; "Non . . . fatis" is from lines 66–67 of Book VI of the *Aeneid:* "I do not ask for kingdoms not due me by my destiny." In these words of Aeneas is justified Alessandro's arrogance! "Incerti . . . ferant": "Uncertain where Fate will carry us" is from line 8 of Book III. Such is the situation of the Trojan survivors after the fall of their city. The last inscription, from lines 66–67 of Ode 4, Book III, of Horace, read: "Vis consili expers mole

On the other side, on the west, opposite the return of Cosimo, appeared the auspicious nativity of the Most Illustrious Duke Cosimo, as a new beginning of a happier century. The architrave showed this clearly, having in its round a Phoenix, with these letters: MAGNUS AB INTEGRO SAECLORUM NASCITUR ORDO. Below: FORTES CREANTUR FORTIBUS. On the side toward the loggia: IAM NOVA PROGENIES. On the other, common to this and to the following painting: REDEUNT SATURNIA REGNA.[71]

In the second painting was seen the creation, or rather election, of His Excellency to the office of Duke. Mercury's caduceus was in the architrave, accompanied by these words: SEQUIMUR TE SANCTE DEORUM. Below, at the feet of these electors: IMPERIOQUE ITERUM PAREMUS OVANTES.[72]

The third and twentieth books of Livy provided the subject for the third painting, which followed on this side, being opposite the Entry of Leo. It showed three proud Capuan ambassadors being expelled from the Roman Senate because of their audacious demand for something that was not due them, as the words written below described: PETENTIBUS PER ORATORES CAMPANIS ALTERUM ROMAE CONSULEM SENATUS ILLIS PER LICTOREM DISCESSUM IMPERAT. In the little round of this architrave was a winged horse, with this motto:

---

ruit sua / vim temperatam dii quoque provehunt": "Brute force bereft of wisdom falls of its own weight to ruin; the very gods make greater force tempered [with wisdom]."

[71]Cosimo had been born on June 12, 1519, in Florence. "Magnus . . . ordo," "Redeunt . . . regna," and "Iam . . . progenies" are, in that order, from lines 5, 6, and 7 of Vergil's Fourth Eclogue, in which the pagan poet was commonly believed to have predicted the coming of Christ: "A new revolution of the centuries is being born. / [The Virgin is returning to the earth] and with her the reign of Saturn. / A new race of mortals [is now being sent from Heaven]." These lines were thought by many people to be inspired in the same way as Holy Scripture, and to quote them in connection with the birth of a secular prince was to carry flattery very, very far. "Fortes creantur fortibus" is from Horace, Book IV, Ode 4, line 29: "The brave are born of the brave," another reference to the Duke's warrior father.

[72]On January 5, 1537, the Council of Forty-Eight confirmed Cosimo as Head of the Republic. On June 21, in the presence of the Council, he was given the still somewhat equivocal title, Duke of the Republic. The term *duca,* a cognate of both *doge* and *duce,* was still sufficiently undefined, at least in some minds, to permit its association with republican institutions. The ceremony of June 21 is doubtless the ceremony referred to here, though Cosimo was confirmed by the Emperor as hereditary Duke only in September. "Sequimur . . . deorum": "We follow you, Holy One of the gods" is from line 576, Book IV of the *Aeneid.* "Imperioque . . . ovantes" is from the next line: "And we obey you again with joy." Aeneas is speaking to a god who has appeared to him in a dream.

CAECIDIT TREMENDAE FLAMMA CHIMERAE. On the right side, where the ambassadors where fleeing: DURA FUGAE MALA.[73]

There was shown in the other painting the taking of Montemurlo, with the Egyptian owl above the lance of Pyrrhus, in the round of the architrave, and letters saying: IMPROVISA LOETI VIS RAPUIT RAPIETQUE GENTES. On the right side: FRACTI BELLO FATISQUE REPULSI. Below: NIL DESPERANDUM TEUCRO DUCE, ET AUSPICE TEUCRO.[74]

In the painting coming next, opposite the Coronation of the Emperor, was seen His Excellency, invested with all the ducal insignia by His Majesty, and in the round of the architrave was seen a magpie with bay leaves in its mouth—a sign, according to Horus Apollo, of whoever acts according to the oracle's orders. And there was this motto: NIL SINE TE MEI PROSUNT HONORES. Below: TUA CAESAR AETAS SIGNA NOSTRO RESTITUIT IOVI. On the right side: BENE APUD MEMORES. On the left: GRATES PERSOLVERE DIGNAS.[75]

---

[73]This painting depicted an incident recounted by Livy in Chapter 6, Book XXIII, of his *History of Rome*. When the citizens of Capua, an Italic ally of Rome, heard about Hannibal's victory at Cannae in 216 B.C., they tried to take advantage of the situation by requiring as condition to their aid that a Capuan be appointed one of the consuls of Rome. An enraged Roman Senate had the Capuan ambassadors escorted from the city. Vasari explains (III, 298, of his *Lives*) the rather recondite contemporary allusion. The Capuan ambassadors were to be compared with the Florentine cardinals Ridolfi, Gaddi, and Salviati, who had come from Rome soon after Cosimo's accession in order to question his rule. "Petentibus . . . imperat" is adapted from Livy: "To those seeking through the Capuan ambassadors the [office of] second Roman Consul, the Senate orders, through a lictor, departure." "Caecidit . . . chimerae" is from lines 15–16 of Horace's Ode 2, Book IV: "The flame of the frightful chimera fell." Thus the cardinals' blustering came to nought. "Dura fugae mala" is from line 28 of Ode 13, Book II: "The hard pains of flight."

[74]In July, 1537, at Montemurlo, forces loyal to Cosimo decisively whipped the republican exiles' army led by Filippo Strozzi. Pyrrhus, King of Epirus, had led an army into Italy in the third century B.C. We have been unable to discover the emblematic significance of his lance and of the Egyptian owl.

"Improvisa . . . gentes" is from Horace, Book II, Ode 13, lines 19–20: "The unexpected force of death has seized and will seize peoples." Thus may be consoled the relatives of democrats killed at Montemurlo! "Fracti . . . repulsi" is from line 13 of Book II of the *Aeneid:* "Broken by war and rejected by fate"—a description of the desperate plight of the Greeks besieging Troy before they came upon the stratagem of the Trojan horse. "Nil . . . Teucro" is from Horace's *Odes,* Book I, Ode 7, line 27: "There is no cause to despair with Teucer as leader and under his auspices." Teucer, a Greek leader in the Trojan war, is compared to Alessandro Vitelli, Cosimo's general, or perhaps to the Duke himself.

[75]The subject of this painting is puzzling, for Cosimo had not seen the Emperor since assuming power. Despite the language of Giambullari's description, the tableau must simply

The last contained the proxy marriage in Naples of His Excellency and the Most Illustrious Donna Eleonora of Toledo, and there were in the round of the architrave two crows, ancient symbol of weddings, with these words: BONA CUM BONA NUBIT ALITE VIRGO. On the side: DIIS AUSPICIBUS ET IUNONE SECUNDA. Below: BONI CONIUGES BENE VIVITE, BREVI LIBEROS DATE.[76]

Around under the paintings ran a continuous border of novel, very beautiful tapestries, of which there is no need to speak.

I don't want to say any more about the stage setting for the comedy in order not to take away its beauty with my inappropriate words. Even those who saw it can hardly imagine it. Therefore I go back to the opposite loggia, hung with gold-fringed crimson satin from the bottom of the vault to the floor. In this loggia's middle lunette was a very natural portrait of the old Cosimo the Great,[77] adorned with clusters and arcs of little festoons that accompanied it in two big rounds. There was also the new ducal insignia of entwined anchors and their motto: DUABUS.[78]

---

have shown Cosimo arrayed in his ducal regalia, authorized by the Emperor, but not conferred in person.

Horus Apollo was the supposed ancient author of a book of *Hieroglyphica,* the discovery of which in the fifteenth century had had much to do with the development of the mode of emblems. (See section on Emblems and Classical Inscriptions.) The emblem of the magpie with bay leaves is indeed illustrated in a Latin edition of his work published in Lyon in 1541. "Nil . . . honores" is from lines 9–10 of Ode 26 of Horace's Book I, in which the poet speaks to his muse: "My praises without you are worth nothing." "Tua . . . Iovi": "Your age, O Caesar, has restored to our Jove the insignia" is part of lines 4–6 of Ode 15 of Horace's Book IV. The passage is a warm eulogy of Augustus, to whom Charles V is here compared. "Bene apud memores": "well remembered" is from line 539, Book IV, of the *Aeneid.* "Grate . . . dignas" is from line 600 of the epic's first book; Aeneas is speaking to Dido: ". . . [it is not in our power] to render worthy thanks [for your good deeds]."

[76]Cosimo had sent two representatives, Luigi Ridolfo and Iacopo dei Medici, to Naples so that they could marry Eleonora in his name. "Bona . . . virgo" is from Catullus' Poem 61, lines 19–20. The whole passage is translated: "Junia marries Manlius, as beautiful as the inhabitant of Idalis, Venus, when she came to the Phrygian judge [Paris]; *she gives herself to her husband, a perfect virgin, under perfect auspices.*" "Diis . . . secunda" is a paraphrase of line 45 of Book IV of the *Aeneid,* translated: "Under the auspices of the gods and with a favorable Juno." "Boni . . . vivite," from lines 233–234 of Catullus' Poem 61, means: "Good couple, live well"; "Brevi liberos date," from lines 211–212 of the same poem, means: "Give children quickly."

[77]Cosimo il Vecchio, called *pater patriae,* 1389–1464.

[78]This device is the subject of a very interesting speculation in the "Ragionamento" of Ludovico Domenichi appended to Paolo Giovio's *Dialogo delle imprese* (157–58). Following is a translation of the principal remarks: "I don't know whether I shall be presumptuous, trying to guess and to penetrate into the very high conceptions of Princes, but

And on the eastern side the portrait of Leo X, with the two Most Reverend Cardinals Iulio dei Medici and Luigi dei Rossi[79] around the seat, so naturally figured that they seemed alive to people who knew them. The same was true for the portraits in the other painting, that is: Clement VII, with the Most Reverend Ippolito and the Most Illustrious Alessandro dei Medici,[80] placed on the western façade, or we mean "face."

Under this loggia was the table of the Bride and Groom, with great table extensions on each side, the length of the courtyard. There were seated more than a hundred of the first gentlewomen of the entire nobility, with those dresses and adornments appropriate for such wedding celebrations.

The courses of the great banquet were infinite, with many sorts of food in each course. I do not describe the particulars in order not to lose time for such an unimportant thing; it is enough to say that there lacked nothing appropriate to such a high prince.

The sumptuous banquet finished, there appeared before the tables an Apollo, dressed in crimson taffeta covered with golden tocca, with a belt almost of rainbow hue.[81] He had an ancient mantle of the same cloth, gathered above the left shoulder. He had a bow on his shoulder and a quiver at his flank. His shoes were of crimson satin, with an ingenious ancient-style knot of golden tassels in the form of two lions' heads. He was crowned with grcen laurel, above very long golden hair. Holding a lyre in his left hand and a little bow in his right, he came, in the midst of a choir of Muses dressed in this way:

The first was in very blond cloth, girded with a green olive branch and having a number of clus-

though I know nothing for sure I say that in my judgment he wanted to show that he has steadied his most happy state by two supports, so that he probably has to fear nothing. The two supports and props, if I am not mistaken, may be (1) the grace and favor of the invincible Emperor Charles V, and (2) the safety of the impregnable fortresses of his domain." The interpretation is ingenious and would be convincing if there were not the fact that Cosimo obtained control of Tuscan fortresses only in 1543. Perhaps the second anchor stood simply for some such general conception as "security at home."

[79]Cardinal Giulio dei Medici was the future Pope Clement VII. Cardinal dei Rossi had been one of Cosimo's sponsors at his baptism.

[80]Ippolito and Alessandro, cousins and both illegitimate, had represented Clement VII in Florence while he ruled from Rome. The two young men quarreled, and Alessandro is generally considered to have been responsible for Ippolito's death in 1535.

[81]Apollo, to whom classical tradition assigns many qualities, appears in the pageant (1) as god of the sun, and (2) as god of music and poetry.

ters and streamers. Her curly hair was scattered with thyme flowers, with a few bees around them, and she wore a hat of the same cloth but in an old-fashioned style, adorned with crystals and beryls and with garlands of chaste tree, with a chameleon as a crest. From her neck hung a string of pearls. There was a horned beetle on her breast, which was draped with the skin of a panther. Her buskins were of the ancient style, covered with catskin, with a crab on each foot. She had in her right hand a *trombone* and, in the other, a *taninera,*[82] as painters say, where, in a blue field, could be read in gold letters: THALIA.[83] And at the top there was a red ball, as in the *taninere* of all the others.

[82]This word appears in no dictionaries, but if one judges from context it seems rather clearly to have meant a tablet shaped like an artist's palette. Each of the Muses carries one with her name written on it.

[83]Thalia is the Muse of festivals and of pastoral and comic poetry. We have not translated the names of musical instruments carried by personages in the pageant; they are defined in the section, The Instruments.

Vasari's drawing for the costume of a Muse in the 1565 celebrations for the wedding of Prince Francesco —Courtesy Uffizi Gallery, Drawings Department

The second was dressed in greenish-yellow cloth, having two entwined serpents as a belt and a hyena's skin slung across her shoulder. Her long hair, scattered with marjoram flowers, hung from under a winged hat, rich with agates and topazes, garlanded with lesser burnet, with a parrot as crest. There hung from her neck a number of finely worked pieces of yellowish-green glass, and she had old-fashioned buskins made of monkey-skins, with the heads of the animals under her knees. In her right hand she held a *dolzaina* and in the left the *taninera,* in which many dogwood berry leaves, a groundsel tree, and a nightingale accompanied her gilded name EUTERPE[84] in the blue field.

The third, more playful than the others and accompanied by many odors, was dressed in splendid cloth, with a number of streamers of tocca. On the cloth was a white goatskin, and she had as a belt the famous girdle of Venus, as described by lapidarians. Her golden tresses were arranged by a master hand, scattered with myrtle flowers, below an attractive hat in the ancient style, of tan satin with gold and emeralds, crowned with roses and with a red branch of coral for its crest. She had buskins of rabbitskin on her nude flesh, with the rabbits' heads on her feet. The skins were bound around her legs by the paws under the knees and at the ankles. She held in her right hand a *violone* and in the left the *taninera,* with swallows and wagtails, on which, in the midst of pomegranate flowers and damask roses, on a blue field, one could read: ERATO,[85] in gold letters.

The fourth, pompous in a richer dress, was attired in gold-sewn crimson silk, belted with fresh heliotrope. The dress was decorated with various precious stones, that is, chrysolite, sun's eye, eaglestone, oriental jasper, *pantaura.* She had the little skin of a lion cub across her breast and at the bottom of her dress a flounce of gold with all the musical instruments marvelously depicted. Above her loose hair, strewn with jessamines and having a well-composed garland of cedar, this lady constituted the ornament and basis of five layers of organetti, which, put together, provided her with a hat and crest. Her pretty buskins were of lynxskin and had on each foot a bright beetle. She carried in her right hand a *piffero* and in the other the *taninera,* adorned with peonies and verbenas, with two cynocephali,[86] having between

[84]Muse of music.
[85]Muse of lyric poetry.
[86]Egyptian dog-faced men.

them the name: MELPOMENE.[87]

The fifth was dressed in crimson satin, with many streamers of gold tocca, red and rust-colored. Her belt was of scammony and aconite, above the leopardskin. Her red hair was under a sort of helmet of red satin, with a raised iron visor, sewn all over with amethysts and diamonds and, above this, serving as a crest, a woodpecker. Her ancient-style buskins were of wolfskin, with a small artificial head on the back of each foot. She had in her right hand a *flauto* and in the other the *taninera,* with the gilded name CLIO[88] in the blue field, crowned with butcher's-broom.

The sixth was in a splendid yellow cloth, designed with a number of clusters and Moorish knots of cloth sewn with pure silver. Her belt was a slender vine branch. There hung from her shoulders an old stagskin. Her hair was loose under an ancient-style helmet made of yellow cloth, strewn with sapphires and hyacinths, crowned with oak, with an eagle as crest. Her very white stockings were of lambs' skins, with their little gilded heads on the calf of the legs, bound together in front with clever weavers' knots of gold tocca. She had in her right hand a *leuto* and in the left the *taninera,* on which one read TERPSICHORE,[89] between two partridges inside a garland of ears of grain and corn.

The seventh was dressed in gold embroidered cloth sewn with black silk, so that it seemed to be burning lead. The cloth was strewn with *camoini* and black jaspers, and a sort of knapsack of hare-skin was slung over her shoulders. Her hair was partly wrapped around her head and partly over her shoulders, crowned with mandragora leaves, under a pyramid-shaped hat, which was covered with the same cloth found in her dress and which had, in a well-designed upper part, three rows of angelic countenances with wings. These seemed to be successively smaller. Between one row and the other were seen whirls of little spangles gathered in Moorish knots, with numerous but small golden tassels. There was a rich chair of fire and gold on the crest of the pyramid. Her boots seemed to be of lead, and they had on each foot a little tortoise fixed in such a way that it made a fine buskin. In her right hand she carried a *storta* and in the other the *taninera,* with two little pine branches dressing the blue space in which was written: POLYMNIA.[90]

---

[87]Muse of tragedy.
[88]Muse of history.
[89]Muse of dancing.
[90]Muse of singing and rhetoric.

The eighth was all blue, dressed in a beautiful taffeta sewn with golden stars, with various figures of the forty-eight celestial images, each one in the proper place, adorned with its particular stars. She had slung over her shoulders a zodiac, with its secret images, properly matching the rest of the dress. Her hair was blue, as were the *mazocchio*[91] and hat on her hair. These were sewn with golden stars, with, for crest, a Cupid holding his face in his hand but with the eyes revealed. She had a *cornetta* in her right hand and in the left the *taninera,* with the name: URANIA.[92]

The last was completely white, dressed in snowy Rheims linen, which was sewn all over with celestial characters and divine writing of reddish black color, as the Cabalists say the first letters were.[93] Upon this was an outer dress of very fine silver tocca that, next to the white below, seemed a true crystal. The hair and ornaments of this lady were of the same color and tocca. A little ancient hat had, embroidered on its *mazocchio,* fifteen characters of the first fixed stars, these standing out in the same reddish black color. Above was a very white Capricorn as a crest. The buskins were of the same cloth, with other letters and figures, different from those mentioned above. This one, I say, had a *ribechino* in her right hand and, in the other, the *taninera* with her name: CALLIOPE.[94]

When this fine company had arrived in the high presence of the ladies and gentlemen, Apollo, sweetly playing, sang the following stanzas, composed by our Giovanni Battista Gelli:

Dal quarto Ciel' dove co'l mio dorato
Carro, girando al Mondo io dò la luce,
Vengo hor tra voi: da quello amor tirato,
Ch'io portai sempre valoroso DUCE
Alla nobile stirpe, onde sei nato;
C'hoggi sovr'Arno piu ch'ogn'altra luce:
Et tien' per suo vessillo & caro segno

[91]The *mazocchio* was apparently a headdress shaped like a ring, which could be worn with or without a cap in the middle.

[92]Muse of astronomy.

[93]Central to the beliefs of the Cabalists was their conviction that the letters of the Hebrew alphabet, given by God, had mystical (and numerical) significance. Cabala was a Jewish tradition of mystical thought that was believed to have its beginnings with Moses. It had come into Western Europe through medieval Spain. Like the Hermetic tradition, of Alexandrian origin, to which it bears a close relationship, Cabala intensely interested some Renaissance philosophers. Of these the most important before 1539 had been Pico della Mirandola, protégé of Lorenzo il Magnifico.

[94]Muse of eloquence and heroic poetry.

Le verdi fronde del mio sacro legno.
Io son' colui, che co'l mio aspetto lieto
Fo vive queste cose inferiori;
Onde si mosse il figlio di Iapeto
A volermi furare i primi honori.
Et questo è delle Muse il santo Ceto,
Ch'accendon' sempre i generosi cori
A gloriose imprese; & sono scorte
A chi per fama vuol' vincer' la Morte.
Et veggend'hoggi insieme celebrarvi
Le sacre Noze in amoroso zelo,
Volendo di mia vista lieti farvi
Lasciati ho i miei corsier' liberi in Cielo:
Et vengo con costoro ad honorarvi
Sotto questo mortale aereo velo:
Et con la luce mia, che vi mantiene,
Porgervi quanto io mai posso di bene.
Et perche del futuro io son presago,
Che il lucido occhio mio vede ogni tempo,
Tal che de vostri studi ogn'hor m'appago,
Come ei sien' preda et di Morte, et di tempo:
Onde veggiendo quanto ogn'huomo è vago
D'intender quel che dee recargli il tempo:
Parte dirò di quel che in Ciel si vuole
Che di voi sorga, & della vostra Prole.
Dentro al bel sen' di Flora origine hebbe
La Regia stirpe donde, nato sei,
Da un'altro COSMO, a cui non poco debbe
Che l'arricchì di mille alti Trofei.
Questi lei tanto & sè per fama accrebbe
Che ascritto fu fra i maggior semidei:
Et sì fur l'opre sue chiare & leggiadre,
Che morto lo chiamò la Patria padre.
Di costui nacque poi quel santo Alloro,
Premio delle alte & valorose imprese,
Sotto'l qual vide Flora il secol' d'oro,
Che'nsino al Ciel le frondi sue distese.
Questi co'l suo saver' dall'Indo al Moro
Cotal' dell'amor' suo le menti accese,
Che in sin' donde i miei raggi son piu ardenti
Devote al nome suo venner' le genti.
Nacquero poi di questa sacra pianta
Molti altri rami, & sì crebbero à gara;
Che l'alma Roma la sua sede santa
N'ornò come di cosa illustre & chiara.
Ma perche il Suol' terrestre non si vanta
Di cosa alcuna eterna, benche rara;
Quando la Parca il fil troncar' ne volse,
Ogni alto ramo a questa pianta tolse.
Ma hor (vostra Mercè) coppia si bella
Risorge à tanta stirpe un nuovo Germe,
Che le perdute frondi rinnovella;
Et rende vive le sue parte inferme:
Et COSMO per principio ha come quella;

Ma con radici assai piu salde & ferme:
Et crescerà con tanto piu valore,
Quanto è di quello il COSMO suo maggiore.
L'Aquila altera, dentro al verde seno
Di questa nobil' pianta, fara'l nido,
Di legni & d'herbe piu Salubri pieno,
Che degli Indi ò Sabei ne porga il lido:
Et ne difenderà dal rio Veneno
D'ogni Animal' mortifero & infido
Le verdi fronde; e i frutti cari & belli
Da i piu selvaggi, & piu rapaci Uccelli.
Ben si può gloriar la bella Flora,
Che di suo stato tenga il freno in mano
Si bella Coppia, COSMO & LEONORA;
Dal Cielo graditi sovra l'uso humano:
Faranno queste verdi piante anchora
Si bei fior', che d'appresso & di lontano
Ne vinceran, co i lor soavi odori
Di Tesifone & d'Iride i furori.
Quanto lieta ella sia, che piu non teme
Di fortuna l'orgoglio acerbo & fero,
Vedrete hor che verran' con ella insieme
E i santi numi del suo largo Impero,
Pien' d'alta sicurtà, di ferma speme,
Portati da desio pronto & leggiero
Che gli have accolti d'ogni vostro intorno
A rallegrarsi di si lieto giorno.

Voi sante muse in questa al Ciel' devote,
Tutte infiammate di divino Amore,
Il sacrato Hymeneo con dolci note
Cantate liete con sincero Core:
Hymeneo, quel, che solo & santo puote
Di duoi far un sol cor' col suo valore;
C'hoggi venga propitio à vostri prieghi,
Et con dolci legami ambi duoi leghi.

(From the Fourth Heaven,[95] where, going around with my gilded chariot, I give light to the world, I come among you, drawn by that love which I always bore, valiant Duke, toward the noble race from which you were born. Today, over the Arno, it shines more than any other light and takes as its standard and cherished sign the green leaves of my sacred wood. / I am he who with my happy face gives life to things below, whence moved the son of Iapetus to try to rob me of first honors.[96] And this is the sacred rank of the

[95]According to the Ptolemaic astronomy (poetically illustrated in Dante's *Paradiso*), the sun lay in the fourth of nine concentric spheres surrounding the earth. Copernicus was to publish his *De revolutionibus orbium caelestium* in 1543, just four years after the wedding, but his theories would gain wide acceptance only after Galileo, in the early seventeenth century.

[96]The son of Iapetus was Prometheus, who, in revolt against Jupiter, climbed into the sky and stole fire from Apollo's chariot, that is to say, from the sun.

Muses, who always fire generous hearts to glorious enterprises and who are the guides of anyone who wishes, through fame, to conquer death. / And today, seeing sacred matrimony celebrated here in amorous zeal and wishing to make you happy by seeing me, I have left my steeds free in the sky; and I come with the Muses to honor you under this mortal, aerial veil and with my light, which sustains you, to offer you everything good that I possibly can. / And because I am a seer of the future, my lucid eye seeing all time—so that I am concerned with your affairs every hour, albeit they are the prey of Death and of time—therefore, seeing how eager every man is to hear what time is to bring him, I will tell you a part of what Heaven wishes to issue from you and from your seed. / Inside the beautiful breast of Flora[97] the kingly stock of which you were born had its origin from another COSIMO,[98] to whom she owes not a little because he enriched her with a thousand exalted trophies. This man increased her and himself so much through fame that he was inscribed among the major demigods. And his works were so shining and so pleasing that when he was dead his homeland called him father. / From him was born then that holy laurel,[99] prize of high and valorous enterprises, under whom Flora saw the Golden Age and that raised its unfolded leaves up to Heaven. This man, with his knowledge from the Hindu to the Moor, so fired minds with love of him that peoples as far as the places where my rays are most burning became devoted to his name. / There were then born from this sacred plant many other branches, and they grew one faster than the other, so that beneficent Rome adorned its Holy Seat with them as with an illustrious and shining thing.[100] But because the terrestrial ground boasts nothing eternal, however rare, when the Fate decided to break her thread, she took every high branch from this plant.[101] / But now, thanks to you, beautiful

[97]Flora had been an Italic goddess of agriculture and of the harvest, but it is her name alone that makes of her the figuration of Florence.

[98]Cosimo il Vecchio.

[99]A play upon the words *alloro* (laurel) and *Lorenzo.* Il Magnifico, 1449–1492, was in fact the grandson, rather than the son, of Cosimo. It is interesting to see that, already in 1539, his reign was looked on as a golden age of the past.

[100]An allusion to the Medici popes Leo X and Clement VII.

[101]Atropos, the eldest of the three Parcae, was believed to cut the thread of human life with her scissors. The legitimate male line of the main branch of the Medici family had been extinguished with the death of Lorenzo, Duke of Urbino, in 1519, its illegitimate male line with the assassination of Duke Alessandro in 1537. The female line survived, it is true, in the person of Catherine des Médicis, wife of the future King Henry II of France.

couple, there arises from such a great stock a new sprout that renews the lost leaves and gives life to infirm parts. It, like the other one, has COSIMO as beginning, but with rather more solid and firm roots; and it will grow with all the more energy because its COSIMO is greater than the other. / The proud Eagle[102] will make its nest inside the green breast of this noble plant, full of more salubrious woods and grasses than those offered by the shores of the Hindus and the Star-Worshippers. It will defend the plant's green leaves from the evil venom of all poisonous and faithless animals, and its precious and beautiful fruits from the most savage and most rapacious birds. / Beautiful Flora can well exult that the rein of its state is held in the hands of such a beautiful couple: COSIMO and ELEONORA, more pleasing to Heaven than is usual for humans. And these green plants will also make such beautiful flowers that, near and far, they will overcome with their sweet odors the furies of Tisiphone and Iris.[103] / You will see how happy she is, no longer fearing the bitter and fierce pride of fortune, now that there will come with her the holy deities of her wide empire, full of high security, of firm hope moved by a prompt and swift desire that has gathered them from all around to rejoice in such a happy day. / You, Holy Muses, devoted to this lady in Heaven, all inflamed with divine love, happily, with sincere heart, sing to the sacred Hymen.[104] Sing to Hymen, to him who, alone and holy, can make one heart of two with his power—that he come today in answer to your prayers and tie both of them with sweet bonds.)

Then the Muses, most sweetly singing, pronounced the following *canzone* for nine:

Sacro & santo Hymeneo
 Il Ciel ti chiama, Arno ti pregha, & Flora
 Alle Noze di COSMO & LEONORA:
 Vien dunque ò dolce Dio,
 Vieni Hymeneo, ò Hymeneo, Io.
Vien desiato bene, al santo offitio,
 Prendi la face, e'l velo,
 Che l'un' accenda, & l'altro copra Amore:
 Fa segno hoggi col Cielo

[102]The Emperor, who will draw sustenance from the Medici house and, in return, defend it from enemies.

[103]Tisiphone was one of the Furies who carried out divine vengeance on mankind. Iris was a messenger of the gods who cut the thread detaining the soul in the body of dying people. The two represent in this context simply death, which has felled all men in the main line.

[104]God of marriage, often represented as a young man carrying a torch and a veil.

Che te lieto dimostri, & sì propitio
Che dentro ad ambi duoi si regga un Core.
Celeste alto vapore
Al tuo santo spirar quinci esca fuora
Amor lascivo, et Nemesi, & Pandora.
Vien dunque ò dolce Dio
O Hymeneo, Hymeneo Io.
Deh porgi al Ciel, è a lor tua dolce aita;
Onde Pianta rinasca
Simile al tronco Avito, ornata & rara
All'ombra cui si pasca
Et Arno, & Flora in piu quieta vita;
Dolce appagando ogni lor doglia amara.
Fate gelosi à gara
Chi di piu alta Prole orna & ristora
Quella stirpe, che'l Cielo, e'l mondo honora.
Vien dunque, ò dolce Dio
Vien Hymeneo, ò Hymeneo, Io.

(Sacred and Holy Hymen, Heaven calls you, Arno entreats you and Flora to the wedding of COSIMO and ELEONORA: come thus, O sweet god, come Hymen, O Hymen, Io. / Come, desired good, to the holy office, take the torch and the veil, the one to light up and the other to cover love. Make a sign today with Heaven that will show yourself happy and so favorable that one heart will reign in both. High celestial emanation, at your holy sighing let there now depart lascivious Love, Nemesis, and Pandora.[105] Come thus, O sweet god, O Hymen, Hymen, Io. / Offer to Heaven and to them your sweet aid, with which may be reborn a plant like the ancestral trunk, ornate and precious. In its shade may both Arno and Flora graze in a quieter life, it sweetly appeasing their every bitter pain. Make people compete jealously to see who can adorn and restore this stock with higher offspring—this stock that honors Heaven and the world. Come thus, O sweet god, come Hymen, O Hymen, Io.)

[105]Nemesis, goddess of vengeance, and Pandora, known for her box of evils, represent here only misfortune—unless in mentioning the first Gelli wished to allude to die-hard republicans.

CANTUS
Sa- cr'et san- to Hime-ne-
CANTUS SECUNDUS
Sa- cr'et san- to Hime-ne- o,
CANTUS TERTIUS
Sa- cr'et san- to Hime-ne- o
ALTUS
Sa-
ALTUS SECUNDUS
Sa- cr'et san- to Hime-ne-
TENOR
Sa- cr'et san- to Hi- me- ne- o,
TENOR SECUNDUS
Sa- cro et san- to Hi- me- ne-
QUINTA PARS
Sa-
BASSUS
Sa- cro et san- to Hime-

5
o il ciel ti chi- a- ma Ar- no ti
Sa- cr'et san- to Hime- ne- o il ciel ti chi- a- ma
il ciel ti chi- a- ma, il ciel ti chia- ma
cr'et san- to Hime- ne- o il ciel ti chia- ma Ar-
o il ciel ti chia- ma Ar- no
sa- cr'et san- to Hime- ne- o il ciel ti chi- a- ma
o il ciel ti chi- a- ma, il ciel ti chia- ma,
cr'et san- to Hime- ne- o il ciel ti chia- ma
ne- o il ciel ti chia- ma Ar- no ti prie-

10
prie- gha et Flo- ra
Ar- no ti prie- gha et Flo-
Ar- no ti prie- gha et Flo- ra
no ti prie- gha, Ar- no ti prie- gha et
ti prie- gha et Flo- ra, Ar- no ti prie- gha et Flo-
Ar- no ti prie- gha, Ar- no ti prie- gha et Flo- ra
ti- chi- a- ma Ar- no ti prie- gha et Flo- ra
Ar- no ti prie- gh'et Flo-
gha et Flo- ra

15
a le noz- ze di Cos- mo et Le- o- no- ra
ra a le noz- ze di Cos- mo
a le noz- ze di Cos- mo a le noz- ze di
Flo- ra a le noz- ze di
ra a le noz- ze di Cos- mo et Le- o- no- ra, a le noz-
a le noz- ze di Cos- mo et Le- o- no- ra
a le noz- ze di Cos- mo et Le- o- no- ra, a le noz- ze di
ra a le noz- ze di
a le noz- ze di Cos- mo et Le- o- no- ra

20
vien dun- que o dol- ce Di- o o
et Leo- no- ra vien dun- qu'o dol- ce Di- o
Cos- mo et Le- o- no- ra o i-
Cos- mo et Le- o- no- ra vien dun- qu'o dol- ce Di- o
ze di Cos- mo et Le- o- no- ra vien dun- que o dol-
vien dun- que o dol- ce Di- o
Cos- mo et Le- o- no- ra vien dun- qu'o
Cos- mo et Le- o- no- ra vien dun- qu'o dol- ce Di-
vien dun- qu'o dol- ce Di- o o

25
i- o, o i- o vien Hi- me- ne- o, o Hime- ne- o, o
o i- o, o i- o vien Hi- me- ne- o,
o, o i- o vien Hi- me- ne- o, o Hi- me- ne- o,
o i- o vien Hi- me- ne- o, o
ce Di- o o i- o, o i- o vien Hi- me- ne-
i- o vien Hi- me- ne- o, o Hi- me-
dol- ce Di- o o i- o,
o o i- o vien Hi- me- ne- o, vien
i- o, o i- o vien Hi- me- ne- o, Hi- me- ne- o

30
i- o.
o Hi- me- ne o i- o.
i- o, o Hi- me- ne- o i- o.
Hi- me- ne- o i- o, i- o.
o, o Hi- me- ne- o i- o.
ne- o i- o.
o Hi- me- ne- o i- o, i- o.
Hi- me- ne- o, o Hi- me- ne- o i- o, i- o.
i- o, o Hi- me- ne- o i- o.

35
Vien de- si- a- to be- ne al san- t'of- fi- ti- o pren- di
Vien de- si- a- to be- ne al san- t'of- fi- tio
Pren- di la fa- ce
Vien de- si- a- to be- ne al san- t'of-fi- ti- o
Vien de- si- a- to be- ne al san- t'of- fi- tio pren- di la
Pren- di la
Vien de- si- a- to be- ne al san- t'of- fi- tio
Vien de- si- a- to be- ne al san- t'of- fi- tio pren- di la
Vien de- si- a- to be- ne al san- t'of- fi- tio

40
la fa- c'el ve- lo et l'al- tro co- pr'a- mo-
che l'un ac- cen- da et l'al- tro co- pr'a- mo- re,
el ve- lo che l'un ac- cen- da et
che l'un ac- cen- da et l'al- tra co- pra a- mo- re et
fa- c'el ve- lo che l'un ac- cen- da et l'al- tro co- pra a- mo- re
fa- c'el ve- lo che l'un ac- cen- da et l'al- tro co- pra a- mo-
che l'un ac- cen- da et
fa- c'el ve- lo et l'al- tro co- pr'a- mo-
che l'un ac- cen- da

45
re fa se- gn'hog-gi col cie- lo, fa se- gn'hog-gi col
et l'al- tro co- pr'a- mo- re fa se- gn'hog- gi col cie-
l'al- tro co- pr'a- mo- re
l'al- tro co- pr'a- mo- re fa se- gn'hog- gi col cie- lo
et l'al- tro co- pr'a- mo- re fa se- gno hog- gi col cie- lo fa se- gn'hog-
re fa se- gn'hog-gi col cie- lo, fa se- gn'hog-gi col
l'al- tro co- pra a- mo- re fa se- gn'hog- gi col cie-
re fa se- gn'hog- gi col cie-
et l'al- tro co- pr'a- mo- re fa se- gn'hog-gi

50
cie- lo che te lie- to di- mo- stri et si pro-
lo che te lie- to di- mo- stri, che te lie- to di- mo-
che te lie- to di- mo- stri, che te lie- to di- mo- stri
che te lie- to di- mo- stri, che te lie- to di- mo- stri
gi col cie- lo che te lie- to di- mo- stri, che te lie- to di-
cie- lo che te lie- to di- mo- stri, che te lie- to di- mo- str'et
lo che te lie- to di- mo- stri
lo che te lie- to di- mo- stri
col cie- lo che te lie- to di-

55
pi- tio che den- tr'ad am- bi du- oi si reg- g'un co- re
str'et si pro- pi- tio che den- tr'ad am- bi du- oi si reg- ga
et si pro- pi- tio
et si pro- pi- tio si
mo- str'et si pro- pi- tio che den- tr'ad am- bi du- oi si reg- ga
si pro- pi- tio che den- tr'ad am- bi du- oi si reg- g'un co-
et si pro- pi- tio che den- tr'ad am- bi du- oi si
che den- tr'ad am- bi du- oi si reg- g'un
mo- str'et si pro- pi- tio si reg- g'un co- re

60
ce- le- st'al- to va- po- re al
un co- re ce- le- st'al- to va- po- re
si reg- g'un co- re ce- le- st'al- to va- po- re
reg- g'un co- re ce- le- st'al- to va- po- re al
un co- re ce- le- st'al- to va- po- re al
re ce- le- ste al- to va-po-
reg- g'un co- re ce- le- st'al- to va- po- re al
co- re ce- le- ste al- to va- po- re
ce- le- ste al- to- va- po re

65
tuo san- to spi- rar quin- c'e- sca fo- ra a-
quin- c'e- sca fo- ra
al tuo san- to spi- rar a-
tuo san- to spi- rar quin- c'e- sca fo- ra
tuo san- to spi- rar quin- c'e- sca fo- ra a-
re quin- c'e- sca fo- ra
tuo san- to spi- rar quin- c'e- sca fo- ra a- mor la-
al tuo san- to spi- rar quin- c'e- sca fo- ra
al tuo san- to spi- rar quin- c'e- sca fo- ra a-

70
mor la- sci- vo, a- mor la- sci- vo et Neme- si et Pan- do-
a- mor la- sci- vo, a- mor la- sci- vo et Neme- si
mor la- sci- vo, a- mor la- sci- vo et
a- mor la- sci- vo a- mor la- sci- vo et
mor la- sci- vo a- mor la- sci- vo, a- mor la- sci- vo et Ne-
a- mor la- sci- vo, a- mor la- sci- vo et Neme- si,
sci- vo, a- mor la- sci- vo et
a- mor la- sci- vo, a- mor la- sci- vo et Ne- me-
mor la- sci- vo, a- mor la- sci- vo et Neme-si et Pan- do-

75
ra vien dun- que o dol- ce Di- o
et Pan- do- ra vien dun- qu'o dol- ce Di-
Neme- si et Pan- do- ra vien dun- que o dol- ce Di- o o
Ne- me- si et Pan- do- ra vien dun- que, dun- que o dol-
me- si et Pan- do- ra vien dun- qu'o dol- ce Di-
et Neme- si et Pan- do- ra vien
Pan- do- ra vien dun- que, vien dun- que o dol-
si et Pañ- do- ra vien dun- qu'o dol- ce Di-
ra vien dun- qu'o dol- ce Di-

80
o i- o, o i- o, o Hi- me- ne- o, o Hi- me-
o o i- o, o i- o, o Hi- me-
i- o, o i- o, o Hi- me- ne- o, o Hi- me-
ce Di- o o i- o, o i- o, o Hi- me-
o o i- o, o Hi- me- ne-
dun- qu'o dol- ce Di- o o i- o,
ce Di- o o Hi- me- ne- o, o
o o i- o, o Hi- me- ne- o
o o i- o, o i- o, o Hi- me- ne- o, o Hi- me-

85
ne- o, o i- o vien dun- qu'o dol- ce Di- o
ne- o vien dun- que o dol- ce Di- o o
ne- o i- o, vien dun- que o dol- ce Di- o o i-
ne- o i- o vien dun- que, vien dun- qu'o dol- ce Di- o
o i- o, vien dun- que, dun- que o dol- ce
o i- o, vien dun- que, vien dun- qu'o
Hime- ne- o o i- o, vien dun- qu'o dol- ce Di- o o
o Hi- me- ne- o i- o, vien dun- qu'o dol- ce Di- o o
ne- o i- o, vien dun- que o dol- ce Di-

90
o i- o, o i- o, o Hi- me- ne- o
i- o, o i- o, o Hi- me- ne- o, o Hi- me- ne- o
o o i- o, o Hi- me- ne- o, o Hi- me- ne- o
o i- o, o Hi- me- ne- o, o
Di- o o i- o, o i- o, o Hi- me- ne- o
dol- ce Di- o o i- o,
i- o, o Hi- me- ne- o, o Hi- me-
i- o, o i- o, o Hi- me- ne- o, o Hi- me- ne- o
o o i- o, o Hi- me- ne- o, o

95
o Hi- me- ne- o o i- o.
o i- o.
i- o, o Hi- me- ne- o i- o.
Hi- me- ne- o i- o, i- o.
i- o, o Hi- me- ne- o i- o.
o Hi- me- ne- o i- o.
ne- o i- o.
i- o, o Hi- me- ne- o i- o.
Hi- me- ne- o, o Hi- me- ne- o i- o, i- o.

The sweet singing of the Muses being finished, there appeared the beautiful Flora, with five nymphs around her and two rivers for her company, and behind her a large cortege, as you will see below in the proper places.

She was dressed with rich brocade and, under her gilded belt, was adorned with a wide frieze, in which were seen figured the instruments of each liberal and mechanical art. These were divided in learned order, between very beautiful fringes of gold that accompanied the frieze above and below. Under her armored arms, covered with a silver veil, fell turned-back sleeves used as a mantle, all in golden cloth with Red Balls[106] in relief, expertly distributed over it. Above each of her shoulders was a lion's head, from whose mouth issued, besides the arm, that silver veil which covered the gilded steel. Her neck and throat were adorned with a very rich lady's gorget, and above the long hair, sewn with flowers, which hung about her shoulders, was the ducal beret. Its *mazocchio* was adorned with very rich jewels and with gilded spiral points, which appeared above and outside. And she had as a crest, above a gilded little vase, the Imperial Eagle, with its wings partially stretched out as though it wished to hatch the Red Balls, which were visible, gathered under its feathers. Her buskins were of gold-sewn silk next to the skin, with ancient mask buttons among various clusters and bows arranged up each shoe. And as Lady of the others, with a rod in her right hand, she came before all of them, between two Old Men, thus figured:

The one on the right had very long and thick beard and hair, almost tangled, with a big garland of oak. He was nude all over, having across him a mantle of pale taffeta. His belt was of tree branches, and he was shod with reeds. He carried a great horn of plenty, pouring out water copiously, and in the main mouth of it was written: ARNO.

The other, who seemed younger and was on his left, wore hair and a beard of moss. He was covered with a thin mantle of silver tocca strewn with black tadpoles. He had moss buskins and held in his arm a little vase. The latter was con-

[106]Six red balls appeared on the Medici coat of arms and were, in everyone's mind, the symbol of the family. In Florence Medici partisans were wont to shout "Palle, palle, palle!" in opposition to the republicans' cries of "Libertà!" The combination of the red balls with the Imperial Eagle affords a plastic metaphor that is, at the least, baroque.

tinually pouring and had written, inside its mouth: MOGNONE.[107]

Shortly after Flora came a nymph dressed in red and yellow taffeta with many streamers of gold tocca. And above her loose-hanging hair she wore an antique hat, with a crest of a golden cup from which were drinking in company a fox and a wolf.

With her was a lady dressed in purple, whose bodice of gold tocca bore eight balls in front and eight behind. Her very white hair was crowned with a garland of poplar. She carried in her arms a vase pouring water, and inside it were letters saying: SIEVE.[108]

Third came a matron rather than a nymph, dressed in sandstone rock, all in rags and barefoot. She had long hair, braided and woven in a garland of chisels, which were very cleverly worked in. She had as a crest a little pinnacle with a red moon above it. She carried in her hand a crude basin of sandstone, having inside it a carpenter's square, a hammer, and a pair of compasses.

The fourth, girded with green cloth, was dressed with laurel branches, variously bound with bits of gold tocca. And she had a fine pair of buskins composed of laurel leaves.

The last was dressed in yellow and purple. Above a fine nymph's coiffure, she was adorned with many flowers, which, cleverly divided into different garlands, made her pleasing and pretty. She carried in her arm a vase pouring out water, with the name ELSA[109] written on the edge.

At their appearance, Apollo, again playing, started the following stanzas:

Ecco Signor colei, che cotanto ami,
  Ecco la patria tua, Fiorenza, quella
  Che spera all'ombra de tuoi santi rami
  Fuggir gli influssi d'ogni acerba stella:
  Et prega il Ciel, che in si saldi legami
  Leghi voi coppia sovr'ogn'altra bella;
  Che di voi nasca stirpe al mondo tale
  Che spieghi insino al Ciel secura l'Ale.
Et per mostrarti quanto allei sia grato,
  Che in si bel nodo involto hoggi ti sia;
  Del bel contado suo seco ha menato
  Le care et vaghe Nymfe in compagnia.

---

[107]A small stream that comes from near Fiesole, flows through Florence, and joins the Arno within the city.

[108]A tributary that joins the Arno upstream from Florence.

[109]A stream that enters the Arno between Florence and Pisa.

Quella cura have ogn'hor del tuo bel Prato,
Et seco a gara te servir' desia:
Et quanto ogn'altra di belleza eccede,
Le avanza et vince di sincera fede.
Quella che le chiome ha, ch'assembran' neve,
Che pur hor fiocchi in vago colle ameno;
Di Popol cinte, della antica Sieve
La Driada è, che dentro al largo seno
Del bel Mugello tuo l'acque riceve,
Per renderle con Arno al gran Tyrreno:
Et sovr'ogn'altra al Ciel' per gratie renda,
Ch'a tanto grado la sua stirpe ascenda.
Quell'altra che veste ha si stracciata,
Che fatto ha'l volto di pudor vermiglio;
L'antica Fiesole è, che edificata
Fu da Iapeto del gran Noè figlio
Et benche Flora di sue spoglie ornata
Miri con disdegnoso & fiero ciglio,
Pur da tè vinta, et poi dalla belleza
Di quella, piega sua superba alteza.
Quell'altre due tengon la valle ombrosa,
Ch'Arno fa dal Tyrreno all'Apennino:
L'una non men di Biade et Gran' copiosa,
Che l'altra di dolce Olio, et nobil Vino:
L'Ancisa è l'una, patria si famosa
Del Poeta, à cui forse Orfeo ne Lino
Pari non ha pe'l mondo alzato il nome;
Et ben Roma à ragion, gli ornò le chiome.
L'altra, che la fredda Elsa tiene in braccio,
Che bagna il fertil' suo sito fecondo,
Di Certaldo è, là ve nacque il Boccaccio,
Non forse à Arpino ò Padova secondo.
Queste, d'ogni timor deposto il ghiaccio,
Et d'ogni rio sospetto il grave pondo,
Son venute hoggi con la bella Flora
Ad honorarvi, COSMO & LEONORA.

(Here, Milord, is she whom you love so much; here is your homeland Florence, she who hopes, in the shade of your holy branches, to flee the influence of every enemy star. And she prays Heaven that it bind you, couple beautiful above all others, in such solid bonds that there may be born from you into the world a stock that will stretch its wings confidently up to Heaven. / And to show you how pleasing it is to her that you should be bound in such a knot today, she has brought with her, from her beautiful countryside, the dear and pretty Nymphs. This one cares constantly for your beautiful Prato[110] and desires to do her best to serve you. And to the extent that she exceeds every other in beauty, she surpasses

[110]An important town very near Florence on the northwest.

them and outstrips them in sincere faith. / The one who has hair like snow falling even now on some nice pretty hill, hair bound with poplar, she is the Dryad of the ancient Sieve, who receives in her broad breast the waters of your Mugello,[111] in order to return them, with the Arno, to the Tyrrhenian Sea. And she seems, above all others, to be giving thanks to Heaven that her stock ascends so high.[112] / The other, in such ragged dress, whose face is vermilion with modesty, is ancient Fiesole, who was built by Japheth, son of the great Noah.[113] And although she looks at Flora, adorned by her spoils, with a disdainful and proud eye, she bends her proud haughtiness, also vanquished by you and, then, by the beauty of this your lady. / These other two hold the shady valley that the Arno makes from the Apennines to the Tyrrhenian. The one is no less full with corn and grain than the other with sweet oil and noble wine. One of them is Ancisa, the so-famous home of the Poet. Perhaps Orpheus and Linus never raised on earth the name of one equal to him, and rightly did Rome crown his head.[114] / The other, who holds in her arm the cold Elsa, which bathes her fertile, fruitful place, is from Certaldo, where was born Boccaccio. It is not perhaps second to Arpino or Padova.[115] These ladies, having thrown off the ice of every fear and the heavy weight of every evil suspicion, have come today with the beautiful Flora to honor you, COSIMO and ELEONORA.)

Apollo stopped after he had said this, and Flora, having gone up in front of His Excellency with her nymphs, sang the following *canzone:*

Piu che mai vaga & bella
　Ardendo in dolce spene

[111]Name for the valley of the Sieve.

[112]The Medici are represented as natives of the Mugello because of a country house built at Cafaggiolo by Cosimo il Vecchio and occupied also by later members of the family.

[113]Fiesole, on a hill overlooking Florence, had been an important Etruscan settlement before the latter city was founded. Japheth, mentioned here as its founder, was often equated with Iapetus, father of Prometheus. It was common to draw correspondences between biblical and Homeric characters. In the Renaissance nearly every Italian city claimed to have been founded by an illustrious personage of one or the other tradition.

[114]Ancisa, today called Incisa, is a town near Florence. The poet referred to is Petrarch, 1304–1374, who was actually born in Arezzo, but whose father had lived in Incisa. He was given the ancient crown of laurel for poetry at Rome in 1341. Orpheus and his teacher Linus were considered patrons of poetry.

[115]Boccaccio, 1313–1375, grew up in Certaldo, but is thought to have been born in Paris of an illegitimate union between his father and a Frenchwoman. Arpino, south of Rome, was thought to be the birthplace of Cicero and Julius Caesar. Padua was that of Livy.

COSMO, Flora hoggi viene
Ad honorarti come fida Ancella.
Flora la bella che sicura posa
All'ombra tua quieta,
Hoggi piu che mai lieta
Della novella sposa
Rende al Ciel gratie, et à te sommo honore:
Et l'eterno motore
Prega con humil core,
Che di voi sorga anchor' tal Prole, ch'ella
Al Ciel' co'l suo valore
S'alzi per fama sovr'ogn'alta stella.

(Prettier and more beautiful than ever, burning in sweet hope, COSIMO, Flora comes to honor you today as a faithful handmaiden. / Flora the Beautiful, who rests securely in your quiet shadow, today happier than ever because of the new bride, thanks Heaven and gives greatest honor to you. And she prays the Eternal Mover with a humble heart that there may spring from you again such seed that she, through her value, will rise to Heaven in fame, above every high star.)

CANTUS
ALTUS
TENOR
BASSUS
Piu che mai va- gh'et bel- la ar- den- do in dol- ce spe-
Ar- den- d'in dol- ce
Ar- den- d'in dol- ce
Piu che mai va- gh'et bel- la ar- den- d'in dol- ce

5
ne Flo- ra og- gi Cos- mo vie- ne ad ho- no- rar- te co- me fi-
spe- ne Flo- ra og- gi Cos- mo vie- ne ad ho- no- rar- te
spe- ne Flo- ra og- gi Cos- mo vie- ne ad ho- no- rar- te co- me fi-
spe- ne Flo- ra og- gi Cos- mo vie- ne ad ho- no- rar- te co-

11
d'an- cel- la Flo- ra la bel- la che se-
co- me fi- d'an- cel- la Flo- ra la bel- la che se- cu- ra
da an- cel- la Flo- ra la bel- la che se- cu- ra
me fi- d'an- cel- la Flo- ra la bel- la che se-
17
cu- ra po- sa a l'om- bra tu- a qui- e- ta hog- gi
po- sa a l'om- bra tu- a qui- e- ta hog- gi
po- sa a l'om- bra tu- a qui- e- ta hog- gi
cu- ra po- sa a l'om- bra tu- a qui- e- ta hog- gi

23
piu che mai lie- ta del- la no- vel- la spo- sa ren-
piu che mai lie- ta ren-
piu che mai lie- ta del- la no- vel- la spo- sa
piu che mai lie- ta del- la no- vel- la spo- sa ren-
29
d'al ciel gra- tie et a te so- mo ho- no
d'al ciel gra- tie et a te so- mo ho- no-
ren- d'al ciel gra- tie et a te so- mo ho- no-
d'al ciel gra- tie et a te so- mo ho- no-

35
re et l'e- ter- no mo- to- re pri- e- ga con hu- mil co- re
re et l'e- ter- no mo- to- re
re et l'e- ter- no mo- to- re prie- ga con hu- mil core prie- ga con hu- mil co-
41
che di voi sor- ga an- chor tal pro- le ch'el- la al ciel col su- o
che di voi sor- g'an- chor tal pro- le ch'el- la al ciel col suo va-
re che di voi sor- g'an- chor tal pro- le ch'el- la al ciel col suo va-
re che di voi sor- g'an- chor tal pro- le ch'el- la al ciel col suo va-

47
va- lo- re s'al- zi per fa- ma sov- r'o- gn'al- ta stel-
lo- re s'al- zi per fa- ma sov- r'o gn'al- ta
lo- re s'al- zi per fa- ma sov- ra o- gn'al-
lo- re s'al- zi per fa- ma sov- r'o- gn'al- ta
52
la, s'al- zi per fa- ma sov- r'o- gn'al- ta stel- la.
stel- la, s'al- zi per fa- ma sov- r'o- gn'al- ta stel- la.
ta stel- la, sov- r'o- gn'al- ta stel- la.
stel- la, s'al- zi per fa- ma sov- r'o- gn'al- ta stel- la.

The *canzonetta* having been finished and Flora having withdrawn a bit to the side, there came forward Pisa, dressed in red velvet that was adorned with many streamers and clusters. She had an antique coiffure, with a *mazocchio* and a little hat on which sat a fox with a shield under his paw. Upon this shield was the white cross on its usual red field.

Almost as a guardian of this lady came a rustic nymph, dressed in faded red taffeta, who on her disheveled hair had a high mountain with a tower at its summit. With her were two others, of which one was dressed in green from the waist down and all in yellow from there up and carried a goatskin across her shoulders. She was barefoot and had no belt. There were some branches of cork trees and of holm oaks on her head and several goats' heads on her shoulders.

The other was in green damask, with a belt of tender olive branches. She had also a garland of the latter and a number of tocca streamers on her back. She carried white cottage cheese in a well-prepared little basket. She had buskins of green tocca, with a few heads placed on them.

Following them was a triton with long hair and beard and with an extravagant hat sewn from reeds and shells. He had on his forehead a branched horn made like an open hand. From the shoulders to the hands (which seemed like bats' wings), and from the neck to the buttocks, were strips of little wings such as are seen in many fish. These wings also went around him, covering the shameful parts in front and behind, although the forked tail also hid everything behind. On his breast hung a big lobster, hooked with its feet and mouth onto the fleece of the breast. The legs, with webbed feet, had stockings of rushes with many shells attached. He carried in his right hand a large snail shell, full of sea things, and in the left a trident. There came right with him, as an equal, a very delicate nymph, dressed in red taffeta, with a tattered outer garment of gold and silver tocca fringed around the neck with orange leaves, with a silver shell between her breasts. She was covered with a very thin veil and could be seen shimmering all over in a beautiful ornament of the above-mentioned leaves. She was girded so high that there could be seen a fringe decoration composed of golden shells among green leaves of citron, Seville orange, and lemon trees. And there could be seen the beautiful buskins, composed of masterly clusters. Above a fine silver hat she wore a coiffure of three shells, with a red ball among them, and citrons and oranges worked in, all arranged in a strange and beautiful manner.

As soon as Pisa appeared, Apollo began again on his lyre, singing these stanzas:

Del ventre usciti à i gran monti Apennini
La Magra e'l Tebro, con le lor chiar'onde;
Prendon correndo contrari cammini,
L'un dove nasce, & l'altr'ove s'asconde
A voi mia luce; & fanno i bei confini
D'Etruria, giunti alle Tyrrene sponde;
Ove con quel' (come a Natura piacque)
Congiungon le lor chiare & limpid'acque.
Fra questi, presso al marittimo lito
Siede sovr'Arno la famosa Alfea:
Vagheggia il suo leggiadro & fertil sito
Triton', Gorgona, Teti, & Galatea.
Lequali hor tutte il chiaro grido udito
Co i piu bei don', che ciascheduna havea,
Delle alme Noze, con piu salda speme,
Vengon' divote ad honorarti insieme.
Quella si ricca di bei colli intorno
Per Fida guardia allei data da Flora,
L'alta Verrucola è, ch'al nuovo giorno
Prima de raggi miei la cima indora:
Seco n'adduce & di bei pomi adorno
Calci, & di Biade, che la valle irrora:
Per honorarti co piu cari doni,
Ch'a suoi cultor' ne porge utili & buoni.
Ne ti sdegni il mirar' discalza & scinta
Maremma roza & incolta pastorella;
Che pur quanto altra da buon Zelo spinta
De molti suoi Tesor' t'arreca anch'ella.
L'altra d'Oliva inghirlandata & cinta
La Collina è, ch'a si cara novella
Co'l buono augurio à te s'inchina, & porge
Quanto di bene in lei si nutre & sorge.
Ecco Triton' con l'alta sua Gorgona,
Ch'al bel Livorno ha cura, et porta anch'egli
La sua sonora conca, & la ti dona
Con mille Nicchi, i piu vaghi & piu begli.
Teti poi, che d'aranci s'incorona
Et che intreccia d'Argento i bei capegli
Quanto ha, ti arreca; & Pietra santa tiene
Di fuor bella, & piu ricca entro alle vene.

(Having come out of the belly of the great Apennine Mountains, the Magra and the Tiber, with their clear waves, set off in contrary directions—one toward where my light is born to you, the other toward where it hides. They make the beautiful borders of Etruria, having arrived at the Tyrrhenian shores, where, as Nature pleased, they join to that sea their clear and limpid waters.[116] / Between these, near the seashore, sits, on the Arno, the famous Alphea. Her pretty and fertile site is admired by Triton, Gorgona, Tethys, and Galatea.[117] All of these, having heard the clear news, come devotedly together, bearing the most beautiful gifts that each has, to honor you with firmer hope for the holy marriage. / That one, so rich with fine hills, has had given to her by Flora, as a faithful guardian, the high Verrucola,[118] who first gilds its summit with my rays in the new day. She brings with her Calci,[119] adorned with beautiful apples and corn, which sprinkles the valley, in order to honor you with the dearest gifts, useful and good, offered to her farmers. / Nor should you disdain to look upon barefoot, unbelted Maremma,[120] a rustic, uncultured shepherd girl. For she as much as any other is impelled by good zeal, and she also brings you many of her treasures. The other, garlanded and belted with olive branches, is Collina.[121] At such good news, she, with her good wishes, bows to you and offers to you all the good things that are nourished and have their source in her. / Here is Triton with his high Gorgona, who cares for beautiful Leghorn.[122] He also carries his sonorous

---

[116]The Magra and the Tiber, both rising in the mountains and flowing to the Tyrrhenian Sea, roughly form the northern and southern borders of Etruria, present-day Tuscany.

[117]A difficult, conceited passage whose general meaning is, however, clear. Alphea is Pisa. A fourteenth-century geographical encyclopedia in verse, the *Dittamondo* of Fazio degli Uberti, states that the city's name had once been Alphea. (Uberti is quoted by Fra Leandro Alberti in his *Descrittione di tutta Italia e isole pertinenti ad essa,* 28.) Vergil refers to the city as Alphea in the Tenth Book of the *Aeneid,* but he is using a poetic conceit. Greek literature contains allusions to a Peloponnesian city named Pisa situated on the river Alpheus. This river was also personified as a god, and Alphea was probably a goddess bearing some contrived relation to him in a medieval legend about the Italian Pisa's founding. Triton, Tethys, and Galatea are all marine deities and stand here simply for the Tyrrhenian Sea. Gorgona is, on the other hand, the real name of a mountainous island off the Tuscan coast. Because the name also applies to the mythological character Medusa, Gelli feels authorized to mention it with the names of the sea deities. All this pedantry makes for a very slipshod figure.

[118]A strategic peak of Monte Pisano near Pisa. It had once been a strong point of defense against Florence, but when Pisa became subject to the Florentines the latter, of course, took control of the post. They had built a new fort there in the early part of the sixteenth century.

[119]A valley slightly upriver from Pisa.

[120]A general name for the swampy, sparsely inhabited coastal region of Tuscany, especially that near the mouth of the Arno. Later in his reign, Cosimo would sponsor work to make the region more salubrious and productive.

[121]A village near Pistoia.

[122]The main port of Tuscany, whose harbor facilities were to be greatly improved during Cosimo's reign. The island of Gorgona, directly off the coast, is here presented as protector of the port.

conch and gives it to you with a thousand shells, the prettiest and most beautiful. Tethys then, crowned with oranges, her beautiful hair woven with silver, brings you all she has. And she has beautiful "holy stone" outside, and richer in her veins.)[123]

All these nymphs and those of the other companies were bearing presents of the dearest things of their countries. These things were made of sugar and were dyed a natural color. Also of sugar were the plates, basins, and other containers holding the presents. Each was colored silver or gold or another hue, as was appropriate.

When Apollo's singing was finished, Pisa, with her nymphs, began the following *canzonetta:*

Lieta per honorarte,
Ecco Signor' la nobil Pisa antica:
Et ch'io ti sono amica
Non men che serva, bramo hor' di mostrarte.
Queste Nynfe che meco hò, la cura hanno
De miei cari vicini:
Questi son Dei Marini,
Che securo il Tyrren' solcar' ne fanno:
Et per letitia il piu che ponno & sanno
Di tue Noze felici,
Pregan' che vi sien' sempre i Celi amici.
Et prompti siam' (com'hor' si vede) à darte
Di quel, che può ciascun, più larga parte.

(Happy to honor you, here, Milord, is ancient noble Pisa. That I am your friend as well as your servant I now long to show you.[124] / These nymphs I have with me care for my dear neighbors. These are sea gods, who make the Tyrrhenian's lanes safe for us. Through happiness at your fortunate wedding, they pray the best they can that Heaven will always be friendly to you. And we are ready, as you see now, each to give you in great measure of what he has.)

---

[123]Pietra Santa is a town north of Pisa that had been in Cosimo's time an important fortress. The name means literally "holy stone," and a pun is apparently intended, probably with allusion to nearby marble quarries.

[124]Pisa, often an enemy of Florence, had most recently been conquered by an army under the direction of Machiavelli in 1509.

CANTUS
ALTUS
TENOR
BASSUS
Lie- ta per ho- no- rar- te ec- co si- gnor la no- bil
Lie- ta per ho- no-rar- te ec- co si- gnor la no- bil
Lie- ta per ho- no- rar- te ec- co si- gnor la no- bil
Ec- co si- gnor la no- bil

5
Pi-sa an- ti- ca et ch'io ti so- n'a- mi- ca non men che ser- va bra-
Pi-sa an- ti- ca et ch'io ti so- n'a mi- ca non men che ser- va bra-
Pi-sa an- ti- ca et ch'io ti so- n'a mi- ca non men che ser- va bra-
Pi-sa an- ti- ca et ch'io ti so- n'a mi- ca non men che ser- va bra- mo

11
mo hor di mo- strar- te
mo hor di mo- strar- te
mo hor di mo- strar- te que- ste nim- phe
hor di mo- strar- te que- ste nim- phe che
17
de miei ca- ri vi- ci- ni, que-
de miei ca- ri vi- ci- ni, que-
che me- co la cu- r'han-no de miei ca- ri vi-ci- ni, que-
me- co la cu- ra han- no de miei ca- ri vi- ci- ni,

23
sti son dei ma- ri- ni che secu- r'il tir- ren sol- car ne fan- no et per
sti son dei ma- ri- ni che secu- r'il tir- ren sol- car ne fan- no et per
sti son dei ma- ri- ni che secu- r'il tir- ren sol- car ne fan- no et per
che secu- r'il tir- ren per
3
8

29
le- ti- tia il piu che pon- no et san- no di tue noz- ze fe- li-
le- ti- tia il piu che pon- no et san- no di tue noz- ze fe- li-
le- ti- tia il piu che pon- no et san- no di tue noz- ze fe- li-
le- ti- tia il piu che pon- no et san- no di tue noz- ze fe- li-
3
8

35
ci pre- gan, pre- gan che ti sian sem- pr'i ce- l'a- mi- ci
ci pre- gan, pre- gan che ti sian sem- pr'i ce- l'a- mi- ci
ci pre- gan, pre- gan che ti sian sem- pr'i ce- l'a- mi- ci
ci pre- gan, pre- gan che ti sian sem- pr'i ce- l'a- mi- ci
41
et pron- ti sian co- m'hor si ve- de a dar- te di
et pron- ti sian co- m'hor si ve- de a dar- te
et pron- ti sian co- m'hor si ve- de a dar- te
et pron- ti sian co- m'hor si ve- de a dar- te

46
quel che puo cia- scun piu lar- ga par- te, di quel che puo cia-
di quel che puo cia- scun piu lar- ga par- te, di quel che puo
di quel che puo cia- scun piu lar- ga par- te, di che puo
di quel che puo cia- scun piu lar- ga par- te, di che puo
51
scun piu lar- ga par- te.
cia- scun piu lar- ga par- te, piu lar- ga par- te.
cia- scun piu lar- ga par- te, piu lar- ga par- te.
cia- scun piu lar- ga par- te, piu lar- ga par- te.

Pisa finished the *canzonetta* and moved aside. And as Apollo started again with those stanzas which we shall put below, Volterra[125] came forward in her pomp, dressed in red and green velvet, with many ornaments of tocca. And she had an ornate hat, topped by a boat, above which appeared the two-faced head of Janus[126] crowned with green vine leaves. And there were in her company five nymphs in very unusual dress, in that the first, dressed in green, wore on her head, between wild broom and mastic, a kettle with flames under it. And there seemed to be coming out of this kettle a light green gum, which covered her shoulders and almost all the rest of her person.

The next, dressed in light brown, had a similar coiffure, but with a different kind of kettle. It seemed to be melting copper, which, flowing down over her shoulders, made her beautiful in a strange way.

The third, much more extravagant, was seen with two faces and four arms under a single head, which seemed to be covered with earth. She was dressed from the middle forward in very delicate gold cloth, and from the middle backward in very white silver. On each side the hair corresponded in color to the face and dress. And between her hair and the earth of the head there went around a garland composed of minute herbs. This lady seemed to be quite helpless and came with her hands bound together in front and behind.

The next, all yellow-green, crowned with holly and holm oak, wore on her coiffure four little vases like pitchers that, with flame lit under them, were pouring out yellow matter. The lady was dressed naturally in this matter and did not seem at all less beautiful than if art had dressed her.

The last, all white, crowned with willows and tree branches, had also a kettle as headdress, but a kettle of a different kind. She was rich with many icicles that, dripping down from the boiling kettle in the form of water, stayed on her dress and, freezing there little by little, almost appeared to be very white roots. In her hand she carried a horn, full of her white salt.

Of these figures, Apollo spoke in this way:

Sorge in Toscana un'alto et aspro Monte,
Dove Cecina irriga i verdi campi,
Sovr'esso innalza la superba fronte

---

[125]An important hill town south of Pisa.

[126]The mythical first king of Italy, usually represented as having two faces. Subsequent verses will make it clear that Volterra liked to think of him as her founder.

Costei, che par', che'l Ciel con quella stampi;
Volterra detta: et perche dal Bifronte
Iano ha principio, par' di voglia avvampi
Mostrar, quant'ella sia fedele et amica,
Et sovr'ogn'altra nobile et antica.
Ond'è venuta à rallegrarsi teco
Suo Duce, et dirti quanto ella ha piacere
Delle tue Noze: et ha menato seco
Le Nymfe delle sue ricche Minere;
Quelle, che sempre dentro al loro speco
Fan' fuoco, & son fuliginose & nere,
Piene di Cener' fumo, & di sqame;
L'una è del vetriuol', l'altra del rame.
Quelle, ch'ambo le mani hor' legate hanno
L'una è dell'Oro, & l'altra è dello Argento;
Et forse anchor'un' giorno le sciorranno
Per farti piu felice, & piu contento.
Quell'altre due, il zolfo, e'l Sal' ne danno
Sovr'ad ogn'altro grato condimento.
Accetta dunque valoroso Duce
La pronta voglia, c'hoggi à te le adduce.

(There arises in Tuscany a high and rough mountain, where Cecina[127] irrigates the green fields. Above the mountain this lady raises her proud head, this lady whom Heaven seems to stamp as "named Volterra."[128] And because she has her origin in the two-faced Janus, she seems to be burning with the desire to show how faithful and friendly, noble and ancient she is, above all others. / Therefore she came to rejoice with you, her Leader, and to tell you how glad she is of your marriage. She has brought with her the nymphs of her rich mines. These ladies, always burning inside their caves, are sooty and black, full of smoky ashes and of flaked metal. One is of sulphate, the other of copper. / Those who have both hands tied—one is of gold, the other of silver. And perhaps one day their hands will be untied to make you happier and more content.[129] These other two give us sulphur and salt, pleasing above every other condiment. Valiant Leader, accept then the ready will that brings them to you today.)

Apollo stopped, and Volterra with her nymphs sang the following *canzonetta:*

---

[127]A small river flowing toward the sea south of Volterra.

[128]This is apparently a play on the town's name, which might, if a point were stretched very far, be taken to mean "flying town."

[129]This passage seems to express a hope that gold and silver would be found some day in the hills around Volterra. No doubt that would indeed have made the Duke more content.

Ecco Signor' Volterra;
Ecco le Ninfe mie, ch'ad hora ad hora
Gareggiano à chi piu v'ama, & vi honora.
De vostre Noze allegre in sì bel giorno
V'apron' lor ricche vene;
Et ne dan' ciochè lhanno entro ed intorno.
Et questa, che si saggia et lieta viene
Pien' del suo bianco sal' ne porge il corno.
Et con sicura spene
Prega ciascuna il Cielo, et sempre adora,
Ch'eterno viva COSMO & LEONORA.

(Here, Milord, is Volterra. Here are my nymphs, who are ever competing to show who loves you and honors you most. / Happy about your marriage on such a fine day, they open to you their rich veins and give of what they have inside and around themselves. And this one, who comes so modest and joyful, offers to us her horn, full of her white salt. With confident hope each one worships Heaven always and prays that the union of COSIMO and ELEONORA may live eternally.)

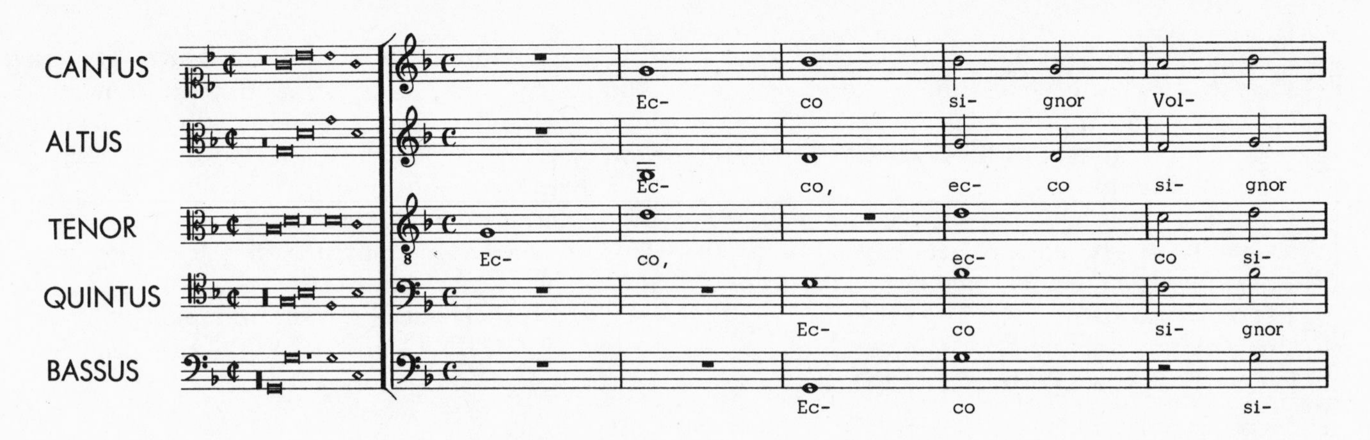
CANTUS
Ec- co si- gnor Vol-
ALTUS
Ec- co, ec- co si- gnor
TENOR
Ec- co, ec- co si-
QUINTUS
Ec- co si- gnor
BASSUS
Ec- co si-

6
ter- ra, ec- co le nim- phe
Vol- ter- ra, ec- co le nim- phe mi-
gnor Vol- ter- ra, ec- co le nim- phe mi- e, ec- co le
Vol- ter- ra, ec- co le nim- phe mi- e, ec- co le nim- phe
gnor Vol- ter- ra, ec-

12
mi- e ch'ad hor ad ho- ra gha- reg- gion
e, ec- co le nim- phe mi- e ch'ad hor ad ho- ra gha-
nim- phe mi- e ch'ad hor ad ho- ra, ch'ad hor ad ho- ra gha- reg- gion a chi
mi- e ch'ad hor ad ho- ra, ch'ad hor ad ho- ra
co le nim- phe mi- e ch'ad hor ad ho- ra
18
a chi piu, gha- reg- gion a chi piu v'a- m'et v'ho- no- ra.
reg- gion a chi piu, gha- reg- gion a chi piu v'a- m'et v'ho- no- ra, v'a- m'et v'ho- no- ra.
piu v'a- m'et v'ho- no- ra, v'a- m'et v'ho- no- ra.
gha- reg- gion a chi piu v'a- m'et v'ho- no- ra, v'a- m'et v'ho- no- ra.
gha- reg- gion a chi piu v'a- m'et v'ho- no- ra, v'a- m'et v'ho- no- ra.

25
Di vo- stre noz- ze al- le- gre in si bel gior- no
Di vo- stre noz- ze al- le- gre in si bel gior- no
Di vo- stre noz- ze al- le- gre in si bel gior- no
Di vo- stre noz- ze al- le- gre in si bel gior- no
Di vo- stre noz- ze al- le- gre in si bel gior- no
31
v'a- pron lor ric- che ve- ne et ne dan cio che l'han den- tro et din- tor-
v'a- pron lor ric- che ve- ne et ne dan cio che l'han den- tr'et din- tor-
v'a- pron lor ric- che ve- ne et ne dan cio che l'han den- tr'et din- tor-
v'a- pron lor ric- che ve- ne et ne dan cio che l'han
et ne dan cio che l'han den- tr'et dan- tor-

37
no pien del suo bian-co
no et que- sta che si sag- gia et lie- ta vie- ne pien del suo bian-
no et que- sta che si sag- gia et lie- ta vie- ne pien del suo bian-
no que- sta che si sag- gia et lie- ta vie- ne pien del suo bian-
no pien del suo bian-
44
sa- le ne por- ge il cor-
co sal' ne por- g'il cor- no, ne por- ge il cor- no, ne por- g'il cor-
co sal' ne por- ge il cor- no, ne por- g'il cor-
co sa- le ne por- ge il cor- no, ne por- g'il cor-
co sa- le ne por- ge il cor- no

50
no et con se- cu- ra spe- ne il ciel prie- ga cia- scu-
no et con se- cu- ra spe- ne il ciel prie- ga cia- scu-
no et con se- cu- ra spe- ne il ciel prie- ga cia- scu-
no il ciel prie- ga cia- scu-
et con se- cu- ra spe- ne il ciel prie- ga cia- scu-
57
na et sem- pre, et sem- pre a- do- ra
na et sem- pre, et sem- pre, et sem- pre a- dona et sem- pre, et sem- pre et sem- pre a- dona et sem- pre, et sem- pre, et sem- pre a-
na et sem- pre, et sem- pre, et sem- pre a- do-

63
ch'e- ter- no, ch'e- ter- no vi- va
ra ch'e- ter- no vi- va Cos- mo
ra ch'e- ter- no, ch'e ter- no vi- va Cos- mo, vi-
do- ra ch'e- ter- no vi- va Cos- mo, vi-
ra ch'e- ter- no vi- va Cos- mo, vi-
70
Cos- mo, vi- va Cos- mo et Le- o- no-
vi- va Cos- mo et Le- o- no- ra, viva Cos- mo et Le- o- no- ra, vi- va Cos-
va Cos- mo et Le- o- no- ra, vi- va
va Cos- mo et Le- o- no- ra, vi- va

76
ra, vi- va Cos- mo, vi- va Cos- mo et
va Cos- mo, vi- va Cos- mo et Le- o- no-
mo, vi- va Cos- mo et Le- o- no-
Cos- mo, vi- va Cos- mo et Le- o- no-
Cos- mo, vi- va Cos- mo et Le- o- no-

82
Le- o- no- ra.
ra, et Le- o- no- ra, et Le- o- no- ra.
ra, et Le- o- no- ra.
ra, et Le- o- no- ra, et Le- o- no- ra.
ra, et Le- o- no- ra, et Le- o- no- ra.

The *canzonetta* of Volterra being finished and Apollo singing again as before, there appeared an ancient nymph, dressed in a youthful habit, with white and red damask. She wore as a crest above her coiffure a bay horse, unbridled, having around his neck a red shield in which was a golden cross. And she had with her a nymph, very well dressed in yellow tocca, with a headdress made of ears of grain.

After this one came three others. One was covered with dark tan under a very green bodice, and her loose hair was covered with a leafy hat of beech branches, on which could be seen, as crest, a sylvan Pipes of Pan.

The other, above a garland of beech, had a large meadow of flowers. She was dressed entirely in green, without any belt or stockings.

The last, yellow and gray, adorned with olives and with apples, was carrying a few goat's cheeses in a long basket.

Apollo said of these:

D'Armenia Aretia con Noè suo sposo,
Che dagli antichi Iano è nominato,
Venne in Toscana: & dove disdegnoso
Torce Arno il muso, à guisa d'adirato,
Arezo pose à piè d' un' monte ombroso,
La dove largo il campo era, & più grato
A Cerere la Dea, ch'apre il bel seno
A chi più l'ama, più di frutti pieno.
Quindi hor' seco n'adduce ogni vicina
Nymfa, & son tutte à suoi terreni amiche
Per honorarti: Quella è Laterina,
C'ha ne bei campi suoi ricche le spiche:
Quell'altra custodisce ogni collina
Del Casentino, & le sue valli apriche;
Et quando il mio splendor' piu'l mondo incende,
Piu dolce & grato à Pastor' suoi si rende.
Quella, che sì selvaggia e'nculta pare,
Di Prato magno tien' lo sceptro, e i regni:
Et larga accio i Pastor' tuoi, possin' fare
Le Capannette ogni hor ne porge i legni.
Quell'altra fa del chianti cultivare
I dolci colli, d'ogni ben' si pregni:
Et per renderti honor' qui tutte hor sono
Con molto & buon' desio, se poco è'l dono.

(Aretia with her husband Noah, called Janus by the ancients, came from Armenia to Tuscany.[130] Where Arno disdainfully twists his muzzle as though in anger, she put Arezzo at the foot of a shady mountain—there where the field was wide and most pleasing to the goddess

Ceres,[131] who gives most generously of the fruits of her beautiful breast to those who love her most. / Now she brings with her every neighboring nymph—all friendly to her domains—in order to honor you. This one is Laterina,[132] who has rich ears of grain in her fields. This other one takes care of every hill of the Casentino[133] and of its sunny valleys. And when my splendor warms the world most brightly, she becomes most sweet and pleasing to her shepherds.[134] / That one, who seems so wild and uncultured, has the scepter of Pratomagno[135] and reigns there. She ever generously offers wood so that your shepherds can build huts. This other one has cultivated the sweet hills of Chianti,[136] so full of every good. And to do you honor, all of them are here now, with strong and good desire, even if the gift is small.)

When these ladies had arrived in front of the Lord and had made the proper bow, they sang the following *canzonetta:*

Come lieta si mostra
  Di cosi bella sposa, Arezo vostra?
Quant'hogg'io colma sia d'amore & speme
  Di Nodo si felice,
Con le mie Nynfe insieme,
Cantando appena dimostrar' ne lice.
Ogni sorte infelice
Sia da voi lunge, ò bella coppia et cara:
Che in vostra luce chiara
Speriam' secure haver' la vita nostra.

(How joyful does your Arezzo show herself for such a beautiful bride? / How overcome I and my nymphs are today with love and hope for such a happy marriage we can hardly show by singing. May every unhappy bit of luck be far from you, O beautiful and dear couple, because we hope to live our lives safely in your clear light.)

---

[130]This curious story is typical both of founding legends and of attempts to correlate Christian and pagan tradition. Arezzo is an important town in southern Tuscany and the birthplace of several great men of the Renaissance, including Giorgio Vasari.

[131]Goddess of the harvest.

[132]A part of the countryside near Arezzo.

[133]The valley of the upper Arno, near Arezzo.

[134]This is apparently a reference to the coolness of the Casentino, most appreciated at noon.

[135]Another pun. Pratomagno is the name of a mountain between Florence and Arezzo, but the word means literally "big meadow." Hence the headdress of a meadow with flowers worn by the personifying character.

[136]The hill country between Florence and Siena, already famous for wine.

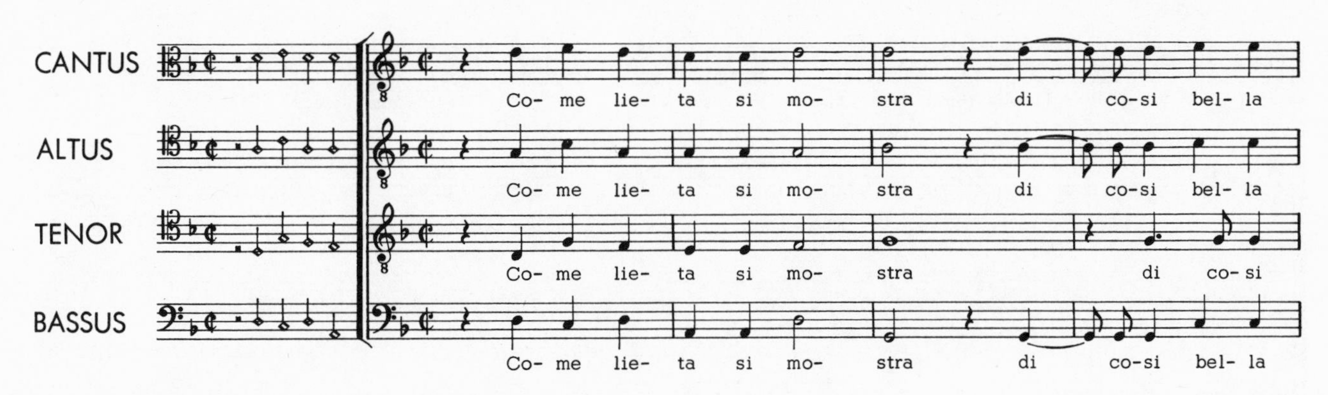
CANTUS
ALTUS
TENOR
BASSUS
Co- me lie- ta si mo- stra di co-si bel- la
Co- me lie- ta si mo- stra di co-si bel- la
Co- me lie- ta si mo- stra di co-si
Co- me lie- ta si mo- stra di co-si bel- la

5
spo- sa A- rez- zo vo- stra
spo- sa A- rez- zo vo- stra
bel- la spo- sa A- rez-zo vo- stra quan- t'hog- gi col- ma sia d'a-
spo- sa A- rez- zo vo- stra quan- t'hog- gi col- ma sia

10
quan- t'hog- gi col- ma sia d'a- mor et spe- me di no- do
quan- t'hog- gi col- ma sia d'a- mor et spe- me di no- do si fe-
mo- re et spe- me di no- do si fe- li-
d'a- mor et spe- me di no- do si fe- li-
15
si fe- li- ce con le mie Nim-ph'in sie- me can- tan- d'a- pe-
li- ce con le mie Nim-ph'in- sie- me can- tan- d'a- pe-
ce con le mie Nim-ph'in- sie- me can- tan- d'a- pe-
ce con le mie Nim-ph'in- sie me can- tan- d'a- pe-

20
na di mo- strar n'e li- ce
na di mo- strar n'e li- ce o- gni stor- t'in- fe-
na di mo- strar n'e li- ce o- gni stor- t'in- fe-
na di mo- strar n'e li- ce o- gni stor- t'in- fe-
26
sia da voi lun- gi o bel- la cop- pi'et ra- ra ch'en vo-
li- ce sia da voi lun- gi ch'en vo-
li- ce sia da voi lun- gi o bel- la cop- pi'et ra- ra ch'en
li- ce sia da voi lun- gi ch'en vo-

32
stra lu- ce chia- ra spe- rian se- cur ha- ver, spe- rian se- cur ha-ver
stra lu- ce chia- ra spe- rian se- cur ha- ver
vo- stra lu- ce chia- ra spe- rian se- cur ha- ver la vi-
stra lu- ce chia- ra
37
la vi- ta no- stra, spe- rian se- cur ha- ver la vi- ta no- stra.
la vi- ta no- stra.
ta no- stra, spe- rian se- cur ha- ver la vi- ta no- stra.
spe- rian se- cur ha- ver la vi- ta no- stra.

Apollo, as usual, after the singing of these, again began playing and singing the following *stanze*. And a lady dressed in red and white damask, who was wearing as crest a winged white lion with a book in his paw, came before the Lord with three companions. One was girded in green and gray, with a garland of marsh reeds interwoven with many ears of grain, and she wore buskins, also of reeds. The other one, dressed in red and white, wore a red, unbridled horse above a headdress of vine leaves. The last, dressed in purple and gray, had no particular sign, but wore, like the other nymphs, a headdress of ancient-style tocca, with many streamers on her person.

Fra'l Tebro & l'Arno, dove il Trasimeno
Lago, del Roman' sangue Hannibal' tinse,
Che mal poi seppe porre à quello il freno,
Et la vittoria usar' sì come ei vinse;
Verso il Ciel' s'alza un vago colle ameno,
Sovra il qual d'alte mura intorno cinse
Costei, c'hor lieta il core & se ti dona,
Crotone Egittio, & la chiamò Cortona.
Quella di ricche & bianche spighe adorna
Hà cura all'alte chiane, à i fertil' piani:
Et quando il mio splendor' a voi ritorna
Si specchia in quelle: & con le dotte mani
Sè parimente, e i dolci campi adorna;
Per poi di biade colmi, & di bei Grani,
Renderli à suoi cultor' cortese e amica,
Mercede & premio d'ogni lor fatica.
Quell'altra, ch'è dalla sinistra mano;
Che di riccheza & di beltà l'eccede,
La patria fu del tuo Politiano,
Che sì gran' fama all tua stirpe diede.
L'altra di Castiglione il ricco piano,
Che simil' forse l'occhio mio non vede,
Governa: & ciascheduna humile & pia
Tue sante Noze di honorar desia.

(Between the Tiber and the Arno, where the Trasimeno Lake was stained with Roman blood by Hannibal [who then could not stop and exploit victory as he had won it],[137] there rises toward Heaven a nice, pretty hill. On it, Croton Egyptus surrounded this city [who now happily gives you her heart and herself] with high walls

---

[137]Trasimeno is a large lake in southeastern Tuscany, north of Perugia. Near there, in 217 B.C., Hannibal and the Carthaginians inflicted a severe defeat upon Rome and then failed to press their advantage.

and called her Cortona.[138] / That one, adorned with rich, white ears of grain, takes care of the high pools and the fertile plains. And when my splendor returns to you, she looks at herself in these pools and similarly adorns herself and the sweet fields with her clever hands. In order then to make these fields heavy with corn and grain for their farmers, she is kind and friendly, the recompense and prize of all their labors. / This other one on the left hand, who exceeds her in riches and beauty, was the home of Politian, who gave such great fame to your family.[139] The other one governs the rich plain of Castiglione,[140] whose equal perhaps my eye does not see, and each one humbly and piously desires to honor your holy marriage.)

Cortona now, with her company, sang the following words:

Non men' ch'ogn'altra, lieta hoggi Cortona
COSMO, le sante Noze
Antico Amor'ad honorar' ne sprona.
Ma come potrò mai con le parole
Mostrarti à pieno il Core?
Et far' quanto d'honore
Desio ne scorge à cosi bella Prole?
Prendi dunque il desio, prendil' Signore;
Che non piccolo è il don', di chi'l Cor' dona.

(No less than any other, COSIMO, happy Cortona is spurred today by ancient love to honor the holy marriage. / But how shall I ever be able to show my heart fully to you with words? Or to do as much honor as I desire to such handsome offspring? Take, then, my wish, take it, Milord, for not small is the gift of her who gives her heart.)[141]

---

[138]Another founding legend. Croton was an Italic warrior supposed to have been killed in single combat by Hercules. According to the fourteenth century *Dittamondo* of Fazio degli Uberti, Hercules founded a town on the tomb of his slain foe and named it in his honor. Cortona is south of Arezzo. (Uberti is quoted by Alberti in his *Descrittione di tutta Italia e isole . . .*, 62).

[139]Angelo Poliziano, 1454–1494, one of the most distinguished men of letters at the court of Lorenzo il Magnifico, had been born in Montepulciano, not far from Cortona.

[140]Between Arezzo and Cortona.

[141]The Italian phrase "chi'l Cor' dona" affords a play on the city's name.

CANTUS
ALTUS
TENOR
BASSUS
Non men ch'o- gn'al- tra lie- ta, non men ch'o- gn'al- tra
Non men ch'o- gn'al- tra lie- ta, non men ch'o- gn'al- tra
Non men ch'o- gn'al- tra lie- ta, non men ch'o- gn'al- tra
Non men ch'o- gn'al- tra

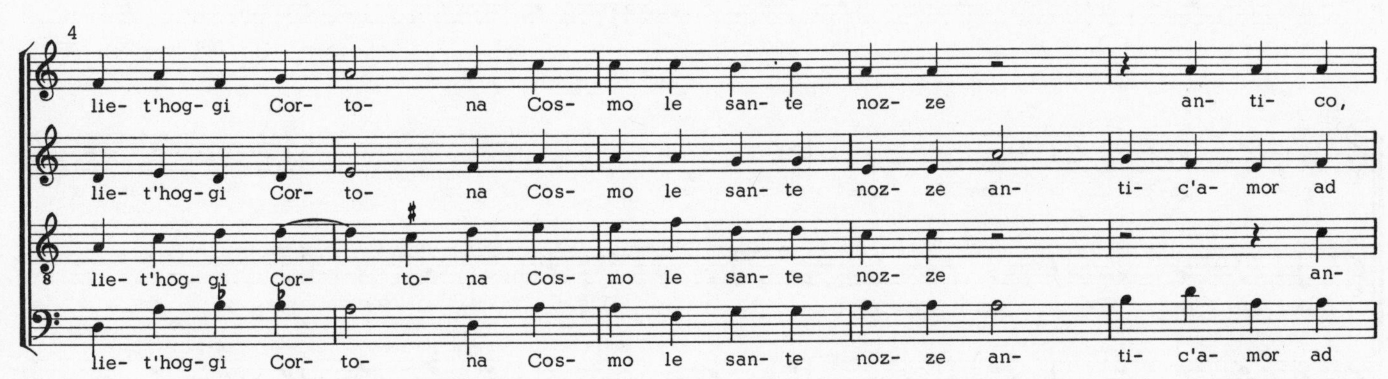
4
lie- t'hog- gi Cor- to- na Cos- mo le san- te noz- ze an- ti- co,
lie- t'hog- gi Cor- to- na Cos- mo le san- te noz- ze an- ti- c'a- mor ad
lie- t'hog- gi Cor- to- na Cos- mo le san- te noz- ze an-
lie- t'hog- gi Cor- to- na Cos- mo le san- te noz- ze an- ti- c'a- mor ad

9
an- ti- c'a- mor ad ho- no- rar ne spro- na. Ma co- me
ho- no- rar, ad ho- no- rar ne spro- na. Ma co- me
ti- co a- mor ad ho- no- rar ne spro- na. Ma co- me
ho- no- rar ne spro- na, ne spro- na. Ma co- me
15
po- tro ma- i con le pa- ro- le mo- strar- t'a
po- tro ma- i con le pa- ro- le mo- strar- t'a pie- n'il co-
po- tro ma- i con le pa- ro- le mo- strar- t'a pie- n'il co-
po- tro ma- i con le pa- ro- le mo- strar- t'a pie- n'il co-

20
pie- n'il co- re et far quan- to d'ho- no- re de- sio ne
re, il co- re et far quan- to d'ho- no- re de- sio ne
re et far quan- t'et far quan- to d'ho- no- re de- siq ne
re, il co- re et far quan- to d'ho- no- re de- sio ne
25
scor- ge a co- si bel-la pro- le
scor- ge a co- si bel- la pro- le
scor- ge a co- si bel- la pro- le pren-
scor- ge a co- si bel- la pro- le pren- di dun-

30
che
pren- di dun- que il de- sio, pren- di si- gno- re che
di dun- que il de- sio, pren- di si- gno- re che
que il de- sio, pren- di, pren- di si- gno- re che
35
non pic- ciol e'l don di chi'l cor do- na, di chi'l cor do- na.
non pic- ciol e'l don di chi'l cor do- na, di chi'l cor do- na.
non pic- ciol e'l don di chi'l cor do- na, di chi'l cor do- na.
non pic- ciol e'l don di chi'l cor do- na, di chi'l cor do- na.

This *canzonetta* being finished, Apollo started his singing again, telling the ladies and gentlemen about another nymph, already appearing with another company constituted in this way:

The principal nymph, in red and white damask, was strangely adorned with clusters and streamers, with an ancient-style hat. The hat had as crest a bear holding in his paws a chessboard in the two aforementioned colors. She was carrying on her arm a little horn of plenty, pouring out water continuously but in small quantity. On the extreme rim of the horn could be read: BRANA.[142]

With her, almost as an equal, came a bearded, naked old man, with a long, untidy bunch of hair under a garland of chestnut. He had a little mantle slung across his shoulder. It was of natural water color. He was shod with grass and moss, with various bindings of reeds. He also wore on his arm a twisted horn of plenty, on which appeared this name: OMBRONE.[143]

Behind these could be seen a little old woman, dressed in coarse gray cloth, barefoot, and with a headdress of leaves and husks of chestnuts. And with her was a beautiful young girl, covered with thin green and blue sendal cloth, with a number of bows and clusters of yellow and white tocca. She was delicate and pretty and wore a fine headdress cleverly made of silken rosebuds, with a silver fish on the crest.

Last came, lone and pensive, a man dressed in black satin, with a mountain on his head. On the mountain was a tower, through the door of which one could see a great fire burning. He seemed, by his appearance, to be coming to ask pardon for a great fault committed by him.

About these figures Apollo spoke thus:

Sopra la Brana ove piu facilmente
  Passar' si può la grande Alpe Apenina;
  Dove già combattendo arditamente
  Perdè la vita il fero Catilina;
  Siede Pistoia; et piange amaramente
  Le sue discordie, et la Civil' ruina:
  Pur'hoggi, posto il freno all'empie parti
  (Tua Mercè) lieta viene ad honorarti.
Quel' ch'ella ha seco con sì bianche chiome
  Ombron'è, che le bagna il fertil piano,
  Et poscia perde in Arno et l'acqua, e'l nome,
  Non molto al vago tuo Poggio lontano.

---

[142] A stream at Pistoia, a town to the northwest of Florence.
[143] A stream near Pistoia.

Quella, c'ha sì le spalle curve et dome,
L'Oreada è, che l'alto Cutigliano
Regge; et governa l'alte sue montagne;
Et le pasce di Latte, et di Castagne.
L'altra, la valle tien', che da Natura
Ricca è di Seta, et d'Animali, et piante:
Et sol brama honorar', ne d'altro ha cura,
Hoggi le Noze tue sacrate et sante.
Quel'; che vien' poi lor dietro in veste oscura,
Montemurlo è, che in voce assai tremante
Quant'ogn'altro, per fama al ciel ti estolle;
Et perdon' chiede del suo Ardir' si folle.

(Over the Brana, where one can cross the great Apennine Alps most easily, where in time past the fierce Catiline lost his life fighting bravely,[144] sits Pistoia. She bitterly weeps for her discord and civil ruin. Yet today, a bridle having been put on the evil parties, thanks to you, she comes happily to honor you.[145] / The man with her, with such white hair, is the Ombrone, who bathes her fertile plains and then loses in the Arno both his waters and his name, not very far from your pretty Poggio.[146] That lady, who had such curved and gentle shoulders, is the Oreada, who reigns over the high Cutigliano and governs its high mountains, feeding them on milk and chestnuts.[147] / The other holds the valley, which by nature is rich in silk, in animals, and in plants. Today, having no other concern, she wishes only to honor your sacred, holy marriage. This man who comes behind them in dark dress is Montemurlo, who, in a rather trembling voice, extols your fame to Heaven as much as any other. And he asks pardon for his mad burning.)[148]

Here Apollo stopped, and Pistoia with her company sang the following *canzonetta:*

---

[144]Catiline fell in battle near Pistoia in 62 B.C., after Cicero had exposed his conspiracy.

[145]Since the middle of the fourteenth century Pistoia had often been torn by strife between two parties: the Cancellieri and the Ranciatichi. Cosimo wished to impose a *pax florentina* so he might govern more effectively, and he eventually succeeded in doing so. Just at the time of the wedding celebrations, after Gelli's lines were written, there was, however, a new outbreak of violence. See Giambattista Adriani's *Istoria dei suoi tempi,* I, 105–6.

[146]The country house Poggio a Caiano, where the Duke and Duchess had stopped on their way from the coast.

[147]Oreada is a mountain nymph, Cutigliano a mountain town near Pistoia.

[148]A poignant reference to Cosimo's victory over the republicans at Montemurlo in 1537.

Ecco la fida Ancella,
Che stanca un tempo da si ria tempesta
(Tua mercè) fuor dell'onde alza la testa.
O pietoso Nettuno, ò saggio Dio,
Che co'l tuo bel tridente,
Fra cosi altera gente,
Fatto hai queto ogni affetto acerbo, et rio:
Siati accetto il desio,
Ch'assai vince il saver di ringratiarte,
Et di sempre honorarte,
Con la tua sposa, et mia secura stella.

(Here is the faithful handmaiden who, having been tired some time from such an evil storm, now, thanks to you, raises her head out of the waves. / O charitable Neptune, O wise god, who with your fine trident have calmed all bitter and evil feelings among such proud people,[149] please accept the desire, which is greater than my ability, to thank you and to honor you, with your wife and my secure star.)

[149]Cosimo is compared to Neptune because he has calmed civil strife, as the god calmed the waves.

CANTUS
Ec- co la fi- da an- cel- la che
ALTUS
Che
TENOR
Ec- co la fi- da an- cel- la che stan-
BASSUS
Che

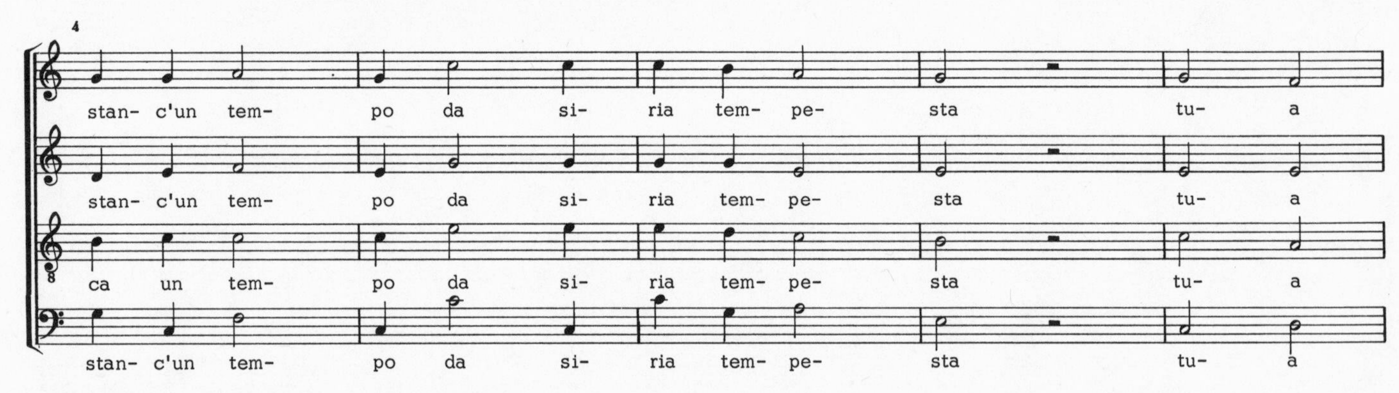
4
stan- c'un tem- po da si- ria tem- pe- sta tu- a
stan- c'un tem- po da si- ria tem- pe- sta tu- a
ca un tem- po da si- ria tem- pe- sta tu- a
stan- c'un tem- po da si- ria tem- pe- sta tu- a

9
mer- ce fuor de' l'on- de al- za la te- sta.
mer- ce fuor de'l'on- de al- za la te- sta.
mer- ce fuor de' l'on- de al- za la te- sta.
mer- ce fuor de' l'on- de al- za la te- sta.
14
O pie- to- so Nep- tun- no o sag- gio
O pie- to- so Nep- tun- no o sag- gio
O pi- e to- so Nep- tun- no o sag- gio
O pie- to- so Nep- tun- no o sag- gio

19
di- o che col tuo bel tri- den- te fra co-
di- o che col tuo bel tri- den- te fra co- si al- te- ra
di- o che col tuo bel tri- den- te fra
di- o che col tuo bel tri- den- te fra
24
si al- te- ra gen- te fat- t'hai que- t'o- gni af- fe-
gen- te fat- t'hai que t'o- gni af- fe- t'a- cer-
co- si al- te- ra gen- te fat- t'hai que- t'o- gni af- fe- t'a- cer-
co- si al- te- ra gen- te

29
t'a- cer- bo et rio sia- ti ac- cet- t'il de- sio ch'as- sai vin- ce
bo et rio sia- ti ac- cet- t'il de- sio ch'as- sai vin-
bo et rio sia- ti ac- cet- t'il de- sio ch'as- sai vin-
ac- cet- t'il de- sio ch'as- sai vin-
34
il po- ter di rin- gra- ti- ar- te. Et di
ce il po- ter di rin- gra- ti- ar- te. Et di
ce il po- ter di rin- gra- ti- ar- te. Et di
ce il po- ter di rin- gra- ti- ar- te. Et di

39
sem- pr'ho- no- rar- te con la tua spo- sa et mia se- cu- ra stel-
sem- pr'ho- no- rar- te con la tua spo- sa et mia se- cu- ra stel-
sem- pr'ho- no- rar- te con la tua spo- sa et mia se- cu- ra
sem- pr'ho- no- rar- te con la tua spo- sa et mia se- cu- ra
44
la.
la, et mia se- cu- ra stel- la.
stel- la, et mia se- cu- ra stel- la.
stel- la, se- cu- ra stel- la.

There appeared finally another company, led by a tall old man, who, shod with reeds and canes, wore over his nude body an adapted mantle of faded blue taffeta. And over his long hair, which fell onto his breast and over his shoulders, he wore a garland of oak, with a big trophy as crest. And he held in his right hand a horn, generously pouring out water, on the extreme rim of which could be read in antique golden capitals: TIBER.

Behind him was an ancient lady, dressed entirely in beech branches. She wore on her head a headdress like a mountain, which seemed to be divided in the middle by a very deep valley. And between this headdress and her head was a garland of beech and fir leaves. She had on each shoulder a bear's head, and her boots seemed to be made from cracked stones, covered with that rust or outgrowth often seen on them.

With this lady, almost as a partner, was another, very emaciated, dressed in rocks and fir branches, who wore on her head a very big stone with the natural form of the Vernia Rock.[150] And she had on each shoulder a wolf's head. All her poor ornaments were of beech and fir branches, which came out from between the vivid stones of the dress she was wearing. Thus ungirded and unshod she came ashamedly forward. After this one came a beautiful and well-dressed pair of young girls. One of them, like a veil seamstress, had her boots, her dress, and her headdress made of veils, with so many festoons and bows that their vividness made the spectators close their eyes. The other, not so pretty, was dressed in red and green, her blond hair being covered by a simple garland of vine leaves. And she had a number of flowers on her whole person.

Finally, there appeared a lady who seemed almost tired from a long journey, dressed in the Romagnuola fashion, and with her dress girded very high. She had her head and throat wrapped around several times with towels. She had on her head a basket, from which dangled some chicken necks, and in her right hand was a rustic basket of eggs, without any other adornment.

On their arrival, Apollo, playing divinely, sang the following stanzas:

Questi (Signor') ch' è di si bianco pelo,
Et di mille Trofei porta Corona,
Et par' superbo, che comandi al Cielo,
É frate ad Arno, et figlio à Falterona:
Et pur'acceso dal nativo zelo

[150] A peak in the mountains east of Florence.

Hoggi la vecchia sua Roma abbandona
Et viene ad honorarti, & darne segno,
Che per Patria conosce il tuo bel regno.
L'antica Madre sua è seco anch'ella,
Che fu de figli suoi sempre gelosa;
Et va lor dietro in questa parte e'n quella
Vestita à fronde, & spesso ancor' nevosa.
Quell'altra, che par' quasi sua sorella,
La casta & fredda Vernia è, che non osa
Molto le ciglia alzare, & si vergogna;
Che piu chieder che darti le bisogna.
Di quelle due la prima assai trapassa
Con la bella arte sua, la dotta Aragne:
Quell'altra, del vin', Còo & Lesbo passa,
E'l Tebro intra lor parte le campagne.
Romagna l'ultima è, che stanca et lassa
N'assembra pe'l passar' l'alte Montagne:
Et di rendervi honor' ciascuna è vaga
Ch'alta speranza sue fatiche appaga.

(This one, Milord, who wears a crown of such white hair and of a thousand trophies, and who seems so proud that he gives commands to Heaven, is brother of the Arno and son of the Falterona.[151] And kindled by native zeal today he abandons his old Rome and comes to honor you and to show that he recognizes your beautiful realm as his homeland. / With him is also his ancient mother, who was always jealous of her sons. She follows them here and there, dressed in leafy branches and often still snowy. This other one, who seems almost to be his sister, is the chaste and cold Vernia, who dares not raise her eyes much and is ashamed because she has to ask you for more than she can give you. / Of these two, the first quite surpasses with her beautiful art the learned Arachne.[152] The other surpasses Cos and Lesbos[153] in wine. The Tiber divides the countryside between them. Romagna is the last; she seems to us tired and weary for having crossed the high mountains.[154] And each one is eager to do you honor, because high hope appeases their troubles.)

[151]Falterona is a tall mountain east of Florence on whose slope the Arno has its source. The Tiber actually arises on Mount Fumaiolo, a little farther east, but calling the two rivers brothers and Falterona their mother does not stretch the point too much. The mountain may be said to follow her sons because she is visible at great distances.

[152]A human seamstress who is supposed to have challenged Minerva to a sewing contest. Having lost, she was changed into a spider.

[153]Aegean islands famous for their wines in classical times.

[154]Romagna lies across the Apennines and is thus not a part of Tuscany. Cosimo's grandmother Caterina Sforza had held a fief there at Forlì, but in 1539 the province was part of the papal possessions.

The Tiber then with his company sang the following *canzonetta:*

Ecco Signore il Tebro,
  Ecco il Tebro, Signora,
  Ad honorarvi, COSMO & LEONORA.
Se la mia nobil figlia
  A quanto gira il sol con la sua spera
  Pose il freno & la briglia:
  Questa, che di lei nacque, per voi spera
  Non men' di lei, di ricche spoglie ornarse:
  Et superba et altèra
  Sovra l'altre innalzarse:
  Onde al pari del Tebro, et Roma, ancora
  Vada la fama al Ciel' d'Arno et di Flora.

(Here, Milord, is the Tiber, here is the Tiber, Milady, come to honor you, COSIMO and ELEONORA. / If my noble daughter[155] put rein and bridle on the earth for as far as the sun turns with its sphere, this lady, who was born from her, hopes through you, no less than she, to adorn herself with rich spoils and, proud and haughty, to rise above the others. So that, like the Tiber and Rome, the fame of the Arno and of Flora may now go up to Heaven.)

[155]Rome.

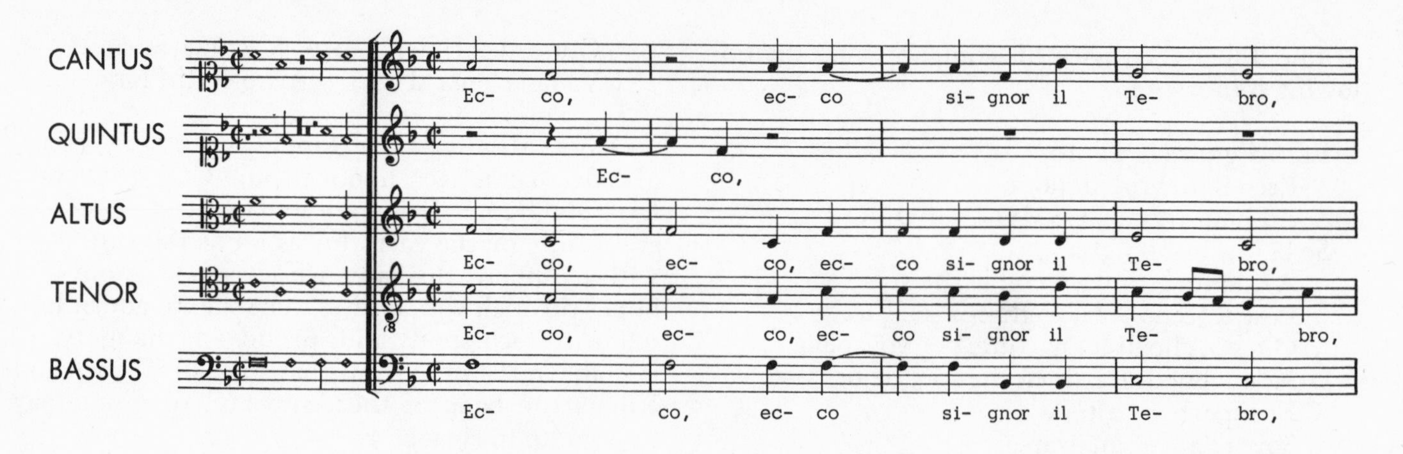
CANTUS
Ec- co, ec- co si- gnor il Te- bro,
QUINTUS
Ec- co,
ALTUS
Ec- co, ec- co, ec- co si- gnor il Te- bro,
TENOR
Ec- co, ec- co, ec- co si- gnor il Te- bro,
BASSUS
Ec- co, ec- co si- gnor il Te- bro,

5
ec- co, ec- ch'il Te- bro si- gno- ra ad ho- no- rar- vi Cos-
ec- co ad ho- no- rar- vi Cos-
ec- co, ec- co, ec- ch'il Te- bro si- gno- ra ad ho- no- rar- vi Cos-
ec- co, ec- co, ec- co il Te- bro si- gno- ra ad ho- no- rar- vi Cos-
ec- co, ec- ch'il Te- bro si- gno- ra ad ho- no- rar- vi Cos-

11
mo et Le- o- no- ra, et Le- o- no- ra. Se
mo et Le- o- no- ra, et Le- o- no- ra.
mo et Le- o- no- ra, et Le- o- no- ra. Se
mo et Le- o- no- ra, et Le- o- no- ra. Se
mo et Le- o- no- ra, et Le- o- no- ra. Se
17
la mia no- bil fi- glia a quan-to gi- r'il sol con
la mia no- bil fi- glia a quan-to gi- ra il sol
la mia no- bil fi- glia a quan-to gi- r'il sol con la
la mia no- bil fi- glia a quan-to gi- r'il sol con

23
la sua sphe- ra po- s'il fre- n'et la bri- glia que- sta
con la sua sphe- ra po- s'il fre- n'et la bri- glia que- sta
sua sphe- ra po- s'il fre- n'et la bri- glia que- sta
la sua sphe- ra po- s'il fre- n'et la bri- glia que- sta
29
che di lei nac- que per voi spe- ra non men di
che di lei nac- que per voi spe- ra non men di
che di lei nac- que per voi spe- ra non men di
che di lei nac- que per voi spe- ra

35
lei di ric- che spo- glie, di ric- che spo- glie or- nar- se et
et
lei di ric- che spo- glie, spo- glie or- nar- se et
lei di ric- che spo- glie or- nar- se et
et

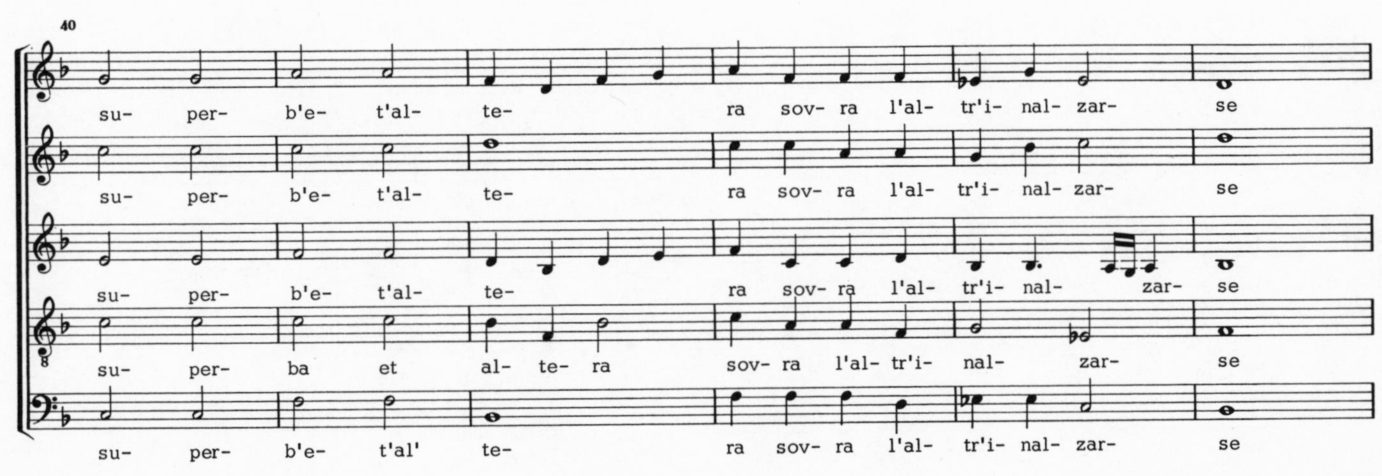
40
su- per- b'e- t'al- te- ra sov- ra l'al- tr'i- nal- zar- se
su- per- b'e- t'al- te- ra sov- ra l'al- tr'i- nal- zar- se
su- per- b'e- t'al- te- ra sov- ra l'al- tr'i- nal- zar- se
su- per- ba et al- te- ra sov- ra l'al- tr'i- nal- zar- se
su- per- b'e- t'al' te- ra sov- ra l'al- tr'i- nal- zar- se

46
et Ro- m'an-cho- ra n'an-
n'an-
on- d'al pa- ri del Te- bro et Ro- m'an-cho- ra n'an-
on- d'al pa- ri del Te- bro et Ro- m'an- cho- ra n'an-
on- d'al pa- ri del Te- bro et Ro- m'an- cho- ra n'an-
52
dra la fa- m'al ciel d'Ar- n'et di Flo- ra, d'Arn'et di Flo- ra.
dra la fa- m'al ciel d'Ar- n'et di Flo- ra, d'Arn'et di Flo- ra.
dra la fa- m'al ciel d'Ar- n'et di Flo- ra, d'Arn'et di Flo- ra.
dra la fa- m'al ciel d'Ar- n'et di Flo- ra, d'Arn'et di Flo- ra.
dra la fa- m'al ciel d'Ar- n'et di Flo- ra, d'Arn'et di Flo- ra.

Apollo then took leave for himself and for the Muses, in this way:

Ecco alto Duce, il tuo devoto Impero
Ecco di Flora le fedeli Ancelle:
Et come il Cor' ti dan' puro et sincero
Con le piu care lor' doti, et piu belle:
Amale come Padre, & giusto, & vero,
Che gli humil' prieghi lor' sovra le stelle
N'otterran' da chi il mondo, e'l ciel governa,
Vita, Prole, & honor, con pace eterna.
Voi tutti hor dunque lieti in festa, e'n gioco
Danzando insieme & rigirando intorno
Accesi d'amoroso & dolce foco
Finite questo illustre & chiaro giorno.
Io perche qui piu star non pate il loco
Al santo offitio, al mio bel carro torno;
Et con queste salendo al Cielo, anchora
COSMO N'andren' cantando, et
LEONORA.

(Here, High Leader,[156] is your devoted Empire; here are the faithful handmaidens of Florence. And since they give you their pure and sincere hearts with their dearest and most beautiful dowries, love them as a father, just and true. For their humble prayers above the stars will obtain from Him who governs the world and Heaven, life and issue and honor, with eternal peace. / You who are thus all happy in celebration, dancing together and turning around, kindled by amorous and sweet fire, end this illustrious and clear day. I, because the nature of the place does not allow me to stay any longer, return to my sacred duty, to my beautiful chariot. And going back up to Heaven with these ladies, of COSIMO we shall still be singing, and of ELEONORA.)

This having been said, they departed, and all the ladies with these gentlemen retired to the first *cortile* to dance, according to the custom of marriage festivities, and thus they joyfully ended that day.

The following Wednesday evening, which was the ninth [of July], there was a rich supper under the loggias of the first *cortile*. There, with

[156]The form *duce,* used here instead of *duca,* may simply be conceived as a variant of the latter, of which it is a cognate. Probably, however, it was meant to mean "leader" or "captain," as *dux* in Latin, and not to be a formal title of nobility.

Their Excellencies, came the whole state, with the flower of the beauties of the city.

I do not have to say any more about the quality of the banquet, for one can easily divine it from the place, the time, and the nature of the guests. It is enough to say that, the courses of the meal being finished, the happy bride and groom passed into the second *cortile,* described by me above. In its sky were newly suspended a good number of playful cupids, with bows and arrows and a lighted torch in the hands of each one. With these they lighted the place and cavorted in various postures above the fine, honored company.

All the guests being seated here and admiring the stage setting, little by little from the eastern side they saw appear in the sky of the stage a Dawn. She wore, over a red and flowered cloth, very fragile gold and silver tocca with stripes. It was very clear and transparent. Her wings were white and vermilion, with an infinite variety of color. Her buskins were skillfully woven of flowers. She held an ivory comb in her hand, and, combing her long hair, she sang these words:

Vattene Almo riposo, ecco ch'io torno
    Et ne rimeno il giorno.
Levate herbette & fronde
    Et vestitevi Piaggie et Arbuscelli:
    Uscite, ò Pastorelli,
    Uscite ò Nymfe bionde
    Fuor del bel nido addorno,
    Ogn'un' si svegli & muova al mio ritorno.

(Depart, blessed Repose, for here I am again, bringing back the day. / Rise up, grass and leafy branches, and dress yourselves, slopes and shrubs. Come out, O shepherds; come out, O blond nymphs, from your beautiful, adorned nest. Let everyone wake up and bestir himself on my return.)

CANTUS
Vat- te- n'al- mo ri- po- so ec- co ch'io tor- no, ec- co ch'io tor-
ALTUS
Vat- te- n'al- mo ri- po- so ec- co ch'io tor- no, ec- co ch'io tor- no, ch'io
TENOR
Vat- te- n'al- mo ri- po- so ec- co, ec- co, ec- co ch'io tor-
BASSUS
Vat- te- n'al- mo ri- po- so ec- co ch'io tor- no, ec- co ch'io tor-

4
no et ne ri- me- n'il gior- no, et ne ri- me-
tor- no et ne ri- me- n'il gior- no, et ne ri- me- n'il gior- no, et ne ri- me- n'il
no et ne ri- me- n'il gior- no, et ri- me- no, et ne
no et ne ri- me- n'il gior- no, et ne ri-

8
n'il gior- no. Le- va- te, le- va-t'her-bet-t'et fron- de et
gior- no. Le- va- te, le- va-t'her-bet-t'et fron- de et
ri- me- no il gior- no. Le- va- te, le- va-t'her-bet-t'et fron- de et
me- no il gior- no. Le- va- te, le- va-t'her-bet-t'et fron- de et
12
ves-ti- te- vi piag- ge et ar- bo- scel- li u- sci- te, u- sci- t'o pa- sto-rel-
ves-ti- te- vi piag- ge et ar- bo- scel- li u- sci- te, u- sci-t'o pa- sto-rel-
ves-ti- te- vi piag- ge et ar- bo- scel-li u- sci- te, u- sci-te, u- sci-t'o pa- sto-rel-
ves-ti- te- vi piag- ge et ar- bo- scel- li u- sci- te, u- sci-t'o pa- sto-rel-

16
li, u- scit'o Nimphe bi- on- de fuor del bel ni- d'a- dor-
li, u- scit'o Nim- phe bi- on- de fuor del bel ni- d'a- dor-
li, u- scit'o Nimphe bi- on- de fuor del bel ni- do a- dor-
li, u- scit'o Nim- phe bi- on- de fuor del bel ni- d'a- dor-
19
no o- gnun si sve- gli, si sve- gli et muo- va al mi- o ri-
no o- gnun si sve- gli, si sve- gli et muo- va al mi- o ri-
no o- gnun si sve- gli, o- gnun si sve- gli et muo-v'al mi- o ri-
no o- gnun si sve- gli, o- gnun si sve- gl'et muo-v'al mi- o ri-

22
tor- no, o- gnun si sve- gli, si sve- gli et muo- va al mi- o ri-
tor- no, o- gnun si sve- gli, o- gnun si sve- gli et muo- va al mi-o ri-
tor- no, o- gnun si sve- gli, o- gnun si sve- gli et muo-v'al mi- o ri-
tor- no, o- gnun si sve- gli, o- gnun si sve-gl'et muo-v'al mi- o ri-
25
tor- no, al mi- o ri- tor- no.
tor- no, al mi- o ri- tor- no.
tor- no, al mi- o ri- tor- no.
tor- no, al mi- o ri- tor- no.

Her sweet song was accompanied by a *grave cembalo* of two registers, by an *organo,* by a *flauto,* by an *arpe,* by *voci di uccegli,* and by a *violone.* These delighted the ears and the souls of listeners with incredible sweetness.

The words and ideas and the costumes of this and of all the other *intermedii* of the comedy to be recited later were by our Giovanni Batista Strozzi.

Behind the Dawn, little by little one saw rise in the sky of the stage setting a sun, which, moving slowly, made us aware, act by act, of the hour in the play's day. Thus, it finally disappeared near the end of the fifth act, just a little before Night appeared. The words of Dawn being finished, there began this comedy, composed by our Antonio Landi. Its characters are these:

A Happy Arrangement
or
What You Will
Comedy
by Antonio Landi

Characters of the Comedy:

Demetrio, a young man
Libano, a manservant
Travaglino, a matchmaker, or go-between
Lesbia, a nurse
Leandro, a young man
Currado, a manservant
Messer Ricciardo, lawyer, an old man
Lamberto, an old man
Mona Cassandra, wife of the lawyer
Lucia, a servant girl
Mona Cornelia, an old servant woman
Cammillo, a young man
Manoli, a Greek, husband of Lesbia
Giorgetto, a boy

Prologue

Now that I am here, I am relieved of a great doubt as to whether this comedy will be a success or not. I had armed myself to defend it, but, seeing who its spectators are to be, I think that I shall win the victory without drawing a sword. This, because I know that you ladies like all things that have a sweet end (thus suiting your good nature), and this play is, as you will see, full at the end of peace and marriages, both of which are very sweet things. Nor are you so critical that when a thing works out right[157] it must always

[157] The Italian phrase, "quando una cosa s'accosta al dovere," is puzzling. Another translation, less likely, is, "when a thing touches upon morality."

bore you a little. There is no need, then, to excuse the play or to defend it on your account. One can, rather, be wary of some evil tongues, more apt by nature to condemn than to do or to recognize truth. I understand that they have already started to be offended. Some of them are moved by envy and by a presumption that one should seek their opinion in all things. We, like most people, consider this opinion to be weak and barren and have not sought it for this comedy. There are others who, at a tender age, when they were favored and flattered by everyone, grew used to having approval for everything they did; now, having this habit, they cannot easily discard their ways of offending everyone and condemning everything with little reason and less salt. But they might come in handy for someone who needed a subject for another comedy, since their actions are full of appropriate material, more worthy of laughter than that of our play. You will soon see who these people are, without my describing them to you further, and you will discern clearly how different they are from the discreet, right-minded persons by whom we are quite willing to have our play gainsaid and criticized. But I am sure that these latter people, seeing the play to be so richly adorned, will be so dazzled that they will not notice spots where it deserves to be condemned. Similarly, it often happens for one of you ladies that, though she not be perfectly beautiful in every respect, yet, because of her grace, majesty, and rich clothing, she makes everyone who sees her judge that she is flawless. Thus, you will yourselves be today the second adornment of our story and will make it marvelously charming and pleasing to everyone. In this way, thanks to you, whatever defects it may have will not be so easily noticed and recognized. But it seems to me that some of you are half indignant because I said that you will be our second and not our first adornment. Now, do you want me to show you the first? Turn your eyes around, and, if you can bear so much brilliance, you will soon find it. Two brilliant lights, one of which with its lively rays makes you shining and beautiful. The other adorns and rules not only you but also your dear homeland with his rare grace and his virtues, which are not human but indeed celestial.[158] If I wished now to extend myself in his immortal praises, I am sure that you of hearing them and I of telling them would never consider ourselves satiated. However, since such

[158]This is perhaps the point in the celebrations at which flattery of the Duke becomes most abject and shameless.

an undertaking is so lofty and so difficult, we shall save it for a more appropriate time, when we can fitly celebrate not only these two but also His Caesarean Majesty, who is the origin and the reason of all our repose. Let's now get back to our story, which is called "Il Commodo," a phrase that should delight everyone. Nor should you be too curious about the origin of this name but be content that it is such, as I could be happy with many things without seeking their etymologies. It may also be called "La Commodità," so that everyone has the choice of calling it either "Commodo" or "Commodità." One is a masculine name, the other feminine; let each person take the one that suits him better, the one that better "accommodates" him.[159] Do not expect to hear the plot all at once, but I'll give you part of it. You'll get the rest in bits from the comedy. Thus, receiving it little by little, it will enter into you more easily, without confusing you. The part you'll get from me is this: Demetrio, who will be the first to appear on stage, has been sent by Rinaldo Palermini from Palermo to Pisa (which for today is this setting you see) into the house of Lamberto Lanfranchi, a citizen of the city. He falls in love with Porfiria his sister, without knowing either that she is his sister or that Leandro is his brother. You will see this Leandro, then, in love with the daughter of a lawyer. How they all learn each others' identities at the end and what happens to their loves as well as to the other loves herein, you will see without my telling you any more. There remains only to tell you that the author excuses himself to all, because, though you will soon be led to laugh, he has not, for this purpose, gone so far as to offend decorum. Nor, in order to make someone dislocate his jaws from laughing, has he thought it proper to show you a Parasite so dishonest that he might disgust many other people. Nor has he shown you a man so foolish as to believe (let's say) that he can be severed and then put together again.[160] Nor certain other things—you know what I mean —too remote from truth. Thus, you will not see

[159]The Italian title is purposely enigmatic. Our two English titles, "A Happy Arrangement" and "As You Will," correspond to two possible interpretations.

[160]The Parasite was a stock character inherited from Plautus. Landi may be referring (1) to Ligurio of Machiavelli's *Mandragola,* (2) to Gastrinio of Grasso's *Eutychia,* or (3) to the priest Ser Iacopo of Lorenzino dei Medici's *Aridosia,* presented just three years earlier in Florence. The last is a strong possibility, because any disparagement of Lorenzino in the presence of Cosimo would have been in excellent taste. The second exaggerated character referred to—the incredibly foolish man—is without any doubt Calandro of Bibbiena's *Calandra.*

such things or such people in this comedy, but you will recognize clearly the most common natures of old men, of young men, of masters, and of servants, of married ladies, and of young girls. You can verify these natures in your own houses any day. Therefore, may all of you deign to give us kind attention, and we shall try to do you honor for the favor you grant us.

ACT I

Demetrio, alone:

Quite true is the saying that no one in this world can call himself happy. How often do we see a young man, noble, rich, and wise, endowed with everything good, while, if the secret of his heart were known, there is no one more unhappy or more unfortunate than he. Today all this is exemplified more in myself than in any other, because I am young, healthy, and handsome and do not lack money—or even company, since everybody is glad to be around somebody who can spend freely. In sum, since I came to this city, there has been nothing that has not made me appear fortunate. In spite of all this, I find myself to be the most unhappy, the most tormented young man there is in Pisa, even in all the world. This is because for some time I have been wildly in love with a girl of this city. In this love I encounter every day so many disappointments and so many difficulties that I still have not found any means of winning anything other than a look—and that only at rare intervals. But perhaps it is just, and Love is taking revenge on me in this way, since before I knew what her power was, there was no one who scorned her more than I. When I used to hear of a lover so desperate that he fell to crying and couldn't sleep or take food, becoming pale and weak because of his great suffering, I laughed at him and made fun of his condition a thousand times a day. And when I heard that there were some who stayed outside at night in the rain, in the cold, and in the wind, sometimes sitting for hours on a little wall, and who ran a thousand dangers, either in climbing a very high wall or in jumping from a high window—when I heard of these people, I said that they were all crazy and out of their minds and that it hardly seemed possible. Now I don't talk that way any more because I know from experience that I was wrong and that this is a sickness like the others—indeed, the worst of all—and that whoever is touched by it must give in. Anybody who is pierced by love clear to the bone, as I am, must (whether it suits him or not) always get what he can without taking into account either honor or practicality. He must procure something new every hour, something which, if it may not advance him toward the final goal, will at least keep him in hope, weak and vain though this hope may be. He must content himself sometimes with a glimpse of his lady, sometimes with a brief encounter, sometimes even with a false imagining that feeds his soul. Oh, my sad life! I certainly came here under a bad star. What worse thing could happen to me than to find myself bound by love in this way without having in sight any outlet for my desires? With great trouble I manage to see her whom I love so much, once a week. I came out of my house this morning at this hour because, this being a holiday, she must go to a Mass. Thus, I may perhaps meet her either in church or outside. If this is granted to me I shall draw sustenance on it for a little while. Oh, poor Demetrio, to what a condition are you reduced? I sent Libano ahead so that he could be on the watch and could come tell me what he finds out, because he is usually a good spy, if I'm not wrong. But here he is, coming to me, and he seems quite cheerful. Oh, Libano, what news do you bring me? Tell me right away, whether it is good or bad.

Libano, a servant; and Demetrio

Libano:

You are making too much fuss; speak softly so you won't be heard. Your Porfiria is in the church, at that altar by the side door.

Demetrio:

What do you think I should do—go into the church or wait for her outside? Who is with her?

Libano:

She is with that middle-aged lady of hers by whom she is usually accompanied.

Demetrio:

Is it possible that you have never managed to find out who that lady is—of what class, whether she is her governess, or servant, or who she is? You are not trying hard enough. Don't you see what shape I'm in? Anything new that I found out would give me some foothold; everything is useful to me.

Libano:

You are letting yourself by governed too much by passion, and you want to go so fast in this thing that you're hurting your own cause. These things require time and opportunity—for him who doesn't want a result that is the contrary of his aims. Don't you know that a bitch dog who is in a hurry has blind puppies?

Demetrio:

You can talk, because you don't have a toothache and you must never have been in love.

Libano:

Maybe I have. Now do it this way: This morning, go into the church and stay at a distance so that everyone will not see what you're doing and why you're there. Because you must not act as do some foolish admirers who wait in ambush and rush right up to the face of their ladies and who, if they pass by the house when she is at the window, stalk up and down there all day long, hanging around. Often in the evening, then, they are so worn out that somebody else, without any preparation, reaps the reward.

Demetrio:

All right, that's enough. You always want to instruct me. I'm going on.

Libano:

Listen a little while longer. Don't go so fast; you seem out of your mind. You're forgetting yourself, if you will excuse me for saying so. Remember, I say, to stay at a distance from her, and don't heave those passionate sighs. I tell you again: You are hurting your own case. I shall stay here outside the church, waiting for her to come out, and I shall go along with her, ingratiating myself, seeking some occasion to speak to that lady of hers. You listen here, and then wait for me in the cloister, or go on home, which would be better, and I'll meet you there.

Demetrio:

I have understood and shall do as you say.

Libano:

How little patience he has, and how delirious he has become. Is it possible that he be so blinded by his desire that often he doesn't hear or see a thing that is necessary to him, not even those things which help him? He was scarcely able to listen to me long enough to hear what I am going to do and where I shall meet him, while, if I had failed to tell him those things, he would have looked for me all over Pisa, running here and there like a madman. And, if he had not found me right away, he would have blamed it all on me. And I have to be a mind reader with him; if

I am told that, in working for his sake, I have done well, then I am praised; if, another time, I show him the best thing to do, and he doesn't do it and suffers from not doing it, then I am the one who is cursed, and I have lost all the esteem deriving from the good things done. But I must have a great compassion for him, sometimes giving in and sometimes standing up to him (lest I do worse) with a lot of lies, maneuvering him like a top. If one didn't act in this way with lovers like him, one couldn't get along with them. This morning is one of those when I should have liked to be able to tell him something encouraging, because he is unusually worked up. Who is that fellow knocking on the door of the Lady? I don't recognize him yet, but from a distance he seems to be a person of low class. He is about to go away. Oh, there is Porfiria with that lady, coming out of the church—our friend was able to admire her only a short time. That fellow is tearing down the door again. How ignorant he is! What a lack of discretion! Good Lord![161] The old woman is signaling to him; if Demetrio saw him he would fly off the handle. Wow! There he is, following the ladies; you see he couldn't control himself. I'm going to tell him that he is about to make a big blunder.

Libano and Demetrio

Libano:

Demetrio, get away from here. Go home. Go on, I tell you.

Demetrio:

They haven't seen me. Let me alone. What does it matter?

Libano:

You are going to give yourself away. Go home, and I'll contrive to hear what that fellow says to the servant woman. He's been beating on their door for some time.

Demetrio:

Do you know him? Who is he?

Libano:

Now that he has turned this way I recognize him. By Heaven,[162] he is a go-between who arranges marriages. Go on, I'll easily be able to take advantage of this, because I know him well.

---

[161]The 1566 edition of the play, perhaps showing influence of the Counter Reformation, omits the phrase "Good Lord": "Per dio che . . .".

[162]In the 1566 edition, "By Heaven": "Per Dio" is changed to "For sure": "Per certo".

Demetrio:

I'm going, but see whether you can find out what he's after.

Libano:

If I hadn't sent him away, he'd have been like a robin hanging around the owl.[163] Oh, she is a beautiful girl; you are right, Demetrio.

Lesbia, a servant; Travaglino, a go-between; Libano, aside

Lesbia:

Porfiria, go on up; I want to stay here to find out what this fellow wants who has been knocking on the door so hard.

Libano:

She could hardly wait to get the girl out of my sight. I enjoyed looking at her too, you old spoil-sport!

Lesbia:

Welcome, what did you want?

Travaglino:

I have almost knocked this door down, beating on it so long, and no one has answered. I wanted Leandro; where could I find him?

Lesbia:

I'm not surprised that you got no answer. When we are not at home, Currado is never there, or else he hides in some place where he couldn't even hear artillery, and that other good-for-nothing servant must have slipped out too. But what did you want from Leandro?

Travaglino:

I wanted to talk to him about a good deal.

Lesbia:

Good for you?

Travaglino:

For him, I say.

Lesbia:

Heaven grant that it be so. But this isn't a day for deals or business.

Travaglino:

Tell me, please, where he is.

Lesbia:

I'm not a seer and can't guess where he is, but

[163] This strange expression is taken from the sport of bird-hunting, so popular in medieval and Renaissance Italy. Owls were sometimes used to attract smaller birds, who seemed to be fascinated by their big eyes.

if you'll wait a while he can't be long coming. He went out before we did, saying that he would be back before long and that if anyone came for him he should wait here a little.

Travaglino:

He knew that I might come, and I'm surprised that he went out so early. We'll wait for him here; do you really think that he'll be back soon?

Lesbia:

Didn't you hear me? How many times do I have to tell you? Are you deaf?

Travaglino:

Don't talk ugly to me, because, as I told you, I'm here for his business and in his interest.

Lesbia:

I think I know who you are. What do you want with him? To talk about some patrimony?

Travaglino:

You mean "matrimony."

Lesbia:

It's enough that you know what I mean.

Travaglino:

And you might be right, for that is my trade.

Libano:

Keep your ears peeled, Libano.

Lesbia:

I figured so. You certainly have a fine trade.

Travaglino:

Ours certainly is a fine skill, better than that of the tailor, who has as equipment scissors, needle, thread, and thimble, while, except for words, we have no equipment or body.

Libano:

Or soul.

Lesbia:

I know what you are like. You just charm and deceive and have more tricks than May has leaves. The poor girls often find themselves undone at your hands because they don't know what is due them but have to take what is given to them and must manage the best they can. Oh, it is poor unfortunate girls hungry on Saint Nicholas' Eve that you need![164]

Travaglino:

You know what I have to tell you; marriages

[164]According to a popular story, three indigent girls, about to be sold into prostitution by their fathers, were provided with dowries by Saint Nicholas on the eve of his name day.

are made first in Heaven, so don't talk that way. But you must know this: If Leandro does as I advise, he will accept the opportunity for his sister that I bring, as I have already urged him before.

Libano:
May God help you, Demetrio.

Lesbia:
This girl will make the fortune of whoever gets her, because he will see that she is well brought up and could run a city, much less a house. But don't think that he is reluctant to marry her off; rather, he can hardly wait, so that he can carry on around the house as he likes and have a thousand capers and debauches. I know that if you take her away from us he will have parties day and night.

Libano:
That is not welcome news.

Travaglino:
Then we'll give him a wife and he'll be quiet.

Libano:
Sick, you mean.

Lesbia:
Perhaps that would be the best thing and would bring peace to his whole household. But I think he has something else in mind now.

Travaglino:
We'll win him over, too, when we see an opportunity for him. But tell me, how long have you been with him?

Lesbia:
Oh, for so long that I hardly remember. But why do you ask me about it, why do you need to know?

Travaglino:
I tell you, I'd like to find out where Leandro and Porfiria came from and who their father really was, because many say they are definitely the children of Gherardo Sismondi and others say that he had adopted them.

Lesbia:
Those who say that they aren't his children, whose do they think they are?

Travaglino:
They don't have in mind anybody of lesser lineage than Sismondi's own, because the qualities of Leandro show his worth. There is, however, this doubt, and you, having been so long with them, must know the whole truth.

Lesbia:
For what purpose do you want to know this?

Travaglino:
For a good one, and in Leandro's interest. Please give me some information.

Lesbia:
I am not used to mixing in other people's business, not even in that of my masters.

Travaglino:
When it can help and not harm them it is not wrong. Truly, I beg you, are they the children of Gherardo?

Lesbia:
If they are not the children of Gherardo, they are of much nobler blood, since you insist that I tell you.

Travaglino:
And from where? Are they perhaps from some famous city of Greece?

Lesbia:
From the most famous one there is.

Travaglino:
Where, Constantinople?

Lesbia:
You guessed it right away; they are from that city, and from one of the noblest houses there.

Travaglino:
Didn't I tell you that many people had this idea? I'm going to tell you more. I've often heard it whispered by someone who knew him well that Gherardo couldn't have children because when he was little he had had a sickness, before he went to the island of Scios, so that he couldn't beget. But not everybody is so curious, and the big dowry this girl is reputed to have keeps them from thinking about such questions. And to how many people does it happen that, dazzled by the brilliance of gold, they without hesitation let others load them down with bad merchandise?

Lesbia:
You say nothing of the girls who are ruined, thinking to make their fortune, and who have a bad time and suffer ever after.

Travaglino:
That's enough about that. You must be from those parts, since you know exactly who your masters are.

Lesbia:

I am indeed from that country too, but don't make me talk about that because I should like never to think about it again.

Travaglino:

Why? People usually enjoy talking about their homeland.

Lesbia:

Yes, when there is reason to be glad, but whoever has lost at home his property and flesh, as I have, doesn't like to talk about it.

Travaglino:

What did you lose there?

Lesbia:

What *didn't* I lose there? I lost there some of my masters and my husband, so that when I think about it I am moved and can hardly keep from weeping. Oh, poor unfortunate woman, how much better for me it would be if he were alive! But now I have already done my grieving and lost hope some time ago.

Travaglino:

Don't give yourself so much pain, because, if your husband isn't here, we can get another one for you—and younger than that one would be—especially since you must have a lot.

Lesbia:

A lot of what?

Travaglino:

What do you think I mean? Money and property. I swear that if you have as much as forty ducats, I shall venture to find you a young man. Though you have a few wrinkles, he will manage to find your joints.

Libano:

With a stick, and a well-padded one.

Lesbia:

I don't need your husband; let's talk about something else.

Travaglino:

And even if you don't want a husband, there'll be no trouble finding someone to fill the same need, if you'll just cooperate.

Lesbia:

I'm sure of that. See how you got around to the subject. This is what you-all are good for, and these are the fine matches you make. Often, under the guise of matchmaking, you cause the downfall of poor girls—and maybe you do some of the dirty work yourself.

Travaglino:

Imagine that we are made of flesh and blood, too, and we like good things, though we aren't any of those perfumed dandies. When we can't make a deal one way we try another.

Libano:

A fine deal, I'm sure.

Lesbia:

Yes, I know what you mean. But if you get some men like those in the house, they will cheat you in the name of Charity. In truth, today you have to be careful of everybody. There was a time when I could have been cheated even by monks, but since I heard about a certain scandal near here I know all about them. You can be sure that they won't take me in any more, because I think that they would do anything for money. Honor the righteousness of good men, because there must be some.

Libano:

Few, by God.

Travaglino:

Let's stop this trifling talk, because I see Leandro. Go into the house, for I need to talk to him alone.

Lesbia:

I'm going. Oh, Lord, if I could hear a little I'd find out what kind of match he has in mind, but I am too far away to be able to hear them.

Libano:

I'm going to leave here so they won't get suspicious of me. I'll go over by the bridge, where I know that this matchmaker will pass later, since I often see him on the other side of the river. I'll try to win him over, to get as much information as possible to give Demetrio, though up to here most of the news is bad.

Travaglino and Leandro

Travaglino:

Leandro, I'm glad to see you. I've been waiting here a half hour to talk to you.

Leandro:

What is there new? Tell me.

Travaglino:

The match for your sister that I told you about; it's almost in the bag, except for one difficulty.

Leandro:

What is that?

Travaglino:

Lamberto, the father of Cammillo, would like that, to the two thousand ducats left as a dowry to her by Gherardo, you add three hundred more, exactly the value of the entire marriage gift you said she'd have.

Leandro:

What old man's avarice is this? A betrothal seems like a sale of leather or of cloth, there is so much bargaining.

Travaglino:

I'll tell you what the cause of it is. No one makes money on dowries today, because the ladies want so many dresses, so much jewelry that it's astounding.

Leandro:

And the ladies themselves often suffer from this state of affairs. A young man figures up his assets and, not wanting to be less generous than his peers, foresees so many expenses that he doesn't dare take a wife.

Travaglino:

We are not about to change the world, and I like for everyone to be able to act as he wishes. I like for him who has money owed him to be paid and for right to be the same for the poor and for the rich, as indeed it is. Everybody, in this way, will be careful to spend what he can, and anybody who does otherwise will suffer from it. Once married, the young man will have to keep her in style, especially since she is beautiful and people are used to seeing only hags in this city. He will naturally fall in love with her when she is in his house and will be generous to her, even giving her hen's milk if she asks for it. Moreover, as I told you, he has already shown not a little infatuation for her.

Leandro:

I see your point of view, but he shouldn't quibble about an extra three hundred ducats.

Travaglino:

You are right, and if it depended on him alone —I am more than sure—he would even take her naked and barefooted, as long as it were quickly, and for a dowry he would be content with the usual trousseau that goes to ladies of her station, if nothing else.

Leandro:

On whom does it depend, then?

Travaglino:

The avarice of the old is great; the further they go along in life the thirstier they are for money. They seem to be afraid of losing the world, and they want to stir up things and to run everything in their own way. They are all suspicious, especially Lamberto, who has always held this young fellow down—he still takes him around with him, though he's twenty years old.

Leandro:

I know all that, and I don't want to let myself be done out of this extra money, especially since I was once advised by a fine man that I should avoid marrying into the family of people who consider the dowry the most important thing. It is easy to see that they will be good relatives as long as it's in their interest but will betray you without any hesitation once a little money is involved.

Travaglino:

Such things are forgotten quickly. If you were right, few matches would be made today, because nearly everybody talks about the dowry first. When people are content with the dowry arrangement they can overlook other points of contention.

Leandro:

You see how many family quarrels there are today, caused by money.

Travaglino:

We are off the subject, Leandro. You have so much money available for fixing up your sister. I beg you not to quibble about such a trifle; sometimes you earn three hundred ducats in one night. Go ahead and act now.

Leandro:

It's not that I care a lot about money, but this way of dealing has revolted me; so don't nag me about it any more right now. I'm not afraid that she will lack appropriate suitors. If I were only free of my own worries. They bother me more, and I can't solve them alone.

Travaglino:

What could they be? Have you been trapped, too, like so many others? Tell me something about it, because I might very well be able to help you.

Leandro:

Alas! I'm not clear on anything, but you might be able to help me more than you say.

Travaglino:

Reveal your troubles, and if I can't find a remedy nobody could. Show me your affliction.

Leandro:

I'd show it to everybody, if I could. But my pain, or rather my joy, my bliss, is in the house of the lawyer who lives next door to Cammillo, whom you would like to make my brother-in-law.

Travaglino:

Who could it be? Mona Cassandra, wife of the lawyer? She was a beautiful woman, but now she's past her prime.

Leandro:

The rose is elsewhere. It is Faustina her daughter, to tell the truth, but be careful not to let this news out. I pretend to everyone that it is the mother, so as not to be a burden to the girl.

Travaglino:

I think that the mother would take *your* burden on top of herself gladly, but her daughter seems to me very young. My faith, you want to get them tender and when they've just been taken away from the nurse, and you like to paint in crimson rather than in light red. But tell me: If I could manage to get the lawyer to give her to you as a wife, what would you say? Our chances are improved by the fact that he is very avaricious and that you, perhaps, wouldn't quibble about the dowry.

Leandro:

I wouldn't quibble about the dowry or anything else. Indeed, I would give her a dowry myself, if there were no other way, because money comes and goes, while I don't think there is in all the world another girl so beautiful and graceful as she or one who pleases me more.

Travaglino:

Leandro, I'm not going to lose any time. Good luck, and be of good cheer, because I might be able to kill two birds with one stone. In less than two hours I'll come back to talk to you. Where will you be?

Leandro:

I shall be at home or shall leave word where you can find me, provided that you bring me good news.

Travaglino:

I shall not fail to; be calm.

Leandro:

Goodbye.

Travaglino:

Things are going as I like for them to today, and I hope to cash in double. What pleases me is that I also got some information out of that woman Lesbia. It is to women like her that people who want to find out things should go, because they always have more secrets than a locksmith. I'll work on these two deals, letting all the others ride for today. Help me, tongue, or I'll cut you off. I might be able to live off these two deals for several months, especially if I save the dowry for the lawyer, who was talking about fifteen hundred ducats. He'll have to be generous to me. I also have a foothold in the house, and if I can contrive to talk with the wife while he isn't there and can let her in on it, I know that she will get things started and serve the cause joyfully. He is a handsome young man, and ladies are very anxious for their daughters to have handsome husbands. Come on! Don't waste time.

First Intermedio

The first act being thus finished, there came onto the stage twelve shepherds, two by two, differently dressed and adorned. The first two were dressed as red goats with long fleece, and they had little caps and shoes of the same material. One of them carried in his hand a piece of fresh, leafy cane—or so it seemed from the outside, for inside was a *storta.* The other one carried a shepherd's staff.

The two who came next had vestments of tree bark made into scales, with fringes of ivy and other plants. The shoes and caps were of the same bark, adorned with ivy and flowers. And one of them carried a broken-off branch from a chestnut tree, with chestnuts and leaves. Hidden in it was a *storta,* as above. The other shepherd was going along, weaving a basket of reeds.

Of the third couple, dressed in blue clothes, with matching little caps and shoes, one had a slingshot in his hand, and the other carried the shinbone of a stag, in which lay a *cornetta.*

The first member of the fourth couple was playing another *storta* with all the apparatus of a bagpipe. He was entirely dressed in broom plants woven and held together in various bundles by clasps and cords of the same material. The other, adorned with the same dress, was carrying a vine shoot in his hand. Their caps and shoes were of broom flowers.

The fifth couple were wearing white cloth embroidered with real birds, whose feathers were, however, dyed in several colors. Their shoes were similarly made, but their caps, with new strangeness, were made of a single pigeon, which, with its wings somewhat drooping and with the tail hanging down, made an appropriate roundness for the cap, the neck and head being raised above the forehead of the shepherd. And one of them had in his hand two goat horns joined together, with a *storta* hidden between them. The other was carrying on his neck a little lamb, which seemed to have been born just a little while before.

The costumes of the last couple were of plaits of straw, with various workings of ears of grain, some of these with tassels and some without. Beautifully arranged, these plaits covered their legs, their knees, and their thighs, and formed on their heads a strange, ancient-style hat, adorned and fringed with various grasses. And one of them was playing that instrument of seven reeds carried by the God of the Countryside.[165] In this instrument was cleverly hidden a *stortina.* The other shepherd who came along with him was weaving together a straw hat. Each one of these twelve carried a knapsack around his neck. Those of the first couple were of foxskin, those of the second of kid, those of the third of roebuck, those of the fourth of rabbit, those of the fifth of stag, and those of the last of Spanish cat.[166] On their appearance these men were playing the aforementioned instruments. Then they played and sang together the following *canzonetta,* addressing their words to the sun:

Guardane almo Pastore
  Delle sempre fiorite herbose rive:
  Et le gran fiamme estive
  Temprane hoggi, e'l gran' foco, e'l fero ardore,
  Altro da farti honore
  Nulla Habbiam' noi, che questi dolci fiati;
  Et queste voci sole.
  Odile ò biondo Apollo, odile ò Sole.
  Ma care greggi hor via pe'i verdi prati
  A bei Ruscelli amati.

[165]The Pipes of Pan.

[166]We have been unable to find a definition of this term. It may refer to leopards or, perhaps, to hyenas.

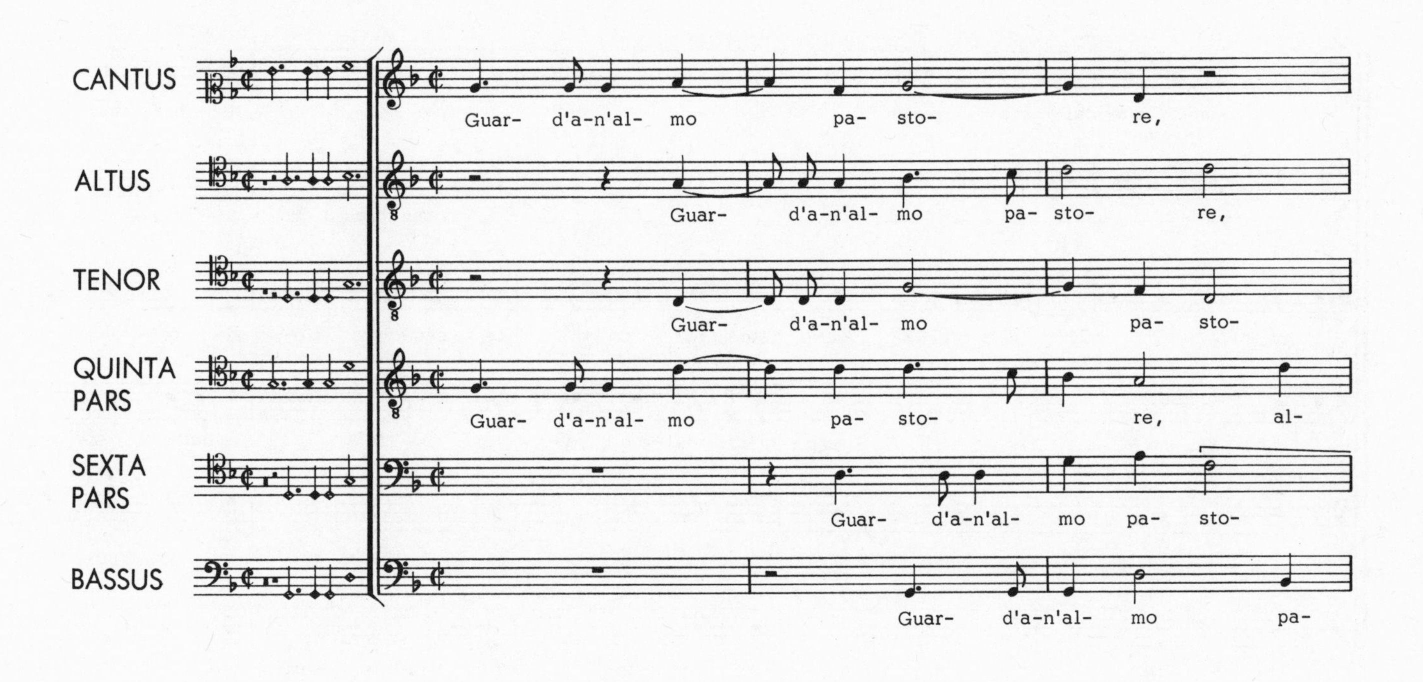
CANTUS
Guar- d'a-n'al- mo pa- sto- re,
ALTUS
Guar- d'a-n'al- mo pa- sto- re,
TENOR
Guar- d'a-n'al- mo pa- sto-
QUINTA PARS
Guar- d'a-n'al- mo pa- sto- re, al-
SEXTA PARS
Guar- d'a-n'al- mo pa- sto-
BASSUS
Guar- d'a-n'al- mo pa-

4
guar- d'a-n'al- mo pa-sto- re del' sem- pre fio- ri- te her- bo- se
guar- d'a-n'al- mo pa- sto- re del- le sem- pre fio- ri- te,
re, guar- d'a-n'al- mo pa- sto- re del- le sem- pre fio- ri- te her-
mo pa- sto- re, guar- d'a-n'al- mo pa- sto- re delle sem- pre
re, guar- d'a-n'al- mo pa- sto- re del- le sem- pre fio-
sto- re, guar- d'a-n'al- mo pa- sto- re del- le sem- pre fio- ri- te,

9
ri- ve, del- le sem- pre fio- ri- t'her- bo- se
del- le sem- pre fio- ri- t'her- bo- se ri- ve,
bo- se ri- ve, del- le sem- pre fio- ri- te her- bo- se ri- ve
fio- ri- te her- bo- se ri- ve, fio- ri- te her- bo- se
ri- t'her- bo- se ri- ve, del- le sem- pre fio- ri- te her- bo- se
del- le sem- pre fio- ri- te her- bo- se ri- ve, del- le sem- pre fio- ri-

14
ri- ve et le gran fiam- m'e- sti- ve, et
her- bo- se ri- ve et le gran fiam- m'e- sti- ve,
et le gran fiam- m'e- sti- ve, et
ri- ve et le gran fiam- m'et le gran fiam-
ri- ve et le gran fiam- m'e- sti- ve, et le gran fiam- m'e-
te her- bo- se et le gran fiam- me,

19
le gran fiam- m'e- sti- ve tem- pr'a-n'hog- g'il gran
et le gran fiam- m'e- sti- ve tem- pr'a-n'hog-
le gran fiam- m'e- sti- ve, e- sti- ve tem- pr'a-n'hog- gi
m'e- sti- ve tem- pr'a-n'hog- g'il gran fo- co,
sti- ve, et le gran fiam- m'e- sti- ve
et le gran fiam- m'e- sti- ve

23
fo- co, tem- pr'a-n'hog- g'il gran fo- co e'l fe- r'ar-
g'il gran fo- ch'e'l fe- r'ar- do- re, e'l fe- r'ar- do-
gran fo- co, tem- pr'a- n'hog- g'il fo- co e'l fe- r'ar-
tem- pr'a- n'hog- g'il gran fo- co e'l fe- ro ar- do-
tem- pr'a-n'hog- g'il fo- co e'l fe- ro ar- do- re
tem- pr'a-n'hog- g'il fo- ch'e'l fe- ro ar- do-

27
do- re al- tro da far- t'ho- no- re
re al- tro da far- ti ho- no- re
do- re al- tro da far- t'ho- no- re
re al- tro da
al- tro da far- ti ho- no- re, al- tro- da
re al- tro da

32
nul- l'hab- bi- am noi che que- sti dol- ci
nul- l'hab- bi- am noi che que- sti dol- ci
nul- l'hab- bi- am noi che que- sti
far- ti ho- no- re nul- l'hab- bi- am noi che que- sti dol- ci
far- t'ho- no- re nul- lo hab- bi- am noi che
far- t'ho- no- re nul- l'hab- bi- am noi che que- sti

37
fia- ti et que- ste vo- ci so-
fia- ti et que- ste vo- ci
dol- ci fia- ti et que- ste vo- ci so- le
fia- ti et que- ste vo- ci
que- sti dol- ci fia- ti et que- ste vo- ci so-
dol- ci fia- ti et que- ste vo- ci so- le

42
le o- di-l'o bion-d'A- pol- lo, o- di-l'o so-
so- le o- di-l'o bion-d'A- pol- lo, o- di-l'o so- le,
o- di-l'o bion- d'A- pol- lo, o- di- le, o- di-l'o so-
so- le, so- le o- di-l'o bion-d'A- pol- lo, o- di-l'o sole o- di-l'o bion- d'A- pol- lo, o- di-l'o
so- le o- di-l'o bion- d'A- pol- lo, o- di-l'o

47
le ma ca- re greg- gi hor vi- a pei
o- di-l'o so- le ma ca- re greg- gi, ma
le, o- di-l'o so- le ma ca- re greg- gi hor vi- a pei ver- di
le, o- di- l'o so- le ma ca- re greg- gi hor
so- .le, o- di-l'o so- le ma ca- re greg- gi hor vi- a
so- le, o- di- l'o so- le ma ca- re greg- gi hor vi- a

52
ver- di pra- ti, pei ver- di pra- ti
ca- re greg- gi hor vi- a pei ver- di pra- ti ai bei ru-
pra- ti pei ver- di pra- ti ai bei ru-
vi- a pei ver- di pra- ti, pei ver- di pra- ti ai
pei ver- di pra- ti pei ver- di pra- ti ai bei ru- scel- l'a-
pei ver- di pra- ti, pei ver- di pra- ti, pei

57
ai bei ru- scel- li a- ma- ti, ma ca- re
scel- l'a-ma- ti ma ca- re greg- gi hor vi- a, ma ca- re
scel- l'a- ma- ti ai bei ru- scel- l'a- ma- ti, ma ca- re
bei ru- scel- l'a- ma- ti, ma ca- re greg- gi hor vi-
ma- ti, ai bei ru- scel- l'a- ma- ti, ma ca- re greg- gi, ma
ver- di pra- ti ai bei ru- scel- l'a- ma- ti, ma ca- re

62
greg- gi hor vi- a pei ver- di pra- ti, pei
greg- gi, ma ca- re greg- gi hor vi- a pei ver- di
greg- gi hor vi- a pei ver- di pra- ti, pei ver- di pra-
a, ca- re greg-gi hor vi- a pei ver- di pra- ti,
ca- re greg- gi hor vi- a pei ver- di pra- ti, pei ver- di
greg- gi hor vi- a pei ver- di pra- ti, pei

67
ver- di pra- ti ai bei ru- scel- li a- ma-
pra- ti ai bei ru- scel- l'a-ma- ti, ma ca- re greg- gi hor vi-
ti, ai bei ru- scel- l'a- ma- ti, ai bei ru- scel- l'a- ma-
pei ver- di pra- ti ai bei ru- scel- l'a- ma- ti, ai
pra- ti ai bei ru- scel- l'a- ma- ti, ai bei ru- scel- l'a- ma- ti,
ver- di pra- ti, pei ver- di pra- ti ai bei ru- scel- l'a- ma-

72
ti.
a ai bei ru- scel- l'a- ma- ti.
ti.
bei ru- scel- l'a- ma- ti, ai bei ru- scel- l'a- ma- ti.
ai bei ru- scel- l'a- ma- ti, a- ma- ti.
ti, ai bei ru- scel- l'a- ma- ti.

(Look upon us, kind shepherd of the ever-flowering grassy banks. Temper for us today the great summer flames, and the great fire, and the fierce ardor. We have nothing with which to do you honor except these sweet pipings and these voices alone. Hear them, O blond Apollo; hear them, O Sun. But, dear flocks, let us away through the green meadows to the beloved streams.)

And thus, singing and playing for this last verse, they went away. And coming out alone, Leandro started the second act.

Act II

Leandro, alone:

I wanted to wait for the answer from the matchmaker, to see what hope is permitted me, but I stayed in the house less than an hour and it seemed to me more than a hundred. We'll go over by the lawyer's house, and maybe I'll see the object of my desire, or if not her, somebody else from the house, or failing even that, then at least the walls and windows. People in my shape take comfort in the smallest things. Oh! If what the matchmaker has in mind should succeed and I should have her as a wife, how joyful I would be! How blessed! How eternally happy! What loving looks, what delightful embraces, what sweet kisses, what tender speeches would be ours! Provided, certainly, with every pleasure and free of any jealousy, I wouldn't trade places then with the greatest lord of Italy. But I already see the house, with nobody at the windows, and I know that I shan't be lucky enough today to have the nourishment of a single glimpse. Let me get away from here, because I see two people coming out of the house next door, and I wouldn't like for them to see me. I'll take a walk and come back again to see if I have better luck the second time.

Demetrio, Libano

Demetrio:

O, Libano, is it possible that Fortune has made me her scapegoat and is torturing me[167] every hour?

---

[167]In the 1566 edition, the verb *trafiggere* ("to pierce through") is replaced by *saettare* ("to strike with an arrow"). The first may have been associated with the Crucifixion and so have been judged improper for a comic context in the Counter Reformation.

Libano:

I told you what I learned first from the conversation between that woman and Travaglino the matchmaker and then what I learned from him when I stopped him near the bridge. Because of our friendship and because I told him you would make it all up to him, he poured out everything to me.

Demetrio:

Really, finding out that Leandro is in love and with whom is very interesting to me. In any case, I'd like to try what I told you about.

Libano:

I'd rather you tried just anything else first, because what you want to do is too desperate an act and I can't imagine that anything but a painful end could come of it. Wouldn't it be good to ask for her as a wife, that is, through a friend or a matchmaker?

Demetrio:

How do you expect them to listen to us, since I am a stranger here? People want to marry their daughters to somebody from the same place, even when the dowry is moderate; in this case, it is extraordinarily high, and I am almost unknown here. Then, such things take time, while the match with Cammillo might be settled at any moment, since there is such a small disagreement.

Libano:

You can say what you please; it seems to me a very strange plan, and I shall never advise you to follow it. Nevertheless, I shall not fail to adapt myself to your will, as I always have, and shall help you in every way. Still, think about it carefully, for it is a very important thing.

Demetrio:

I have thought about it enough and have resolved on it. I hope that it will work, because often, when bad luck has you down, doing something desperate brings salvation. And even if things turn out the opposite of what I want, this is not my home and somebody who has money can get along anywhere. Too, I am not the first person who has decided on such an expedient, for I have heard and read about many who have tried similar desperate plans. Also, I'm going to tell you something that I'd forgotten: This morning in church she seemed to be looking at me more pleasantly than usual and to be granting me some favor. In any case, I am resolved to try my luck in this way. And I'll tell you this: As for trying to make friends with Leandro, I don't know how it would help me, because I am so blinded with love that I'm afraid I'd forget myself, talking with him, and he would notice my condition. That wouldn't help us, but would ruin us. Think whether it wouldn't be better, then, for you to do the job instead of me.

Libano:

All right, I'll do it, and I think it'll do me as much good as it would you.

Demetrio:

I don't mean that you should go into Porfiria's house, say, but that you should make friends with Leandro and wheedle him till he confesses to you that he is in love.

Libano:

And then?

Demetrio:

Offer your services to him as I would have done, wholeheartedly. Show him the convenience of our house, and take him up to that attic, behind your room, so he can see the lady—from that little window, you know, that opens up on the lawyer's roof. Show him the whole terrace. What do you think? You seem so pensive and don't answer.

Libano:

I am not so intelligent as to be able to make up my mind that fast, but I will do as you wish, because it comes out the same in the end. Perhaps it is better this way, because sometimes people are franker with somebody of my class than they would be with you.

Demetrio:

I see another good side to it; if I took him into the house I would be more obliged to converse with him and to entertain him than you and would not be free to go see Porfiria at the opportune moment. Even if it all ends in a scandal, it's better that the blame be yours rather than mine, don't you think?

Libano:

I think that always you want to put the trouble on my back so that you can have the honey without the flies. Demetrio, whoever wants a fish has to get wet. But let's not say any more about it; you know that ever since we left Palermo I have never failed to do anything you commanded and, for love of you, have never balked at any danger, so long as I could see you happy and successful in your undertakings.

Demetrio:

I know that well, Libano, and admit it. Be sure that I shall not forget your merits. As long as I live and am prosperous, you will be prosperous too. I want to beg you to do this thing, which seems wise to me also for another reason. Though Cammillo is much in love with her, and, as you heard this morning, they are trying to make a match between him and Porfiria, he might get suspicious if he saw me with Leandro, while he won't pay any attention to you.

Libano:

All this is true, but, tell me, have you thought where we might go if we had to flee?

Demetrio:

I'm not going to think about the doctor before I get sick.

Libano:

But this might be prudent.

Demetrio:

Anywhere I went, if it were far from Porfiria, I would be unhappy.

Libano:

I believe you, but I know that everybody tries to get away from danger. Where, I ask you, would be our refuge?

Demetrio:

In any city where business is carried on. But this isn't the time to talk about such things. There's Leandro going toward the lawyer's house. Hurry, go get into a conversation with him in a natural way, because we mustn't lose this opportunity. I'll go home and stay there till lunch, waiting for you to come tell me exactly what's happened.

Libano:

You're right, and he couldn't come at a better time. I'm going.

Leandro and Libano

Leandro:

I can't stay away from here for half an hour at a time; the harder I try, the less I succeed. My eyes are always pointed this way, my thought is never anywhere else, and my feet bring me here without my realizing it. After so much rain, if the sun would just shine on me once!

Libano:

O Leandro, would you like for me to do something for you? You are in our neighborhood here; do you need something we can help you with?

Leandro:

Thank you, but listen: You're not the lawyer's servant, and, to tell you the truth, I don't remember who you are.

Libano:

No, Sir, I'm not, but I wish I were so I could help you. I work in the house next door.

Leandro:

Where?

Libano:

In Lamberto's house.

Leandro:

Whose? Lamberto Lanfranchi's?

Libano:

Yes, Sir, that's the one.

Leandro:

Ah, I thought I'd seen you come out from over there sometimes. I'm glad to meet you; you work for a real gentleman. But why do you say that in order to help me you'd like to be working for the lawyer?

Libano:

Leandro, I didn't say it by chance. If I work for other people and do so because I can't do anything else, it's not that I don't have a generous heart and even a little cleverness.

Leandro:

I'm sure that you're generous and clever—your manner shows it—but I still don't know why you tell me this.

Libano:

Because I know what you're doing here and what makes you come by here so often. Naturally, living right by here, I see you, and you know how hard it is to hide love.

Leandro:

I don't know what love you might have in mind. It's quite true that I come by here a lot—partly to get some exercise and partly because I like this street and it's a good place to walk.

Libano:

I know that you like the street—not for itself but because of the lawyer's house and even more so because of who is in it. Please don't act surly with me, for I could help you out. I haven't had a chance, till now, to offer you my services and all that I am worth to you. I offer them now. Be so kind as to accept my good will, at least, if you don't need deeds.

Leandro:

I accept it and thank you. Now, since you know so much about my affairs—things which can hardly be denied—please don't go telling other people about them, because you would do me great harm and give me great displeasure.

Libano:

You need fear no harm from me; I'd like to think of something I could do to please you. Since we're on this subject, let me tell you something. However hard you looked, you wouldn't find anybody who could help you more in your love than I can. If you please, I'll tell you how.

Leandro:

I shall be delighted to hear how, since if anybody refuses favors that is a sign that he doesn't like to do them either.

Libano:

Over my bedroom there is a garret with a little window that opens onto the roof of the lawyer. And there is on this roof a little balcony, which they use all day to go from the big room to the bedrooms. This is for your own information, and you can use it in any way you see fit.

Leandro:

Oh, Lord, what is your name?

Libano:

It is Libano.

Leandro:

Oh, Libano, I am very lucky—and you will be very lucky—that we got on this subject this morning. I am already very much obligated to you, because the favors one receives without having asked for them are doubly welcome. And since you went so far with your plan and showed me just how in your help lies the means of my salvation, I beg you to put the plan into action and, if it is possible, to get me into that garret one day. Then ask what you will, money or other things, and you will see that I won't be stingy in anything.

Libano:

I know that you can always remunerate me, and I'm ready to accommodate you even today if you wish. Because of the holiday the house is almost entirely empty.

Leandro:

I accept, and you couldn't give me better news. If I covered you with gold I couldn't repay you sufficiently.

Libano:

If I could suggest something further which you would certainly like, what would you say?

Leandro:

What could I say, except that I were overcome by so much kindness?

Libano:

And if I told you how this other information could help you?

Leandro:

I can't ask you for anything else because, having already offered me such services of your own free will, I know that if you want to do the rest you will do it spontaneously.

Libano:

I can't let you down, because when I start to serve a gentleman like you I can't beat about the bush. I am acquainted with a certain Lucia, servant in the lawyer's house. We know each other so well and are so friendly that I think she'd do anything for me, especially if I promise her that you would grease her palm. She'll be very nice to you. She will come to see you on the balcony and will entertain you and tell a thousand things about the lawyer's house that will be helpful to you.

Leandro:

This is what I need, to get acquainted with her. Please, Libano, speak to her, and promise her what you will, for I will honor all your pledges. Get her to come onto the balcony today, and then the sky's the limit for you and her.

Libano:

Trust to me, for I want you to be satisfied with my services; I'll go all out in your behalf. Where will you go now?

Leandro:

Wherever you like. Tell me what you want me to do, and how long it may be before I can get into the house. I'll do whatever you tell me, because I want to navigate with your compass.

Libano:

Come here at four o'clock, which is about the time that Vespers is sounded. The house is deserted, or there is at most a thieving old woman. She likes to count our mouthfuls and to see how many pieces of food we get, but I'll find some method to get her out of the way, sending her out, or to do some task in the house, or to take care of the chickens or the pigeons, or up in the attic, so that she won't be able to spy on us from any side.

Leandro:

I leave it all to you, because I want you to guide me. Oh, Libano, there is the lawyer, who was to come back about lunch time, and that matchmaker is hanging around him. Do me a favor and give me quickly your cape and your toque, and take my beret and this coat and go home. I'll go up behind them, covered up in this way so they won't recognize me, to hear how they're settling my business, because I know they are talking about me. Then I'd like to check on the matchmaker to see whether he's cheating me. He said he would get the lady given to me as a wife.

Libano:

Don't be sure of it, because they are shysters. Give me the coat and take the cape. Please be careful with it, because it is of Siena cloth. I'll go home, and you, at the appointed time, come wearing those clothes, because you won't look suspicious going into the house in them. I'll signal to you from the little window or from the garden door.

Leandro:

I'll do all that; go on.

Libano:

Up to now this disguise is good, and one can't tell the difference from above. I don't want to wear it at home so it won't be seen. I'll give it to somebody who'll keep it for me and who'll lend me a cape and cloak till I get mine back. I know just where to go, not far from here.

Messer Ricciardo, a lawyer; and Travaglino

Messer Ricciardo:

You want to fool me and to dazzle me with this talk of nobility from Constantinople and other places we can't check on. You're trying to make me believe that hail is candy. Haven't I told you that I'm about to give her to somebody nobler than he? Do you think I don't know Leandro? Has he changed overnight? I can't see that he has anything but property, and I don't want to be like some people, who seek only to give their daughters to somebody rich. You're used to cheating and telling lies, but don't bother me with it any more. Before I give my daughter away I'll think about it very carefully.

Travaglino:

Messer Ricciardo, you have to take opportunities when they come, especially since women are not a merchandise that one likes to keep in stock for a long time. Leandro is a serious young man; he has property and is clever enough not only to keep it but also to increase it. He won't insist on too much dowry, because the decision is his own. When money can be saved, I think you ought to do it. I think I know who your other possibility is. You say that he is noble; granted, but there are a lot of brothers and sisters. Though you imagine him with a title, or on a fine horse with a stirrup holder and page, these are all just expectations. You have to marry your daughter to the personal qualities of a young man and not to his father or his mother or his household.

Messer Ricciardo:

I know what I'm doing, and I don't need your advice. You don't know what I mean, but you're trying to lead me on and worm out my secrets.

Travaglino:

That may be, but I think I know what you mean. In this trade I get pretty sharp. Isn't this right? Where I mean, there is the mother-in-law, who is considered to be the crankiest woman in Pisa. You know how mothers-in-law and daughters-in-law get along—there's never any peace between them, especially when they're bad-natured.

Messer Ricciardo:

You know a lot about what you are saying. You want to seem as if you know everybody in Pisa.

Travaglino:

I'm sorry I said it, but think about it well and try, too, when you can, to save this money for your children.

Messer Ricciardo:

Money is fine, as you say, but the flesh of my daughter is also dear to me and not to be thrown away. I don't want to hurry too much; maybe you think this is a bean sale. Let me sleep on it, and I'll answer you tomorrow.

Travaglino:

Talk it over too with your wife, because she

may know something about one or the other of the young men.

Messer Ricciardo:

I'll consult, rather, with my servant and then with my farm superintendent. Don't you know that women always choose the wrong course? You must be talking that way because you have managed to win over my wife and prime her for me. There's some trick here. I know my folks; you make me suspicious, but I'll find out.

Travaglino:

I said it without thinking and with good intentions, because women are curious, and often when you think they are in church praying they are busy talking. They are more interested in other people's business than in their own, and naturally they find out everything. So don't take offense.

Messer Ricciardo:

I see that you're slicker than a greased pig. You have talked enough. It's as if I were being forced to make this marriage. I'll do it or not do it as God guides me. Now go away, and don't come back to talk to me again about this matter. If I need you I can send for you.

Travaglino:

Messer Ricciardo, you know what luck is like. This is the last thing I'm going to tell you—that delay is often harmful and that you might miss out.

Messer Ricciardo:

I am sick of you. If you don't get away I'll get angry and will never speak to you again.

Travaglino:

You have to think about it some more?

Messer Ricciardo:

Get away, don't you hear me, you pest!

Travaglino, the matchmaker, alone:

You see that I couldn't get anything definite out of him, the grouchy old man. He got so mad that he couldn't see. And because he esteems those messy big law books so much, he considers himself to be the wisest man in Pisa. We'll get him another time, when he's in better humor. It's better to see old men after lunch, because the wine cheers them up and the humor that upsets them is not flowing. A tree doesn't fall down at the first blow. If he thinks about saving the money, that will help; I know how stingy he is.

He might also give in to the nagging of his wife, because when I left her not two hours ago she saw things our way. I think I see her down there by the door. I want to go off toward home, because I haven't stopped since eleven o'clock. In this trade you have to be very patient, solicitous, insistent. One must lie and not take offense at harsh words but act like dogs who, if you beat them, run off and then come back to get some food. Whoever does otherwise wastes his time and wears out his shoes walking through the streets, and his purse is empty and light. How many people are there like that? But I see somebody in that street signaling to me; who in the Devil can it be? Let's go over there.

Messer Ricciardo, a lawyer; Mona Cassandra, his wife; Lucia, a servant

Cassandra:

Hurry up, Lucia, come quickly. Hide this thing under your clothes. See how slow she is!

Lucia:

Here I am, I've hidden it. You didn't want me to come out like a crazy woman, did you? I had undressed, not thinking that you wanted to go out any more.

Messer Ricciardo:

Cassandra, where are you going, what do you want to do at this hour? It's lunch time. Go back in the house. You waited too late.

Cassandra:

What time is it? You came back early. The Mass at the Cathedral isn't finished yet, and the churches must still be full. I've been taking care of the girls. Let me go, and I'll be back right away.

Messer Ricciardo:

Don't you hear that it's late and that I want to have lunch? You're in a big hurry; come back, I say.

Cassandra:

You're the one who is in a hurry. You're like a wolf driven in from the woods by hunger. Let me at least go over there to that convent to speak to Sister Pacifica. I promise I'll be back before the wine is on the table. I'm going for something that concerns you too.

Messer Ricciardo:

For what thing that concerns me too are you going? Out with it.

Cassandra:
I'll tell you when I get back. Let me go.

Messer Ricciardo:
Tell me now, because I want to know now.

Cassandra:
To tell the truth, I'm going to have prayers said for our poor daughter, because I'm afraid that her fate is going to be settled soon—may God make it a good one. For some time I've seen around the house those matchmakers who won't leave you alone. The little birds have also told me that you have set your mind to do something. May God prevent you from doing the worst for her.

Messer Ricciardo:
Wasn't I right in thinking that that pest Travaglino had primed her? Oh, feminine sex, weak and frivolous, how easy it is for man to maneuver you as he pleases! In fact, anybody who knows how to talk well can influence women as he likes. Cassandra, you take on too many worries and want to meddle in things where you are not needed. These are things you should leave to me, since, because of my age, experience, and education, I don't need your advice. You must want to give her to Leandro. If you knew all about him, you wouldn't think of it. Is he anything but a handsome bird with plenty of gold?

Cassandra:
I don't know whether he is a bird or not, but I know that he is a good young fellow, well brought up, and that he is well built and as well provided in other things as anyone. That other one that you said was available is an idler who doesn't know whether he's dead or alive and is used to being led around by the nose. Finally, he's nothing but a little puff of smoke who seems to have been formed from Adam's rib. Now do what you please.

Messer Ricciardo:
You always were frivolous and don't know what you are gabbing about. Busy yourself with preparing her trousseau and with other things in your domain, and let me worry about finding her a husband, and you'll be doing[168] well.

Cassandra:
You think that you're so wise and that because I'm a woman I don't know anything, but we too sometimes know how the world runs.

[168]Both editions seem to read "sai" ("you know"), but it is certainly "fai" ("you do") that is meant.

Lucia:
And are pretty sharp!

Messer Ricciardo:
You are wise, and I don't know any more, granted, but I'm still going to marry the girl to whom I please.

Cassandra:
I don't know what you're going to do; if I thought that you were going to give her to the one you talked about I don't know what I'd do to keep from seeing such an awful thing.

Messer Ricciardo:
Look how she talks, the shameful, arrogant fool. You'll make me *want* to give her to him, and if I have a mind, he'll take her away before tomorrow morning.

Cassandra:
If he takes her away, let me be taken away too.

Messer Ricciardo:
Would to God that you be taken away to the Arno River. See how you're making me swear!

Cassandra:
I have spoken.

Messer Ricciardo:
You will tie my hands? You want to be more powerful than I?

Cassandra:
Of course, what do you think? Do you imagine that other people won't have something to do with it?

Messer Ricciardo:
Oh, you shrew, if I weren't in the street I'd teach you a lesson. Get in the house, go on, I may make you say some prayers on various subjects. And you, you damned Lucia, come here, what do you have under your dress? Ah, ah, look, she is hauling off some stuff! I've found you out, these are the prayers! To empty my house and give what's in it to the priests, monks, and nuns, who are like chickens and never get enough. And this wretch was covering up for her. Get in the house, you too, and I'll pay you back for this.

Lucia:
Forgive me, Sir, don't get after me. What can I do; if she orders me to do something, I have to obey.

Second Intermedio

Between the spectators and the stage setting, joined to the latter, was a rather spacious canal, painted inside and around in such a way that it resembled the Arno. In it, on the side toward the sea, appeared suddenly three nude mermaids, each with her two tails minutely worked in silver scales. They had green hair, with novel head-dresses of sea shells and sea snails, having branches of coral above, some white, some red, and some black.

There were in their company three sea nymphs, dressed in light green veiling, their long, blonde hair adorned with pearls and mother-of-pearl shells. Their shoes were cleverly made from sea conches. And each one of them carried a *leuto* hidden in a shell. Playing softly, they accompanied the singing of the mermaids. There were also three sea monsters with antlers on their heads, with long hair and beards of green moss. They were dressed in maidenhair ferns, moss, and algae and had belts of fishskins. Each one of them was playing a disguised *traversa.* The first seemed to be a long fish's backbone, with a head and tail but without minor bones attached to it. The next seemed to be a sea snail and the third a sea marsh cane.

All these together, seeming to be looking for the Most Illustrious Duchess, who had left Naples, came up sweetly singing the following words:

Chi ne l'ha tolta ohyme? Chi ne l'asconde?
Et deh chi ne la mostra
La bella Donna nostra?
Ma come scherzan' l'onde,
Et ridon' l'herbe e i fior, ridon le fronde
Là in quel dolce seren' di Paradiso?
Ivi è certo il bel viso
Et pur gratia & dolceza & pace infonde.
O sempre Arno tranquillo, herbose sponde,
Et chi piu gioia ingombra?
Hor là volianne al ombra.

(Who has taken her from us, alas? Who is hiding her from us? O, who will show her to us, our beautiful Lady? / But, how the waves are dancing, how the grass and flowers are laughing, how the leafy branches are laughing, over there in that sweet serenity of Paradise! There surely is the lovely face, infusing grace, sweetness, and peace. O ever-tranquil Arno, O grassy banks, who is more laden with joy? Now let us fly to the shade.)

CANTUS
Chi ne l'a tol- t'oy- me
QUINTA PARS
Chi ne l'a scon-
SEXTA PARS
Chi ne l'a tol- t'oy- me
ALTUS
Chi ne l'a tol- t'oy- me chi ne l'a- scon-
TENOR
Chi ne l'a- scon-
BASSUS
Chi ne l'a- scon-

4
et deh chi ne la mo- stra la bel- la don- na no-
de et deh chi ne la mo- stra la bel- la
et deh chi ne la mo- stra la bel- la don- na no-
de et deh chi ne la mo- stra la bel- la don- na, la bel- la donde et deh chi ne la mo- stra la bel- la don- na no- stra,
de et deh chi ne la mo- stra la bel- la

8
stra, la bel- la don- na no- stra, la
don- na no- stra, la bel- la don- na
stra, la bel- la don- na no- stra,
na, la bel- la don- na no- stra,
la bel- la don- na no- stra, la bel- la
don- na no- stra, la bel- la don- na no-

12
bel- la don- na, la bel- la don- na no- stra.
no- stra, la bel- la don- na no- stra.
la bel- la don- na no- stra.
la bel- la don- na, la bel- la don- na no- stra.
don- na no- stra, la bel- la don- na no- stra.
stra, la bel- la don- na no- stra.

17
SECUNDA PARS
Ma co- me scher- zan' l'on- de
Et ri- don l'her-b'e i fior
Ma co- me scher- zan' l'on- de et ri- don l'her-b'e i fior
Ma co- me scher- zan' l'on- de et ri- don l'her-b'e i fior ri-
Ma co- me scher- zan' l'on- de
Ma co- me scher- zan' l'on- de et ri- don l'her-b'e i fior

20
ri- don le fron-de la'n quel dol- ce se- ren, la'n quel dol-
ri-don le fron- de, ri- don le fron- de la'n quel dol- ce
ri- don le fron-de, ri- don le fron de la'n quel dol- ce se- ren di
don le fron- de, ri- don le fron- de la'n quel dol- ce se- ren
ri- don le fron- de la'n quel dol- ce se- ren
ri- don le fron- de, ri- don le fron- de la'n quel dol- ce

24
ce se- ren di pa- ra- di- so i- v'e cer- t'il bel vi-
se- ren di pa- ra di- so i- v'e cer- t'il bel vi-
pa- ra- di- so i- v'e cer- t'il bel vi- so, i- v'e cer-
di pa- ra- di- so i- v'e cer- t'il bel vi-
di pa- ra- di- so i- v'e cer- t'il bel vi- so, i- v'e cer-
se- ren- di pa- ra- di- so i- v'e cer- t'il bel vi-

29
so et pur gra-ti'et dol- cez- za
so et pur gra- tia et dolcez- z'et pa- ce in- fon-
t'il bel vi- so et pur gra-ti'et dol- cez- za et pa- c'in- fon-
so et pur gra- tia et dol- cezza et pa- ce, et pa- c'in- fon-
t'il bel vi- so et pur gra-ti'et dol- cez- za et pa-
so et pur gra- tia et dol- cez- za et pa- ce,

35
et pa- ce in- fon- de. O sem-
de, et pa- ce in- fon- de et pa- ce in- fon- de. O
de, et pa- c'in- fon- de. O sem-
de, et pa- c'in- fon- de. O sem- pr'Ar-
c'in- fon- de, et pa- c'in- fon- de. O sem- pr'Ar-
et pa- ce in- fon- de. O sem-

40
pre Ar- no tran- quil-lo her- bo- se spon- de et chi
sem-pr'Ar- no tran-quil- lo her- bo- se spon- de
pr'Ar- no tran- quil- lo her- bo- se spon- de
no tran-quil- lo her- bo- se spon- de, her- bo- se spon-de et
no tran- quil- lo her- bo- se spon- de et chi
pr'Ar- no tran- quil- lo her- bo- se spon- de

45
piu gio- ia'n- gom- bra hor la volian-n'a l'om- bra, hor la volian-n'a l'om-
hor la volian-n'a l'om- bra, hor la volian-n'a l'om- bra, vo-
hor la volian-n'a l'om- bra, hor la volian-n'a l'om- bra, hor la, hor la vo-
chi piu gio- ia'n- gom- bra hor la vo- lian-n'a l'om- bra, hor la vo-lian- n'a l'om- bra,
[♯] ♯ ♮
piu gio- ia'n- gom- bra hor la volian-n'a l'om- bra, hor la, hor la, hor la vo-
hor la volian- n'a l'om- bra, hor la, hor la vo-

49
bra, hor la volian- n'a l'om- bra.
lian- n'a l'om- bra.
lian- n'a l'om- bra, hor la volian-n'a l'om- bra.
hor la vo-lian-n'a l'om- bra.
lian-n'a l'om- bra, hor la, hor la vo-lian-n'a l'om- bra.
lian- n'a l'om- bra, hor la vo-lian-n'a l'om- bra.

Act III

Currado, a servant; and Leandro

Currado:

Leandro didn't come home to lunch and made us wait all morning, servants too. I got the extra food. I wish he would always do that, because I would get more to eat than I usually do and would get to go to the wine cellar more often. They wouldn't pay so much attention to me either, especially since Porfiria and her woman spend a lot of time in their room. My own hussy does what I want her to; we help each other out and cover up for each other when there's trouble. I see somebody over there who looks a lot like the boss. If he weren't wearing a cape, as he is, I'd say it's he, because in the face, in his walk, and every other way it looks like him. Good Lord, it is he! What disguise has he put on? He seems to be out of his head. He went out of the house with a coat and not with a cape. Look at him mooning around. In any case, I'll give him the message I have for him. Oh, master, good day, I almost didn't recognize you; why do you have that disguise?

Leandro:

Mind your own business. What's the matter? What do you want?

Currado:

Chele and Toscanino came from the farm, and they would have liked to settle some kind of accounts with you and to talk to you about some kind of livestock. What shall I tell them?

Leandro:

When did they come?

Currado:

Right at lunch time, don't you know how they do? When they want to have a good feed they come along with pretext of some business, bringing at the most some lettuce that's worth four cents, and with two bows, they have paid the host.

Leandro:

Go home and tell them to come back another time.

Currado:

The more often they have to come back the happier they are.

Leandro:

Listen, be careful not to tell anybody about the

disguise you find me in. But if Porfiria or anyone else asks about me, say that you found me in the Cathedral. Go on; be a good boy.

Currado:

You can be sure that I will. Do you want anything else?

Leandro:

No, go on.

Currado:

Just as long as it took him to go back, that's how long it will take me to tell his secrets. What does it matter to me? I hope the wine cellar is open; and let him stay as long as he wants.

Leandro, alone:

This fellow certainly came at the right time, and those farmers certainly came to talk business at the right time! This was certainly the right day for such things! I've wanted this chance for a hundred years, and never in my life have I been so lucky as I think to be today if I get into that attic. How wise was I not to go to lunch? In any case, I wouldn't have taken a bite that seemed to have any flavor, for love takes away the taste of everything. Libano told me when he left me that I should wait four hours before showing myself again. I don't know how many hours have passed, but it seems a year. As long as I'm not in the house, let me go back to a place where I can at least feed my eyes. I'm burning up worse than snow in the sun. I want to edge over toward Lamberto's house to see whether Libano is signaling to me yet, as he is to do when everybody is out of the house. In this garb I can't be recognized too easily; how wise was I to change clothes this morning! But who are those people coming out of my friend's house? I think it's Lamberto, that old miser, and he has with him his son Cammillo. I'll go, then, around to the back door, because nobody passes by there and I can get in more easily. This big street here is always full.

Lamberto, an old man; and Cammillo, his son

Lamberto:

See what your behavior has been like lately. There is no relative or neighbor who doesn't harangue me a thousand times a day, telling me that I ought to do this and say that and keep you in the house at night. I thought that at this age I could depend on you and rest while you take care of things, but I have more worries and troubles than ever. You have no reason to act like that.

Cammillo:

My Father, you have worries and troubles because you want them and not because I create them. I don't think I have ever done anything that brought you harm or shame.

Lamberto:

You don't think you're doing me harm by squandering everything I have with this, that, and the other? And that's not all; even goods are going out of the house—without limit—and God knows where.

Cammillo:

How unlucky I am, never to have been able to spend two scudos at home or elsewhere without your raising a fuss and complaining to the whole neighborhood. It is quite true that as one grows older he forgets everything and no longer remembers what his life was like.

Lamberto:

If you knew what my life was like at your age —what kind of behavior, manners, friends I had —you would see how different things are today from what they were then, and you would try to imitate people who live in the old way.

Cammillo:

I don't know what kind of manners or friends you had, but I believe that the world has always been the same.

Lamberto:

You believe wrong, and I could tell you some things that might make you change your mind.

Cammillo:

You have already told me these things many other times. I don't mean to contradict you in anything, but I have read that the nature of old men has always been such as to make them praise the past and condemn the present. If the world had been steadily growing worse at every period, life would already have been impossible for centuries.

Lamberto:

I don't know what you have read, but I know what I used to do and now I see what you do.

Cammillo:

Be very wary, for many things may be said by some slanderer—there are so many in this town. There are some big mouths who seem to have no other business besides gossiping and doing harm.

Lamberto:

Eh, Cammillo, Cammillo, do you think that I'm blind? If you don't want things to be found out and talked about, you shouldn't do them. But this is like preaching to the wind. I know many matches that I could make for you if you led a better life. And it would be better for you in all respects.

Cammillo:

I know, too, what chances you have, and I know on whom it depends. But I am so unlucky that I can never have those things that I want; indeed, because you know that I would like to make this marriage, you are putting off the decision so long that somebody else will have the good fortune.

Lamberto:

You think that good fortune is just what you want, and you don't go into things any more deeply. If I thought, however, that giving you a wife would straighten you out, I wouldn't be so hesitant to do what you're thinking about. But I think that you'd be worse than ever.

Cammillo:

Don't believe that of me, because if you do me this kindness you will see me behave in such a way that you won't be sorry for it.

Lamberto:

I shall act as seems best to me, and may God grant that the right way be taken.

Cammillo:

I would like to leave you for today, because I have a few friends who are waiting for me.

Lamberto:

You always have some plan for taking pleasure and for having a good time. Go on, go ahead; just try to get home early so I won't have to wait on you for supper.

Cammillo:

I'll come back early. Do you want anything else?

Lamberto:

Nothing else, except that you think over the things that I have told you.

Cammillo:

Then good day to you.

Lamberto:

Be careful so that God may make you act wisely.

Cammillo:

Well, he certainly preached me a sermon, and he always gets on those topics. I know well that he wasn't a saint either, but now that because of age he can't enjoy things himself he doesn't want me to. But idle pleasure is the last thing I want now; the main thing would be for me to get that girl for a wife.

Lamberto:

People who have grown sons have these troubles. If God grants me enough patience with him, I think I'll go straight to Paradise as a martyr. How many things do I have to bear and pretend not to see? I don't matter much any more because I am old, but I can't help worrying about everything. We shall pray God that He keep the boy safe, and maybe he will become mature with time. But I see there the gentleman in his doorway who seems to be coming to Vespers too. I'll wait for him here so I can sit by him in church. He'll tell me some fine things, because he has a doctor's degree and a fine memory. He always talks about something very interesting.

Messer Ricciardo, Cassandra, and Lucia

Messer Ricciardo:

You heard me: Don't leave the house, because I don't want her to be there alone without one of us, do you hear?

Cassandra:

I heard, and I see that you have little feeling for others and think only about your own concerns. Will you at least let her go where I wanted to go this morning?

Messer Ricciardo:

Where?

Cassandra:

To that convent.

Messer Ricciardo:

Didn't you hear me? No! No! No! I don't want her to go there—do you get it? I don't need to buy so many prayers.

Cassandra:

At least let her go see Don Basilio, my confessor, who is supposed to give me the answer to a question of advice I asked him.

Messer Ricciardo:

I don't want her to go there either. I don't need so much advice that I can make for myself. Every time she wants to set some eggs, or weave a cloth, or do the wash, she wants to get the confessor's advice. I'm sick of it.

Cassandra:

Oh, let her go, because she doesn't have anything else to do in the house and she will come back right away.

Messer Ricciardo:

She who looks can always find something to do in a house. Uncork your ears: I don't want her to go out except with you. If she were old, I wouldn't worry about it.

Cassandra:

You are giving me a hard time on purpose, but I'll do the same to you when I take a mind to.

Messer Ricciardo:

If you argue with me any more you will make me go back in the house and do something wild. Listen, Lucia, if you go out today I'll slap your face so much that it'll be too bad for you.

Lucia:

Sir, I don't want to go, but if Mona forces me to go, what shall I do? She has other means of persuasion besides words.

Messer Ricciardo:

Don't go. If she goes herself, let me settle with her. If you go out of the house today, don't come back.

Lamberto, Messer Ricciardo, and Giorgetto

Lamberto:

It seems he can't get away from that doorway; he starts out and then goes back. If I had thought that he was going to take so much time, I would have gone on. He must have been fussing with his wife, as he often does. Look at him coming along muttering and snorting. He looks like a hedgehog.

Messer Ricciardo:

Having a wife is having hell in this world. In everything else I rely on learning and on laws, but they don't help me a bit with her. She always has more excuses than I have questions. But who is that standing there? Let me take off my glasses; it seems to be Lamberto our neighbor waiting for me. Giorgetto, come here: Go into the church and save a place for us in a pew with this handkerchief. Hurry, before they are all taken, and then go back to the house and see what Cassandra does. I want to find out whether she goes out today, to know whether she pays attention to what I tell her.

Lamberto:

Welcome, Messer Ricciardo, I've been waiting for you here a good while so that we could be together today.

Messer Ricciardo:

I value your company highly. Let's go.

Lamberto:

And I value yours more. Why couldn't you get away from that door?

Messer Ricciardo:

Because whoever has to do with women has to do with the Devil. They always make trouble and are forever filling other people's heads with new worries. I had got up from a nap after lunch, and, imagine, she was all ready to go out and was prancing around in front of the mirror as they all do. They always check themselves in front of the mirror a hundred times before they are satisfied. Since I was still sleepy and, a little before, had had an argument with her, I told her that it wouldn't be good for her to go out and to leave the girls in the care of servants, because you know how they are—you can't trust them as far as you can see them. She started arguing with me and came up clear to the door scolding me. I decided that she wouldn't go, and she won't go, because I want to have my way with her and to win out and to be the master and I don't intend to be run by a woman or for her to wear the pants. What do you say about it?

Lamberto:

I say that you understand the matter well, but that I don't know much about it. My wife gave me this son that I have and then died, so that I had little experience of her.

Messer Ricciardo:

Haven't you ever had a desire to take another one to run your household?

Lamberto:

I have never wanted to get one to manage things, because often a man happens to get one who has to be managed herself. Then, too, when you think that a woman would have to turn the house upside down and rearrange it all, it is clear that they just upset things.

Messer Ricciardo:

To tell the truth, my wife is a pretty good woman and housekeeper, but she too is a little stubborn and proud. She doesn't have a doormat for a husband, though; I insist on supervising her all the time and don't let myself be led around by the nose. But haven't you ever wanted to have some more children, having only one son?

Lamberto:

I don't want to have any more children either, for I can hardly live in peace with this one.

Messer Ricciardo:

And what about that other matter—you know what I mean. How have you managed?

Lamberto:

How do you think? It's like everything else—a matter of getting used to doing without.

Messer Ricciardo:

In your case it's been a matter of getting used to it, but you can be sure that I wouldn't have stayed idle. Do you know that, as old as I am, there still aren't many nights that I don't want to make love to my wife? I have had ten children from her, though only five—two girls and three small boys—are still alive. All of the boys have been born since my sixtieth birthday. Does it seem to you that I've wasted any time?

Lamberto:

No, indeed. But speak to your servant there.

Messer Ricciardo:

Giorgetto, did you save the place?

Giorgetto:

Yes Sir, up there in the choir where you were Sunday.

Messer Ricciardo:

Good. Lamberto, let's go into the church before the service starts. Giorgetto, do what I told you to and report everything to me. Don't hang around the piazzas or on the riverbank gambling. Toward evening, come to get me in the Cathedral, do you understand?

Giorgetto:

Yes Sir, I understand, don't worry. *(Aside.)* If he settles down in the church, you can be sure that I'll be somewhere besides at home. I have some money that, if I'm not wrong, will afford me a good deal of amusement. They are new coins, and I won't gamble them at horseshoes or in similar kids' games but at faro so that I can quickly make some more. Who is that ugly person coming out of Lamberto's house? What an eye that bogey has!

Cornelia, an old woman; Giorgetto, a boy

Cornelia:

What the Devil! In this house one never has an hour to himself. This sickness certainly came at the right time! I had sat down to sew on some of my old clothes when Libano threw himself on the bed screaming and said he was dying of spasms and from pain in the "articles," or "festicles." He sent me to the hospital for some oil of "erion," or "compirion"—I don't know how to say it. I couldn't remember that strange name.

Giorgetto:
Oh, ugly, falseface! Oh, oh, oh!

Cornelia:
What trouble is this? Who is pulling my shawl? Rascal, rascal! Look who is bothering me! Take it easy! Take it easy! He's making faces at me too, can you imagine?

Giorgetto:
Oh, you hag! Oh, oh!

Cornelia:
I'll "hag" you, little criminal. You won't let me alone? You would be wise to go about your own business.

Giorgetto:
Oh, what a funny face! Oh, oh, oh!

Cornelia:
You won't let me go? If I get after you with this stick, I may make you laugh in a different way, little thug!

Giorgetto:
You are trying to scare me. Oh, oh, oh! She can hardly move, and she wants to catch me. I'll bring the other kids to make fun of you.

Cornelia:
By goodness, if he wants the oil, he'll get it himself. I want to go back into the house because I don't want to endure these humiliations for his sake. Let him go to the Devil! I can't even walk with these clogs. A fever on whoever made them.

Giorgetto:
You will certainly do well to go back, because you would scare off people, who would think you were the Devil's wife. But I want to move on too, because if Mona saw me around here it wouldn't take her long to find me something to do. Let me clear out of here and not stand around staring at the sky.

Third Intermedio

Silenus—described by Vergil in his Sixth Eclogue as found sleeping in a cave at noon by Mnasyllus and Chromis and by the very beautiful Aegle—showed us that, as in the comedy, it was noon. Awakened by them, and being begged to sing, he placed between his goatlike legs a tortoise, in which was an excellent *violone,* and, with a bow like an asp, he began sweetly to play and to sing the following *canzonetta:*

O begli Anni del Oro, ò secol divo:
Alhor non Rastro, ò Falce, alhor non era
Visco, ne laccio; et no'l rio ferro, e'l tosco;
Ma sen gia puro latte il fresco rivo;
Mel' sudavan' le querce; Ivano à schiera
Nymfe insieme et Pastori, al chiaro è'l fosco.
O begli anni del Or', vedrovvi io mai?
Tornagli ò nuovo Sol, tornagli homai.

(O beautiful golden years, O divine century! Then there was no rake or scythe; then there was no birdlime or snare, no evil iron or poison. But the cool stream flowed with pure milk; the oak trees exuded honey. Nymphs and shepherds went round in groups together, in daylight and in darkness. O beautiful golden years, shall I ever see you? Bring them back, O new Sun, bring them back now.)[169]

[169]This poem, closely imitated from Vergil, is the only one of those Strozzi wrote for the wedding that appears in the collection of his *Madrigali* published by his sons in 1593.

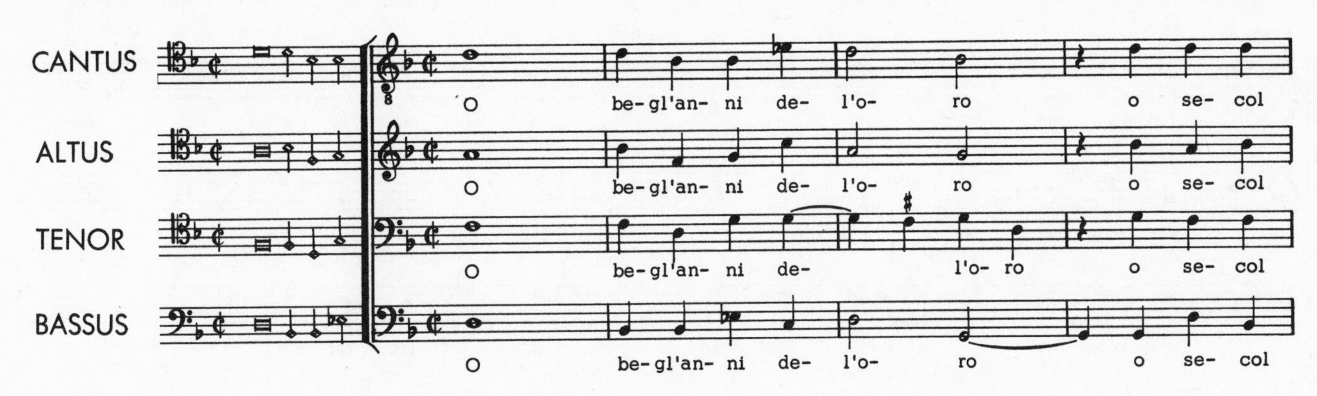
CANTUS
O be-gl'an- ni de- l'o- ro o se- col
ALTUS
O be-gl'an- ni de- l'o- ro o se- col
TENOR
O be-gl'an- ni de- l'o- ro o se- col
BASSUS
O be-gl'an- ni de- l'o- ro o se- col

5
di- vo al- hor non ra- str'o fal- ce al- hor non e- ra
di- vo al- hor non ra- str'o fal- ce al- hor non e- ra
di- vo al- hor non ra- str'o fal- ce al- hor non e- ra
di- vo al- hor non ra- str'o fal- ce al- hor non e- ra

10
vi- sco ne lac- cio et no'l rio fer- r'e'l to-
vi- sco ne lac- cio et no'l rio fer- r'e'l to-
vi- sco ne lac- cio et no'l rio fer- r'e'l to-
vi- sco ne lac- cio et no'l rio fer- r'e'l to-
15
sco ma sen gía pu- ro lat- te il fre- sco ri- vo, il
sco ma sen gía pu- ro lat- te il fre- sco ri- vo, il
sco ma sen gía pu- ro lat- te il
sco ma sen gía pu- ro lat- te il fre- sco ri- vo, il

20
fre- sco ri- vo mel su- da- van' le quer- ce i- va- n'a
fre- sco ri- va mel su- da- van' le quer- ce i- va- n'a
fre- sco ri- vo mel su- da- van' le quer- ce i- va- n'a
fre- sco ri- vo mel su- da- van' le quer- ce i- va- n'a
25
stie- ra Nim- phe in- sie- m'et pa- sto- ri al chia- r'e'l fo- sco.
stie- ra Nim- phe in- sie- m'et pa- sto- ri al chia- r'e'l fo- sco.
stie- ra in- sie- m'et pa- sto- ri al chia- r'e'l fo- sco.
stie- ra in- sie- m'et pa- sto- ri al chia- r'e'l fo- sco.

30
O be- gli'an- ni de l'or' ve- drov- v'io mai,
O be- gli'an- ni de l'or' ve- drov- v'io
O be- gli'an- ni de l'or' ve- drov- v'io
O be- gli'an- ni de l'or' ve- drov- v'io
35
ve- drov- v'io mai tor- na gli nuo- vo sol, tor-
mai, ve- drov- v'io mai tor- na gli nuo- vo sol, tor-
mai, ve- drov- v'io mai tor- na gli nuo- vo sol,
mai, ve- drov- v'io mai tor-

40
na gli o nuo- vo sol, tor- na gli o mai, tor- na gli o nuo- vo
na gli o nuo- vo sol, tor- na gli o mai, tor- na gli o nuo- vo
tor- na gli o mai, tor- na gli o nuo- vo
na gli o nuo- vo sol, tor- na gli o mai,
45
sol, tor- na gli o nuo- vo sol, tor- na gli o mai.
sol, tor- na gli o nuo- vo sol, tor- na gli o mai.
sol, tor- na gli o mai.
tor- na gli o nuo- vo sol, tor- na gli o mai.

Act IV

Demetrio, Libano, Lesbia

Demetrio:

You say that you left him up in the garret, so that I think he won't budge from there all day and we shall be at ease to carry out our plan?

Libano:

I did something more.

Demetrio:

What did you do? I don't know about anything else; I stayed down in my room on the ground floor so he wouldn't see me.

Libano:

I locked him inside, and without this key he can't get out—except through the window. Moreover, if Lucia goes up to talk to him he'll stay until night, thinking he's been there less than an hour. So, concerning him, you needn't have a worry in the world.

Demetrio:

I didn't see come, either, the friend whom you got to reconnoiter the house of the lady. When did he come, and how?

Libano:

Here through the back door, just when Leandro had gone inside.

Demetrio:

And what did he tell you?

Libano:

That the servant had gone out of the house with two peasants. To find out more, he went up to one of them and cleverly ascertained that there was nobody in the house except Porfiria and two women servants.

Demetrio:

All this is fine. But tell me: Do you think I will manage to get in the house?

Libano:

I think that if you do as I said, it will work. If it doesn't, we will think of something else, don't worry. I hope that then you will find things set for the rest. That, and not the entering, seems to me the important thing.

Demetrio:

Oh, something will work out; let's get going. Oh, Libano, I can see part of the house now and am trembling like a leaf and feel myself fainting.

I'm afraid that if I go there I may suddenly pass out or not know what to say.

Libano:
Don't start losing heart before you're on the battlefield—you're not very brave! Poor man; look, his face is as pale as a washed sheet.

Demetrio:
It often happens that someone so much in love loses his head and can't present his case. If I weren't in love, I think I could talk like a Cicero and win her over with a thousand arguments.

Libano:
If women have their Logic and Philosophy down below, why do you need so many arguments? Improvise, and let her know that your hands speak as well as your tongue.

Demetrio:
We are nearly at the door. But, oh, Libano, it won't work; let's go back! I see somebody walking up and down in that alley. Go see who he is, without his seeing you.

Libano:
I think it is Cammillo, from our house. Yes, it is.

Demetrio:
It is he, Good Lord! Didn't I tell you that he was smitten by her too? We are ruined; what do you think we should do?

Libano:
Move away fast so he won't recognize us.

Demetrio:
Alas, alas, oh poor me!

Libano:
What the Devil is the matter with you? You act as if you had been mortally wounded. Don't be so afraid.

Demetrio:
What greater wound, what greater pain could I have?

Libano:
Don't disgrace yourself this way, don't be afraid of your own shadow. Let's think about what to do. You have always been brave; is it possible that love has made your nature change so greatly?

Demetrio:
I'm done for and have lost my mind and hardly know where I am.

Libano:

So it seems. Look out for that money, the necklaces and other jewels that you have on you—where did you put them?

Demetrio:

I have everything in my sleeve, and it's on my arm.

Libano:

Be careful too about that dagger so it won't be seen and you won't get arrested.

Demetrio:

I have it here in a place where it can't be seen, but what are you thinking so hard about?

Libano:

I was thinking about what needs to be done, and I've made up my mind. Wait here, and I'll be back in a minute.

Demetrio:

Come back! What do you intend to do? Don't leave.

Libano:

I'll be right back, don't fear. I want to say something to Cammillo.

Demetrio:

Waiting is a hard thing. He went to meet Cammillo; it seems to me that he's trying everything to get us caught. If we are, the whole plan fails. If he had just told me what he wanted to say to him, but he keeps everything to himself. I hope I won't suffer for it one day and repent for having trusted him too much. But having gone so far in this thing, I have to go the rest of the way. But how many barriers do I have to get by before I get to the goal? How many difficulties are in my way? When shall I attain my desire? Often, when I think I have the thing in the bag it is farther off than ever. That has always happened to me. Oh, here he is. You are back. What did you say to Cammillo?

Libano:

I certainly played a good joke on him. He's running off so fast that he seems to be afraid of getting there late.

Demetrio:

Where, for the Lord's sake?

Libano:

At the home of that friend, where you know he often goes to plant himself. I told him that you are there and very anxious to talk to him.

Demetrio:

But if he gets there and doesn't find me, what will he do?

Libano:

Don't be afraid that he'll leave for that reason; when he sees the cards or the dice in action he will fall like a hawk who has spotted a partridge. You can be sure that he will be there, not just for the rest of the day, but also for the night. He would gamble his share of the sun, especially since he will find there perhaps another little something that he likes, do you get me?

Demetrio:

You're devilishly clever. I'm going.

Libano:

Don't go yet; wait a little.

Demetrio:

Why? I won't wait any more. What's on your mind now?

Libano:

Just let me go about fifty yards over there, before you do anything else. I'll be right back; I've thought of a good idea.

Demetrio:

What idea have you thought of? This seems to me completely irrelevant. What do you want to do?

Libano:

Do what I tell you, and have the patience to wait a little until I come back.

Demetrio:

Listen here: at least tell me where you are going and how long I'll have to wait.

Libano:

Not very long. I don't want to waste any time now telling you more.

Demetrio:

Please don't be long, for without you I am lost. *(Alone.)* That fellow has left me here and wants me to wait for him. I can't guess what he means to do, and, if it weren't for the fact that I have tested him for such a long time and always found him loving and faithful to me, I would suspect some trap—or that he wants me to waste so much time that we would have to give up the plan for today. Until I get there I am in such anxiety that everything seems to work against me. If this chance slipped by I don't think it would ever come back. I can just imagine somebody's telling me that Porfiria has got married. Besides that, I have had to make so many arrangements and lay so many plans that I could never manage again. Libano wouldn't hear of the thing at first, it seeming to him a desperate idea (as indeed it is), but finally he agreed to put all his efforts into it. Leandro can't hinder us; in his house there is nobody but Porfiria and the servants. All these things are so convenient that they don't happen often. But now that I think I am about to carry out the thing, Libano tells me to wait. He's still not in sight—may God help me—yet he didn't seem to be going too far. What the hell kind of a run-around is this? Oh, thank goodness, I think I see him; yes, it's he. He seems to be carrying some kind of bundle under his cape. I still can't figure out what he contrived to do.

Libano:

Here is Leandro's coat. Let's go over here a little piece; I want you to take off your cape and put on this coat.

Demetrio:

What do you mean, Leandro's coat? Where did you get it?

Libano:

Don't be curious about that. Put it on, now, while there's nobody passing to see you. I'll do my best to get two capes on—I certainly won't be cold today. Actually, this will not be too unusual, because there are a good number of people who wear two mantles.

Demetrio:

Now, what shall I do with this coat on?

Libano:

I'll tell you, if you'll be patient. Take this beret too, and give me your hat.

Demetrio:

Please tell me something; I'm all mixed up.

Libano:

You will go, keeping your head low, to Porfiria's door and knock. Whoever is at the window will open up to you right away, thinking you are Leandro. Because now, in every way, you resemble him. So much so that you seem to have been made in a single mold. Anybody who didn't know would take you for him.[170] This way, you will get

[170]Both editions apparently have "vi *correbbe* in iscambio" while "vi *torrebbe* in iscambio" seems to be meant.

into the house; you can be sure that they will open up to you. Do you like this plan of mine?

Demetrio:
I like it, and I want to go knock on the door without waiting any more. You get away from here.

Libano:
Go on. I'll wait for you nearby, if you want me to.

Demetrio:
I do want you to; it'll be good, in case of any accident that might happen. Place yourself where you can see me when I come out of the house.

Libano:
I will.

Lesbia:
Oh, it's the master; I'll open up.

Libano, alone:

They fell for it this time right away. When the servant came to the window she pulled up the latch and my friend has got in. If he can't do his stuff now, so much the worse for him. This has in truth been a desperate expedient, but I couldn't see any other way. He has a package of money and jewels as emergency provisions, since today they are a good medicine for all ills. Then, too, all girls must be anxious to find out at first hand about that pleasure which they imagine can be had with men. So if he doesn't lose his head as he said, I hope that he will enter into port with all sails unfurled. But here's my Lucia; where is she going in such a hurry?

Libano and Lucia

Libano:
Hi! Where are you going, Lucia? Ah, traitress, you pretend not to see me, huh?

Lucia:
Oh handsome hope of mine, I really didn't see you. You're so dressed up today. Why do you have such a fine cape?

Libano:
You see. I have some other things too. Where are you coming from? From doing somebody a favor, eh?

Lucia:
What do you mean, favor? I'm coming back from the convent and was hurrying home before

the lawyer returns, because Mona doesn't want him to know that she sent me out. But what are you doing here?

Libano:
I'm here doing a favor too. But tell me, did you speak to that friend who I told you would be at that window?

Lucia:
What do you think?[171] He talked to me so nicely and gave me so many caresses that I have never seen a more gallant young man. He truly merits all kinds of good things.

Libano:
Be careful not to get spoiled, so that I won't lose you.

Lucia:
You mustn't tease me; you know well that I'm content that you love me.

Libano:
Now that you've left him, what will he do all by himself?

Lucia:
I don't know what he'll do—and he's not so lonely as you think. I've got to go.

Libano:
Come here! What did you say? What do you mean he's not lonely—who's with him? I left him locked in the room; who can have got in there?

Lucia:
Nobody that I know of, but he may have gone somewhere else.

Libano:
What do you mean somewhere else? Could he have got up enough courage to go into your house?

Lucia:
You have guessed it. To tell you the truth, I left him in the middle room with Mona Cassandra.

Libano:
How can this be? Were you so presumptuous and so shameless as to let him come in there?

Lucia:
That's right. He started to beg and to cajole with so many little words and so many tears that I started to tell Mona about it. You know that she

[171]The Italian sentence—"Guarda s'ei ti par dovere?"—is difficult. Another rendering might be: "Do you think it was a chore?"

is so anxious to get him for a son-in-law, too. And she agreed for him to come talk to her. Your friend came on; you can be sure that he didn't waste any time thinking about it.

Libano:
I didn't think he could get out of the room.

Lucia:
Why do you say that?

Libano:
Because I suppose he must have come through that door in the wall dividing the garden, though the door is nailed up and I don't know who would have had the courage to un-nail it.

Lucia:
Eh, you don't seem to be too bright. He would have been lacking in cleverness if he hadn't found another way.

Libano:
How did he go about it then?

Lucia:
How? Do you think he is paralyzed? He lowered himself onto that roof and grabbed hold of one of those hooks on the balcony and came up by the cornice and jumped inside. He was very agile, so that he seemed like our tomcat. How did you manage so many times when you came down for my love?

Libano:
I have taken that way sometimes, and I am used to it. You have helped me too, as you know. But how is it possible that he managed to lower himself there on first try?

Lucia:
Don't you know the power of love? I helped him a little too and held out my hand when he was on the cornice.

Libano:
You did what you should not have done, and you could be the cause of some great scandal. That teaches me to trust women.

Lucia:
Oh you make me sick. Don't butt into this matter. If Mona wanted things this way, why are you afraid—do you think she's crazy?

Libano:
I'm not thinking about her; I'm thinking about myself, because it will always be my fault if there's a scandal. I'm very much worried that my

goose may be cooked. But go on, because I see at a distance the lawyer and Lamberto, who must be coming home.

Lucia:
Uh, you're right. Goodbye.

Messer Ricciardo, Lamberto, Giorgetto

Messer Ricciardo:
Lamberto, let's hurry, because it's getting late and this evening air and the wind that has risen are bad for my head. A person who studies has a weak head, and I'm finding it out.

Lamberto:
The fact is, rather, that whoever has a woman beside him every night gets these troubles; either his head aches or he has gravel in his urine, or the colic, or the gout, or a bad stomach. Why am *I* not bothered by so many things?

Messer Ricciardo:
You are right, but you don't have the consolations that I have either; you don't have anybody to embrace you and to warm you up when it's cold. Moreover, the doctor told me that if I kept away from wine I wouldn't have the gout, but I have never obeyed him.

Lamberto:
You must be sorry for not doing so when the gout makes you yell.

Messer Ricciardo:
I yell when it wants me to—one good mouthful brings on a hundred woes. But, with ten years one way or the other, we all have to get to that. Now I'm nearly seventy, and I've always refused to take care of myself. I eat everything, and in that other matter, too, I have always indulged whenever I felt like it.

Lamberto:
I wish you well at it. These are differences of character; some people get used to one way of life and some to another.

Messer Ricciardo:
Yes, yes. Let everyone follow his own custom. The important thing would be to be able to go back twenty-five or thirty years.

Lamberto:
Every advantage has its disadvantage. We shall get out of the troubles of the world sooner than the young people.

Messer Ricciardo:

The thing to worry about there is whether we may not get into worse troubles. But let's leave off this discussion, especially since it's late and I am worn out. God be with you, Lamberto.

Lamberto:

God be with you. But, Sir, will you do me a favor, if it doesn't inconvenience you? Let me use your servant boy to send him somewhere close on an errand.

Messer Ricciardo:

Willingly. Go, Giorgetto, and do everything he tells you to.

Giorgetto:

Everything?

Messer Ricciardo:

Everything, yes!

Giorgetto:

In truth, I don't know whether I *can* do everything. Here I am. What are your orders?

Lamberto:

Come here. Go to the piazza and see whether you see my son Cammillo. If not, look for him around the bridge. Tell him that he must by all means return home this evening, because I need him to help me to write two letters. And if you see Demetrio—do you know him?

Giorgetto:

Yes, Sir, I know him.

Lamberto:

Tell him to come home early, too, because we have to write to Palermo. That caravel ship which is at Leghorn will sail tomorrow. The weather seems to be getting better. Be sure to tell them, my boy.

Giorgetto:

I will. Do you want anything else?

Lamberto:

No. Hurry back.

Giorgetto and Libano

Giorgetto:

Where the Devil is he sending me at this hour? He could have been patient enough to wait for them to come home to undress. But he gave me the work. I don't have enough of it at home and with the Doctor; I have to do that of the neighbors too. I'll make a round and say I didn't find him. Let him come with me to see whether I'm telling the truth or not. Oh, there's Libano! Let's tell him to do this errand, which is part of his job. Libano, I was looking for your boss and for Cammillo because Lamberto wants them. Tell me where they are.

Libano:
Go on. Say that you found me and that my master will come home in an hour, as he usually does.

Giorgetto:
What about Cammillo?

Libano:
Go look for him. How do I know where he is?

Giorgetto:
I don't know, either. Please, you look for him.

Libano:
I'll look for him. Get out of my way. Quit doing those pirouettes.

Giorgetto:
Libano, boy, you're a good fellow, lend me a carlino.

Libano:
Get away, rascal, aren't you ashamed?

Giorgetto:
Tell me where your boss is and what I should say to Lamberto.

Libano:
Didn't you hear me tell you when he'll come?

Giorgetto:
You could say where he is, too, and tell me where to find Cammillo.

Libano:
If you don't leave, I'll break your head.

Giorgetto:
It was on the tip of my tongue to say that you would run me off.[172]

Libano, alone:

That smart aleck kid certainly came around at the right time! If Demetrio had come out and that good-for-nothing had seen him, it would have been the last straw. You know that, though he's just a boy, he's greedier and more malicious than an adult. It amuses me that Lamberto thinks it possible to find Cammillo when he's started

[172]Both Libano and Giorgetto use the verb *rompere,* and a pun is undoubtedly intended. It escapes us. Moreover, in the absence of stage directions, it is impossible to be quite sure whether Giorgetto's reply is apologetic or insolent.

gambling. I know that it's nearly dawn when he comes home, and then he comes in so slowly and softly that he's like a cat. Nobody hears a door that he touches, because he has oiled them all so they won't squeak. Then he tells his father that he came in early. But if you look at him in the morning you know the truth. Eh, Lamberto, all your efforts are in vain; you are hoeing in the sand, beating your head against the wall. But what's that noise I hear in Porfiria's house? That running and that clatter scare me; what can have happened? You can be sure that everything will go wrong today. Also, Lucia made me fear trouble when she said that Leandro had gone down into the lawyer's house. I can just imagine some disaster, and it will all be laid on my shoulders, because flies always light on skinny horses. Oh, God help us! There is Demetrio coming out without his coat and all bewildered. This is all we needed! He's looking around wildly, like a possessed person. What the Devil is the matter?

Libano and Demetrio

Libano:

Here I am, Master, why are you so upset? You seem half dead, running around that way in your underclothes. What is the meaning of it?

Demetrio:

Alas, my Libano, I am dead indeed; I am ruined.

Libano:

You are without a coat; take your cape and toque. What happened? Are you wounded? Did you fall? What is paining you?

Demetrio:

I can't talk for sorrow. It would be better for me if I were mortally wounded or if I had broken my neck.

Libano:

Tell me how things went. What kind of scandal took place?

Demetrio:

Exactly the opposite of what I expected, the worst possible.

Libano:

Tell me how things are. You know that I never lack ideas and that there's a remedy for everything, except death.

Demetrio:

Let me rest a little and collect myself, and I'll tell everything in detail.

Libano:

Tell me something about this disaster.

Demetrio:

You saw that they opened the door to me, thinking that I was Leandro. When I was half way up the stairs, I saw an open door into a bedroom that was low and very dark. I went in there and lay face down on a little bed. Porfiria appeared and started to talk about some farmers who had come in the morning. I didn't answer her, but gave her to understand that my head ached and that I felt very weak. She came up to me and touched my head and felt my pulse and so on. You can imagine that my suffering increased and that I nearly fainted, feeling myself touched by the delicate hands of this girl whom, before, I had hardly had the grace of seeing once a week, and from a considerable distance, as you know. The tremors given me by my love made her think all the more that I was Leandro, transformed in the clutches of some sudden sickness. I stayed for a while without giving myself away and without speaking, because my ordinary fear was increased by the sight of her. I didn't know what to say or how to go about letting her know who I was. When I would just about have made up my mind to talk, I would get a big shiver, so that it really seemed that I was seized by a great fever. Finally, realizing that time was getting short, once when she was near me, I took hold of her and said to her: "My Porfiria, I am not, as you think, Leandro your brother, I am Demetrio who loves you more than my own life." She didn't let me get any further but turned to run away and started to scream. Holding her firmly by one arm, I stated my case to her with the best chosen words and humblest prayers that I knew, but she screamed so loudly the whole time that two women servants came running. They must have been upstairs, for one is the woman I saw with her this morning. They all started to yell "Thief! Thief!" and to beat their breasts and to tear their hair, and they called for the manservant, probably not remembering that he was not at home. At times they seemed about to open the door and then held back. I begged them to listen to me and showed that I was a friend and not an enemy, but they would never listen to anything I said. Finally, the servants picked up some clubs that were behind the bed, and Porfiria tried to get a dagger that was hanging up on the wall over the little bed. So, not seeing any other wise thing to do, I started down the stairs and came on out. I left them all in despair, doing nothing but weeping.

Libano:

Did you see whether that money would soften them?

Demetrio:

I wish I hadn't tried, because in the scuffle I lost my coat. I was out of my head and don't know where the money and other valuables are now. But all I care about is my personal failure and the shame. Now I realize that I was crazy, and I know that they will tell it all to Leandro and that he will want to get revenge, and he will be quite right.

Libano:

Who would ever have thought that there could be so much cruelty in a woman?

Demetrio:

You understand. I want us to leave this city because I know that by staying here I might lose my life as well as my honor.

Libano:

It's dangerous, and we'd have to be on guard all the time. What worries me is that that coat was left in the house and that they will recognize it, and Leandro knows that he gave it to me, so that I don't see any way of denying. Things couldn't have gone worse. But let's go home, and we'll think of some remedy there. Let's not despair yet; something will turn up.

Fourth Intermedio

The fourth act being finished, in order to show that evening was already drawing near, there came up on the stage eight huntress nymphs with bow and quiver. They were dressed in silver tocca and had very blond hair, adorned with green and red berries and with various wild grasses and garlanded with many flowers. They had flesh-colored buskins with some ermine trimming, very prettily tied with white tocca strips. As though returning from the hunt, they came singing this *canzonetta:*

Hor chi mai canterà, se non canta hoggi;
 Che di sì care prede
 Carche, moviamo il Piede?
O del frondoso bosco;

O delle tenere herbe,
Et voi tutte altre vaghe Nymfe accerbe
Del bel Paese Tosco,
Venite à cantar' nosco:
Et cantando n'andian' la bella Diva;
Anzi il bel Sol, che in sù la fresca riva
Del suo dolce Arno siede;
Et ben'n'ascolta, & vede.

(Now, who will ever sing, if she doesn't sing today, when we move along loaded with such dear prey? / About the leafy wood, about the tender grass, O all you fair, cruel nymphs of the Tuscan country, come sing with us. And let us go singing of the beautiful Goddess, or rather of the beautiful Sun, who sits on the cool bank of his Arno listening to us and seeing us well.)

CANTUS
ALTUS
TENOR
BASSUS
Hor chi mai can- te- ra, hor chi mai can- te-
Hor chi mai can- te-
Hor chi mai can- te- ra, hor chi, hor chi mai
Hor chi mai can- te-
3
ra se non can- t'hog- gi, se non can- t'hog- gi
ra se non can- t'hog- gi, se non can- t'hog- gi
can- te- ra se non can- t'hog- gi, se non can-
ra se non can- t'hog- gi, se non can- t'hog- gi

7
che di si ca- re pre- de car- che mo- vi- a- no'l pie- de, carche di si ca- re pre- de car- che mo- vi- a- no'l pie- de, car-
t'hoggi che di si ca- re prede car- che mo- vi- a- no'l pie- de, carche di si ca- re prede car- che mo- vi- a- no'l pie- de, car-
12
che mo- via- no'l pie- de. O del fron- do-
che mo- via- no'l pie- de. O del fron- do-
che mo- via- no'l pie- de. O del fron- do-
che mo- via- no'l pie- de. O del fron- do-

17
so bo- sco o del- le te- ne-r'her be et voi tut-t'al- tre
so bo- sco o del- le te- ne- r'her- be et voi tut-t'al tre
so bo- sco o del- le te- ne- r'her- be et voi tut-t'al- tre
so bo- sco et del- le te- ne- r'her- be et voi tut-t'al- tre
22
va- ghe nim- ph'ac- cer- be del bel pa- e- se to- sco
va- ghe nim- ph'ac- cer- be del bel pa- e- se to- sco
va- ghe nim- ph'ac- cer- be del bel pa- e- se to- sco
va- ghe nim- ph-ac- cer- be del bel pa- e- se to- sco

27
ve- ni- te, ve- ni- te a can- tar no- sco et
ve- ni- te, ve- ni- te a can- tar no- sco et
ve- ni- te, ve- ni- te a can- tar no- sco et
ve- ni- te, ve- ni- te a can- tar no- sco et
31
can- tan-do n'an-dian la bel- la Di- va an- z'il bel sol
can- tan-do n'an-dian la bel- la Di- va an- z'il bel
can- tan-do n'an-dian la bel- la Di- va an- z'il bel sol, an- z'il bel
can- tan-do n'an-dian la bel- la Di- va an- z'il bel

35
ch'en su la fresca ri- va del suo dol- ce Ar- no sie- de et ben
sol ch'en su la fresca ri- va del suo dol- ce Ar- no sie- de et ben
sol ch'en su la fresca ri- va del suo dol- ce Ar- no sie- de et ben
sol ch'en su la fresca ri- va del suo dol- ce Ar- no sie- de et ben
40
n'as- col- t'et ve- de, et ben n'as- col- t'et ve- de.
n'as- col- t'et ve- de, et ben n'as- col- t'et ve- de.
n'as- col- t'et ve- de, et ben n'as- col-t'et ve- de.
n'as- col- t'et ve- de, et ben n'as- col- t'et ve- de.

Act V

Lucia, Lamberto, Messer Ricciardo, Demetrio, Cassandra, Libano

Lucia:

Oh, my ill-starred life! Oh, poor Mona! Come running, come running, neighbors, Oh, you-all next door, Oh Lamberto, Oh Cammillo, come down right away, because the lawyer is trying to kill my poor mistress!

Lamberto:

What noise is this? What's the matter with you? What has happened?

Lucia:

I say that the master has taken hold of Mona and that he wants to cut her throat. He has pounded her all over and handled her roughly. If we don't get her out of his hands, the poor woman will never be good for anything any more. And yet she hasn't done anything to deserve this.

Lamberto:

What has she done? What is this all about?

Lucia:

I can't tell you all that now. Come help her, come on, and there is a young man shut up in a room who says that he came in from your house. He'll treat him badly, and you will be the cause.

Lamberto:

What do you mean, from our house? If I believed that, I would throw out whoever it is. In my house there is nobody who indulges in such goings-on.

Lucia:

Hurry, because he is trying to throw her down the stairs. Oh, Mona, struggle, get away from him, fight hard! Oh, thank God, run, run down here.

Cassandra:

Eh, Lamberto, don't abandon me, I beg you. When you have heard everything, you will say that I don't deserve being treated this way.

Lamberto:

Mona, come in the house quickly, trust me. Eh, Messer Ricciardo, what are you trying to do?

Messer Ricciardo:

What am I trying to do? What am I trying to do? You, too, will see what I'm trying to do. Where did she go, the rascal, the shameless one?

So this is the way of it! This is the sort of thing that is going on in the house! This is what happens to my honor! I'll give you what you deserve. And you, Lamberto, who had a hand in my shame, I don't know how you have the nerve to talk to me.

Lamberto:

Messer Ricciardo, I don't know what you mean, and if I didn't have respect for you, I'd say that you have become senile. And don't mention my honor or I'll lose patience.

Messer Ricciardo:

It's *my* honor that's been hurt, and if not by you then by somebody in your house. But all this will come out into the open.

Lamberto:

If I find out that it's the fault of someone in my house—which I can't believe—I'll be the first to make a fuss about it.

Messer Ricciardo:

Your words sound good, but I won't be satisfied till I get revenge on that treacherous fellow. I've got him in my clutches, and I'm going to make him pay for what he's doing.

Demetrio:

Don't do that, Sir, just think what a scandal you might cause.

Messer Ricciardo:

Let me alone; I'll treat him as he deserves. If you don't let me go, I'll jump on you too.

Lamberto:

You are too worked up. What the Devil could he have done? Calm down a little and listen to her story.

Messer Ricciardo:

I'll make him confess what he did, in spite of himself. You-all attend to your own business. Let me go, Demetrio.

Demetrio:

I'll let you go, but I want to go back up there with you.

Messer Ricciardo:

I don't want you to come, and I don't need you in my house.

Demetrio:

Do let me come, and if you have the reasons for outrage which you profess, I'll help you get revenge.

Messer Ricciardo:

I don't need your help. Get out, I say, get away, you see that you won't get in.

Lamberto:

Let him go; what the Devil could he do?

Demetrio:

If it's the young man I think, he'll have to show his face to him, and I'm afraid that the lawyer would then have to lower himself and eat humble pie.

Lamberto:

Let's go into the house, and we'll hear from Mona what this mess is, though we have to hear the other side too. We'll back up if they're blaming us rightly, which I can't believe.

Demetrio:

Go on into the house; I'll come in a minute. Libano, go to Salvadore Galletti's house and tell him that I need those letters, because tonight I'm sealing that package that has to be sent away in the morning.

Libano:

I'm going.

Demetrio:

Listen, I just said that because I didn't want Lamberto to hear where I was sending you. You know where I really want you to go.

Libano:

No, Sir, I don't unless you tell me.

Demetrio:

To Leandro's house, and contrive to talk either to the servant or to that woman. It's enough to talk to one, to the first you see. Explain the situation briefly, so that they can help him some way. I'll stay here to see what the lawyer decides to do, for I'm afraid he may do something mean.

Libano:

I'm going. Try to prevent a big scandal, if possible. These are things that can happen to anybody, and you were almost in the same danger today and are still not out of it. If you should be afraid that something really bad is going to happen, you have only to break open that gate that divides our garden from the lawyer's and rescue Leandro and then let him go.

Demetrio:

That's a good idea, and you know this might perhaps be a deed that would cancel out the villainy I did to him today. Now go on, don't lose any more time. If you talk to that woman, call her downstairs and don't let the girl hear, because I don't want her to get any more suffering from me. Don't say that he entered from our house, because we must deny this always.

Libano:

I'm going, and I know what I'm supposed to do.

Libano, alone:

I don't think that since Pisa was founded such strange things have happened in one day as have happened today, and it's all my fault. May God not make me pay for it too, as I fear may happen. Oh, treacherous luck or, rather, my own folly, where have you led me? If I hadn't let Leandro into the garret, none of these scandals would have taken place. But the worst thing was trusting that dizzy Lucia, who has less brains than a goose. Mona is so anxious to get him for a son-in-law that she consented for him to come into the house. Now just try to convince the lawyer that nothing worse happened. This is a net in which we are all caught, and deadly enmity will be born among us, and later people will think about settling the whole thing in other ways besides words. What worries me more than anything else is that coat which was left over there. Now we'll give this news to the first person who answers at Leandro's house, and then I'll go off a way and hang out for a while without showing myself at home, for I know that all the punishment would fall on me. It's better to stay away from the noise for a time until we see how things are going.

Lesbia, a nurse; and Libano

Lesbia:

Who is it? Who is knocking?

Libano:

Friends. Come down.

Lesbia:

Who are you?

Libano:

Come down for something that concerns you.

Lesbia:

Here I am. What do you want?

Libano:

I am very sorry to have to tell you something that will grieve you. The life of your Leandro is in great danger, and you must help him.

Lesbia:

Oh, grief! May God help us! Misfortunes never come one at a time. But who are you? I don't know you. What do you know about the matter?

Libano:

If I weren't sure, I wouldn't tell you. I am your friend; come closer, and I'll tell you what the situation is, because I don't want anyone else in your house to hear it. Leandro was found in the house of Messer Ricciardo, that lawyer who lives next door to Lamberto Lanfranchi, and the whole house is turned upside down. They have shut him up and are threatening to kill him.

Lesbia:

Alas! This is sad news; how did they come to find him there? He couldn't be there as a thief.

Libano:

For now I can't tell you anything except that he is where I said and that you must do something besides cry and beat your breast in the street.

Lesbia:

Show me the house you're talking about, so that I can tell some friends of his who may come help him.

Libano:

Come see it.

Lesbia:

How far is it?

Libano:

A little way from here. Come with me, and I'll show it to you from a distance.

Lesbia:

I am so much upset that I can hardly stand up. Oh, poor Leandro! Oh, unfortunate Porfiria! Oh, wretched me!

Libano:

Not so much noise now. Crying now can help neither him nor you. Think, rather, about whom you can call to help him.

Lesbia:

I don't know whom to call on and don't know where to turn. Alas, what is all this? What are these disasters fallen on us today?

Libano:

You'll make people notice us. What's the use of this crying?

Lesbia:

What is the use of it? Don't I have good reason to cry? Would that I had never been born, alas!

Libano:

Now look over here to the right. See the house down there, that last one with the lattice window?

Lesbia:

We are so far away that I can hardly make it out. Oh, I know which one it is. I went there once to get some fine thread appraised by the lawyer's wife, who is an expert at everything.

Libano:

This evening we'll see whether she is an expert, and she'll need to be good. I have nothing else to tell you. Now you know the house. Think about doing something to get him out. I want to go do another errand that is important for me.

Lesbia:

Oh me, I am afraid that before I find someone they'll do something awful to him. What do you think?

Libano:

I'm not a prophet, but as long as nobody but the lawyer, who is old, is after him, there's not much to fear. But the important thing is to help him right away and not to lose time. Goodbye!

Lesbia:

Please don't leave till I go home and tell his sister.

Libano:

What good would that do? I have a thousand things to do.

Lesbia:

Do me this kindness, since you have already done so much. Because, if I had to find some friend of his and didn't know the house, you might be able to show it to me, or take the trouble of going there.

Libano:

Don't you have your manservant in the house?

Lesbia:

No, I wish he'd break his neck. It would have been good for us if he had been there today. But when Leandro is not in the house he's always gone too.

Libano:

What is the use to you of telling the sister and

wasting this time? Think about some way to help him.

Lesbia:

I don't know what to do. And I am sweating all over from sorrow. Oh what a misfortune, oh what a disaster, oh what a catastrophe! If I don't tell her about it, she will always be able to hold it against me, and rightly. Nor do I really know what friends or relatives might help him. If I tell her about it, adding this suffering to that which she's just had, I'm afraid she may die. Still, he is her brother; I'm going to tell her how things are. May God give her strength.

Libano:

Please do what you have to do fast, because I'm in a hurry.

Lesbia:

Never fear; I'll be right back. But who is that knocking on my door? If it just isn't some other sad news. He seems to me a foreigner and covered with dust. Who in the Devil can he be?

Libano:

It's probably someone bringing letters. Hear what he has to say, and do what you have to do. I'll wait for you right over here.

Lesbia, Manoli, Libano

Lesbia:

Hola! Hola! Whom are you after? What do you want?

Manoli:

Does Gherardo Sismondi live here?

Lesbia:

He used to be here.

Manoli:

And where is he now?

Lesbia:

He's where the majority of souls are.

Manoli:

How long has he been dead?

Lesbia:

More than ten years already. You must not have been in this city before, from what I gather.

Manoli:

I certainly haven't been here. But tell me, isn't Leandro here?

Lesbia:

Oh, yes, Sir, Leandro is here.

Manoli:

Excuse me; I asked over there which was the house of Gherardo Sismondi. They told me this one and didn't say whether he was alive or dead. But, tell me, do you live with Leandro?

Lesbia:

Who are you and why do you need to know this?

Manoli:

I ask you for good reason.

Lesbia:

I believe you. Yes, I do live with him.

Manoli:

You must have been with him for a good while.

Lesbia:

So long that I remember his birth. But I wish I weren't with him now so that I wouldn't have to see what I see.

Manoli:

Tell me, is your name Lesbia?

Lesbia:

Lesbia is my name.

Manoli:

Are you the nurse of Porfiria, sister of Leandro?

Lesbia:

Oh, how do you know everybody, being a stranger?

Manoli:

I know more than you think, and I know you too, now that you have told me so much. I am Manoli your husband, whom you left in the hands of the Turks sixteen years ago.

Lesbia:

Oh, oh, you do surely seem to be he, oh my husband, oh my soul! I still wouldn't have recognized you so soon, you have aged so. Oh, my treasure, I must not seem the same to you, either! Thank God that I have seen you again, because I thought you died so many years ago!

Manoli:

Thank God, as you say. But tell me how Leandro and Porfiria are. Are they both in good health?

Lesbia:

They are both in good health, and Porfiria is safe. I left her a little while ago upstairs in her room. But the same is not true for poor Leandro, because he is in great danger, and you had better come with me to help him.

Manoli:
How is he in danger? What has happened?

Lesbia:
He was caught, I don't know how, in the house of a gentleman of this city who is a lawyer, and they have locked him in, and I don't know what will happen to him.

Manoli:
Alas, what are you saying? This is like a dagger in my heart. Anyway, let's go where he is, because this is so grave a matter.

Lesbia:
Let's do go there. You can see Porfiria when we come back.

Manoli:
But, tell me: Where is the house of Lamberto Lanfranchi, a nobleman of this city?

Lesbia:
I think it's right next to that lawyer's house. Why?

Manoli:
Really? Are you sure that it's there?

Lesbia:
I'm almost certain.

Manoli:
Let's get going, we can do two errands in one trip.

Lesbia:
What business do you have with this Lamberto? Tell me.

Manoli:
Do you know whether he brought back a young foreigner?

Lesbia:
I can't say, but there is somebody who might know. Say, you talk to this fellow about what he needs to know.

Manoli:
Good evening. Do you know where Lamberto Lanfranchi, citizen or merchant of this city, lives?

Libano:
Yes, indeed. Why do you want to find him?

Manoli:
I want to. Tell me, do you know him well?

Libano:
I have seen him several times, and, to tell you the truth, I live in his house.

Manoli:
Oh, by the way, tell me—did he bring back a foreigner?

Libano:
He brought back a young man who is my master.

Manoli:
Where is he from?

Libano:
From Palermo.

Manoli:
What is his name?

Libano:
Demetrio, but why do you need to know?

Manoli:
Lesbia, did you notice that name?

Lesbia:
Yes, Sir, why?

Manoli:
Do you recall ever having heard that name for anybody you know?

Lesbia:
No, Sir, unless you tell me more.

Manoli:
Let me tell you that this Demetrio is the blood brother of Leandro.

Lesbia:
And how do you know? Listen. I seem to remember now that Leandro's brother had a name like that.

Manoli:
The thing is as I have told you.

Lesbia:
Oh, did you hear this new information? Hurry and go call your master, who he says is Leandro's brother, and tell him to come here, because he may be this help and aid we are looking for.

Libano:
All this today seems to me just like a comedy.

Lesbia:
Go, call him right away for his own good.

Manoli:

And for yours, too, please call him.

Libano:

To tell the truth, I hate to go home, because I have a thousand things to do. You can see the house from here, and she knows it. Go knock on the door and have him called down, for it wouldn't be right for me to go there without a good reason.

Manoli:

Now, Lesbia, if you know the house, let's go by ourselves. Many thanks, anyway.

Lesbia:

Let's go.

Libano:

I don't want to show up there, brother or no brother. There's something still worrying me very much. I'll be safe around here, watching how things turn out. If they work out well, I'll show up right away.

Lesbia:

Oh, my good and dear husband, how joyful I would be at seeing you again after so long if it weren't for this trouble of poor Leandro! May God grant that instead of rejoicing together we won't have to weep this evening! I feel my heart fluttering, just as if I had fever.

Manoli:

Don't worry so much till you have seen something worse. Are we nearly there?

Lesbia:

Yes, Sir, here we are. You knock at the door; it'll be better. Seeing you a foreigner and in this dress, they will choose to open up more quickly.

Manoli:

I will. Is this the door?

Lesbia:

This is it.

Mona Cornelia, a servant; Manoli, and Lesbia

Cornelia:

Who is knocking?

Manoli:

Friends. Open up to us.

Cornelia:

What do you want?

Manoli:
Is Messer Demetrio at home?

Cornelia:
Who are you?

Manoli:
I am a friend of his who wants to talk to him.

Cornelia:
Excuse me. I can't open up to you.

Manoli:
It doesn't matter. Call him and that will be enough.

Cornelia:
Tell me your name.

Manoli:
I am someone who needs to talk to him. Call him, please.

Cornelia:
I'm not sure whether he's at home. Wait.

Manoli:
This is always a good way to be safe. Later she can say he is at home or isn't, as is convenient.

Lesbia:
You are right. One should always go slowly in opening the door. I, too, know well what scandals can come from opening up right away.

Manoli:
I wouldn't be surprised if this old woman had been to Ragusa, since she is so suspicious.[173] Oh, here's somebody at the door; maybe it's he.

Demetrio, Manoli, and Lesbia

Demetrio:
Who is calling for me? Oh, good evening, was it you who was asking for me?

Manoli:
Yes, Sir, we are glad to find you. Good evening and a good year to you. Are you Messer Demetrio?

Demetrio:
I am Demetrio, and who are you?

Manoli:
Even if I tell you who I am, you will scarcely

[173]Colloquial expressions that cast slurs on the character of inhabitants of other cities were very common in the Renaissance. Prejudice toward the citizens of Ragusa has survived in the adjective *raguseo,* which today means *grasping* or *avaricious.*

know me. But I know you well and knew you still better from the time of your birth till you fell into the hands of the Turks, when you were scarcely four years old. I was with your father Filemone then and am the husband of this woman, the nurse of Porfiria, who is your sister. And Leandro is your brother.

Demetrio:
Leandro is my brother, and Porfiria is my sister? What wild tale is this?

Manoli:
This is the truth and not a tale. I tell you that Leandro is your brother and Porfiria your sister.

Demetrio:
How sure are you of this?

Manoli:
Surer than I am of being in Pisa.

Demetrio:
I am greatly amazed and don't know what all this means.

Lesbia:
Uh, this fellow looks just like one we chased out. Do you say that this is Demetrio, the brother of Leandro?

Manoli:
This is he. I have so much evidence for both that there's no doubt about it.

Lesbia:
I remember a sign about which I could make no mistake—and another, making two.

Demetrio:
Please tell me what these signs are.

Manoli:
If you are that brother of Leandro, you have under your left breast a mole and, on the narrow part of your right foot, a rather large birthmark.

Demetrio:
In truth, while in a way I wonder whether I'm awake or dreaming, this evidence makes me be quiet.

Manoli:
Messer Demetrio, my dear Master, don't stand there thinking. But if Leandro is in that danger which my wife Lesbia here told me about—and I didn't quite understand her—think about helping him, so that you may recognize each other as the brothers you are.

Demetrio:

Both of you wait for me here. I'll give this news to Lamberto, and, to put an end to this situation, whatever happens, we will enter from our house. There's no lack of a way to get in and liberate Leandro. Don't go away during what follows.

Manoli:

We shall wait for you. If you need help, call.

Lesbia and Manoli

Lesbia:

I'm almost ready to think that this evening, after many troubles, fortune may leave us all happy, but I won't believe it till I see Leandro alive and well—may God grant it!

Manoli:

Be of good faith that all will come out well, for today during my trip, I had a thousand good signs. It seems that fortune always acts that way—when it has led one to the heights, so that he can go no higher, then it has its purpose served by throwing him down. Likewise, when it has put someone else in the depths and done to him the worst it can, then it enjoys raising him up and making him supremely happy. But what noise do I hear in that other house? They must have already passed into it, or must be doing so. I hear doors being unbolted.

Lesbia:

I can hardly wait to see how this thing will end and whether they have done anything mean to Leandro. May God help him! I have already prayed for him in two or three places.

Manoli:

It won't be long before we find out something. I hear more noise. Let's be quiet for a little. Lesbia, do you hear that scraping of feet?

Lesbia:

I hear it, but I want to put my ear a little to this door.

Manoli:

What do you hear?

Lesbia:

Stand still a minute; don't talk. Come here a minute and get next to this hole, but don't touch the bell. Maybe you will hear better than I, because I hear the talking but don't distinguish the words.

Manoli:

I didn't catch a word. But here are some people coming down the stairs. Whether by love or by force, they must have got him out of the hands of that lawyer.

Lesbia:

Oh, there they are! There they are outside. There's that lawyer. I know him—if he has done any harm to Leandro, I'll jump on his back and scratch both his eyes out. Oh, thank God, here are Leandro and Demetrio—I am completely recovered.

Messer Ricciardo, Lamberto, Manoli, Lesbia, Demetrio, and Leandro

Messer Ricciardo:

This must be some wild idea of yours to trick me. I don't know what brothers or foreigners you are talking about. Give me my prisoner.

Lamberto:

Be a little quiet, Sir. And make sure that Leandro stays in the room. Though he's free now on pledge, if he got away, an offense which might have been light would become heavy and we'd all be forced to pursue him until the end of time. Let's examine the truth of this matter. I think I'm in this as much as you, because of the duty you give me, and I want to understand it well. We don't have to give ourselves over to yells—if there's anything in this story it will come out. Demetrio, where is this foreigner? What do you say?

Demetrio:

Here he is. Come forward, please.

Messer Ricciardo:

Get away from me, you pests!

Lamberto:

Demetrio, he's right, move off a little way. We have to examine everything to see whether it's as you told us. Messer Ricciardo, listen. Putting passions aside, let's see whether these are wild tales or the truth. Come here, my good man, and tell us who you are, where you come from, so we will understand. What Demetrio told us is very disorganized and confused and doesn't fit together well.

Manoli:

I'm glad to see you all, and I'll tell you everything in order. First, I am the husband of Lesbia here, the nurse of Porfiria, who is the sister of Leandro, and my name is Manoli. I say that

Demetrio and Leandro are blood brothers and Porfiria the younger sister of both of them. Now I'll tell you how this is. Their father, who was named Filemone and was of the noblest blood in Constantinople, nearly sixteen years ago decided to leave that city and flee the barbarous and insolent rule of the infidels. Sailing toward Cyprus, near Tenedos he was taken by Turkish pirates with his whole family. Later, on the island of Chios, the pirates sold Leandro, Porfiria, and my wife here to Gherardo Sismondi, whom you know to have been a merchant there. Then when they arrived at Patras they sold Demetrio to Rinaldo of Palermo. They didn't do anything with me but promised that if I would serve them twelve or fifteen years they would let me go free. Thus, I was able to ascertain everything that happened to the children of Filemone, my master, who died in the hands of the pirates not far from the island of Chios. Only six months ago I was set free by them, and, remembering the kindnesses received from Filemone, who, as long as he lived, treated me like a son rather than like a servant, I started trying to find out what had happened to his children and to Lesbia, my wife. At Chios I discovered what I wanted to know about Leandro and Porfiria. Then I went to Palermo, where I found the Rinaldo who had bought Demetrio and was informed by him that he had sent him on business here to the house of Messer Lamberto Lanfranchi. So I arrived here and have proof of everything, as you may ascertain and convince yourselves.

Lamberto:

Messer Ricciardo, what do you say about this, what do you think about it? I am amazed.

Messer Ricciardo:

If it's a lie, he told it very well, and I don't know what to think. If that Lesbia of his were younger and prettier, I'd suspect an ulterior motive.

Manoli:

Put aside these suspicions, for I can tell you more if you are not convinced. I have many more proofs than I need, and I am ready here to prove it all, even if you want to go to court and everything.

Messer Ricciardo:

You—what's your name—Lesbia, do you think that this is your husband?

Lesbia:

He is, without a doubt, and though I didn't recognize him at first, it didn't take me long.

Messer Ricciardo:

I don't know what to think, I am so amazed. But this doesn't settle my affair. Brothers or not, what do I care? Let me go back up with my prisoner as you promised me.

Lamberto:

We will keep our promise; wait a little bit. You, Demetrio, and you, Leandro, what do you say about it?

Demetrio:

I am greatly moved, and I perceive that things must be as he tells us, because the kinship of our blood has awakened in me a cordial love for my dear brother.

Leandro:

And I at the same time feel the same affections, and the truth cannot be otherwise, oh Demetrio, my brother.

Demetrio:

Oh Leandro, my brother, how long we have been hidden from each other? I did indeed feel in my soul a natural pity for your dangers—truly the pity for a brother as you were to me.

Lesbia:

Do you imagine that I didn't suffer too at hurting you—you know when—and I really didn't know why.

Demetrio:

Let's forget that for now; everything has come out well. Go, Lesbia, and go, Manoli, to give this news to Porfiria without delay. Tell her that at one stroke you will restore to her two brothers.

Lamberto:

These are certainly amazing things, almost miraculous ones. Listen, Messer Ricciardo, to what I have been planning for our mutual benefit.

Messer Ricciardo:

What do you want me to listen to now?

Lamberto:

Four more words, for love of me, which you may like. Having found out for sure that Demetrio and Leandro are brothers and having been convinced (as I already knew of Demetrio from Rinaldo of Palermo) that they are of the nobility, I would be glad for Cammillo my only son to have as a wife Porfiria their sister with that dowry which was left to her. But with this condition that you, Messer Ricciardo, give Faustina, your elder daughter, to Leandro. You shouldn't reject this, for many reasons, since, especially, it would silence gossip, ending in this way all the trouble you have now. And if you want at the same time to get rid of worries and to rest in your old age, I have enough influence over Demetrio here to make him marry your other, younger daughter later and take her to his house at the proper time. And I will write in such a way to Rinaldo in Palermo, who has great faith in me, that he will be very happy and the dowries will be deposited with me. What do you say about it, Sir? Don't look so doubtful; such things are arranged by God.

Messer Ricciardo:

This is a sudden decision. These things are too important.

Lamberto:

Strong men are recognized by such resolute decisions. What do you say?

Messer Ricciardo:

Truly, I should prefer not to make up my mind so blasted fast, but I'm in such misery that, since you advise me to do it and also offer your services for the marriages, I leave it up to you—if you believe that this will bring me rest and be the best thing for everybody.

Lamberto:

This is the best thing for everybody. I won't wait for Cammillo to say whether he likes it or not, because I'm the boss for that. Nor do I think it necessary to send for the approval of Mona Cassandra, because I have heard that she doesn't want anybody but Leandro as a son-in-law. But you, Demetrio and Leandro, what do you say about this?

Leandro:

For me there can be no greater favor or greater good fortune, for I have come from death back to life and have obtained all that I desired.

Demetrio:

And I am very happy to have gained a brother and a sister today and to have made a satisfactory match.

Lamberto:

Everybody has reason to be glad, and may all profit much from today's proceedings! Here, just when we need him, is Libano, who will go get Cammillo. Oh, Libano, come here.

Libano:

What do you want?

Lamberto:

Go find Cammillo and tell him that we have done as he wished and that Porfiria will be his wife as he wishes. We have found out that she is the sister of your master. Go on, for you will be the first to give him the news. Then come back and you will find out other things which you will like.

Libano:

Good luck to all of you; I'm going. Oh happy day, oh day above all others joyful and festive! From how many troubles do we seem to have escaped!

Messer Ricciardo:

I am weeping from joy, and now I want to embrace and kiss both of you as my sons-in-law.

Lamberto:

Messer Ricciardo, you can later perform these ceremonies more at your ease. Come, let us all go here into my house and we shall give this good news to Mona Cassandra. Then each will go to his own house, for all of us have preparations to make—especially you, Sir, who have a double task. In a few days, then, there will be the proper marriage celebrations, except for Lesbia and Mona Cassandra, who can celebrate whenever they wish. For this evening, spectators, be patient. You ladies get ready for the ceremonies, for, as you see, this year is full of marriages. *Valete & plaudite.*

THE END

This last act was closed by Night, dressed in a black silk veil, with a blue starred headdress, with the moon above her forehead, and with long, dark-brown hair. She had buskins of dark brown and had almost owl-like wings. Having climbed up to the high place where Dawn had shown herself at the beginning, sweetly singing to the accompaniment of four trombones, she uttered the following words:

Vienten'almo riposo: ecco ch'io torno;
  Et ne discaccio il giorno.
Posate herbette & fronde,
  Et spogliatevi piaggie, & arbuscelli;
  Entrate, ò Pastorelli,
  Entrate, ò Nymfe bionde,
  Entro al bel nido adorno:
  Ogn'un s'adagi & dorma al mio ritorno.

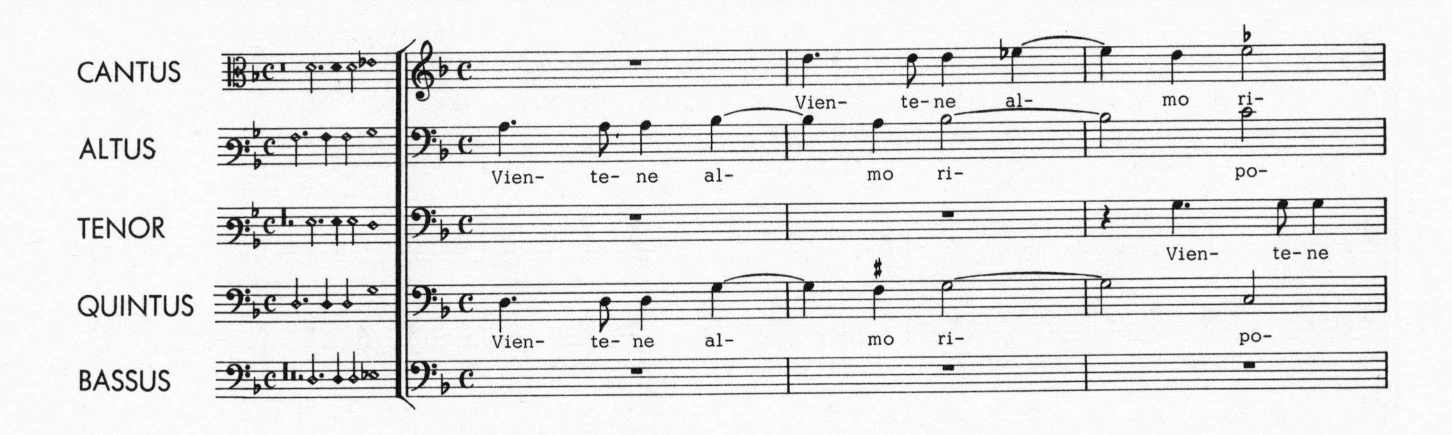
CANTUS
ALTUS
TENOR
QUINTUS
BASSUS
Vien- te- ne al- mo ri-
Vien- te- ne al- mo ri- po-
Vien- te- ne
Vien- te- ne al- mo ri- po-

4
po- so ec- co ch'io tor- no, ec- co ch'io tor- no
so ec- co ch'io tor- no, ec- co ch'io
al- mo ri- po- so ec- co ch'io tor-
so, vien- te- ne al- mo ri- po- so ec- co ch'io tor- no et
Vien- te- ne al- mo ri- po- so ec- co ch'io tor-

9
et ne di- scac-cio'l gior- no, et ne di- scac- cio'l gior-
tor- no et ne di- scac- cio'l gior- no, et ne di- scac- cio'l
no et ne di-scac-cio'l gior- no, et ne, et ne di- scac- cio il
no di-scaccio'l gior- no, et ne di- scac- cio'l gior- no, et ne di- scac- cio'l giorno et ne di- scaccio'l gior- no, et ne di- scac-cio'l gior-
12
no. Po- sa- te, po- sa-t'her-bet- t'et
gior- no. Po- sa- te, po- sa-t'her- bet-
gior- no. Po- sa- te, po- sa-t'her-bet-t'et
no. Po- sa- te, po- sa-t'her-
no. Po- sa- te, po- sa- t'her-bet-t'et

18
fron- de et spo- glia- te-vi piag- ge, et spo- glia-
t'et fron- de et spo- glia- te-vi, et spo-glia-te-vi piag- ge et ar-
fron- de et spo- glia- te-vi, et spo-glia- te-vi piag-ge, et spo- glia- te-vi
bet- t'et fron- de et spo- glia- te-vi piag- ge, et spo-
fron- de et spo- glia- te-vi piag- ge,
23
te-vi piag- g'et ar- bo- scel- li en- tra- te, en-
bo- scel- li, piag- ge et ar- bo- scel- li en- tra- te,
piag- g'et ar- bo- scel- li en- tra- te, en- tra- te,
glia- te-vi piag- g'et ar- bo- scel- li en- tra- te, en-
et spo- glia- te-vi piag- g'et ar- bo- scel- li en- tra-

28
tra- t'o pa- sto- rel- li en- tra- t'o nim-phe bion- de en- tro'l bel
en- tra- t'o pa- sto- rel- li en- tra- t'o nim- phe bi- on- de en- tro'l
en- tra- t'o pa- sto- rel- li en- tra- t'o nim-phe bion-de en- tro'l bel ni- d'a-
tra- t'o pa- sto- rel- li en- tra- t'o nim-phe bion- de en- tro'l bel ni- do, en-
te, en- tra- t'o pa- sto- rel- li en- tra- t'o nim-phe bion-de

34
ni- do a- dor- no o- gnun s'a- da-
bel ni- do a- dor- no o- gnun s'a- da-
dor- no, bel ni- d'a- dor- no o- gnun s'a- da- gi et
tro'l bel ni- d'a- dor- no, a- dor- no o- gnun s'a- da-
en- tro'l bel ni- do a- dor- no o- gnun s'a-

40
gi et dor- ma al mio ri- tor- no,
gi et dor- ma al mio ri- tor-
dor- ma et dor- ma al mio ri- tor- no, al mio
gi et dor- ma al mio ri-
da- gi et dor- ma al mio
46
al mio ri- tor- no, o- gnun s'a- da-
no, al mio ri- tor- no, o- gnun s'a- da-
ri- tor- no, o- gnun s'a- da- gi, o- gnun s'a- da-
tor- no o- gnun s'a- da- gi, o- gnun s'a-
ri- tor- no, o- gnun s'a- da- gi, o- gnun

52
gi et dor- ma al mio ri- tor-
gi et dor- ma, et dor- ma al mio ri- tor- no, al
gi et dor- ma al mio ri- tor-
da- gi et dor- ma al mio
s'a- da- gi et dor- ma al
58
no, al mio ri- tor- no, al mio ri- tor- no.
mio ri- tor- no, al mio ri- tor- no.
no, al mio ri-tor- no, al mio ri- tor- no.
ri- tor- no, al mio ri- tor- no, al mio ri- tor- no.
mio ri- tor- no, al mio ri- tor- no.

(Come, blessed repose, for here I am again, banishing the day. / Rest, grass and tree branches; undress, slopes and shrubs. Go in, O little shepherds; go in, O blond nymphs, to your beautiful, adorned abodes. Let everyone lie down and sleep on my return.)

This singing was so sweet that, in order not to leave the spectators asleep, there came suddenly onto the stage twenty bacchantes, of whom ten were ladies and the others satyrs. Among all these, eight played, eight sang and danced in the middle of the stage, and two on each side played drunk. The satyrs were all nude, with hairy flanks and upper legs, and they had goats' feet. But the ladies were wearing short dress, like the ancient bacchantes, with very thin golden tocca. The instruments of the players were these:

A leather wine bottle, which covered a drum, a tap from a barrel instead of a stick to play it with,

Vasari's drawing for the costume of a bacchante in the 1565 celebrations for the wedding of Prince Francesco —Courtesy Uffizi Gallery, Drawings Department

and a dry human shinbone with a *zufolo* within to accompany the drum.

A stag's head with a *ribecchino* inside.

A goat's horn with a *cornetta* inside.

A crane's shinbone with the foot, having a *storta* inside.

A vine stalk, with a *tromba torta* inside.

A barrel hoop with reeds, having a harp inside.

A swan's beak, with the head and neck, having a *cornetta diritta* inside.

The root and branches of an elder bush, with a *storta* inside.

Those who danced while singing were four satyrs and four ladies, all with various things in the left hand—some with drinking vessels, some with quarters of raw meat, one lady bacchante with a tambourine. Another, almost like a woman from Savoy,[174] had a little satyr around her neck. And all of them had in their right hands small burning torches. The words that they sang over and over were these: "Bacco, Bacco euoe." They had very loud laughter and performed various movements and pranks full of joy and drunkenness as befitted them.

[174]An obscure comparison, unless *savoina* was a name for gypsies as well as for inhabitants of Savoy.

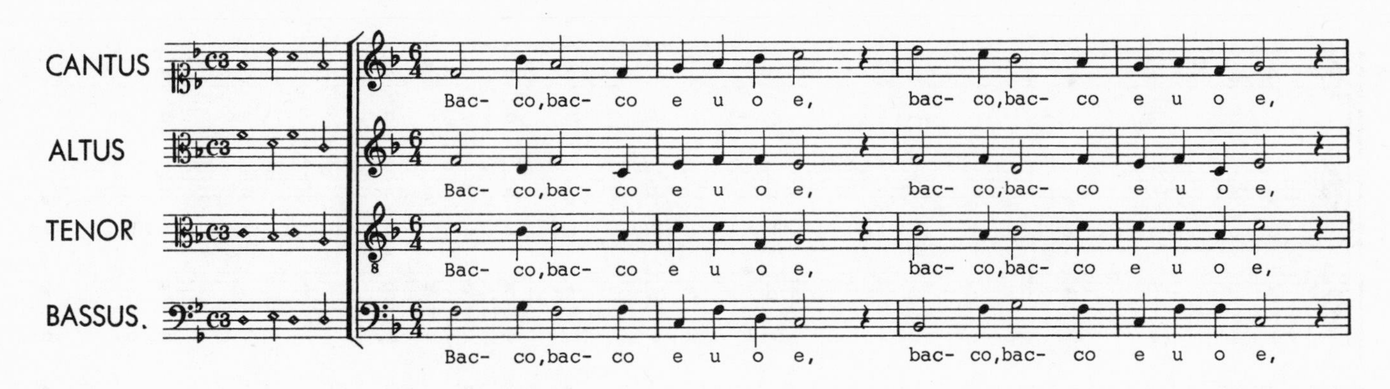
CANTUS
Bac- co,bac- co e u o e, bac- co,bac- co e u o e,
ALTUS
Bac- co,bac- co e u o e, bac- co,bac- co e u o e,
TENOR
Bac- co,bac- co e u o e, bac- co,bac- co e u o e,
BASSUS.
Bac- co,bac- co e u o e, bac- co,bac- co e u o e,

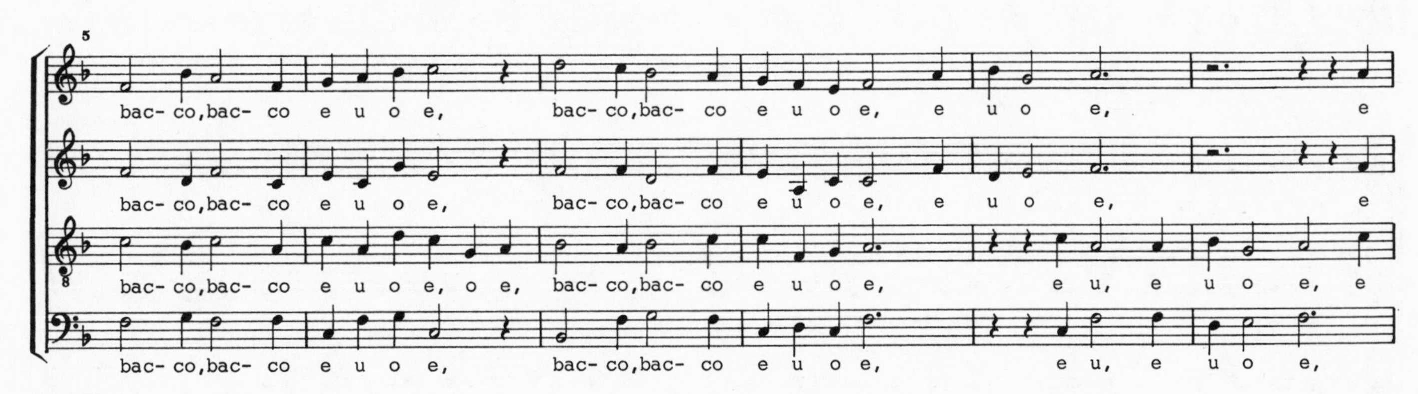
5
bac- co,bac- co e u o e, bac- co,bac- co e u o e, e u o e, e
bac- co,bac- co e u o e, bac- co,bac- co e u o e, e u o e, e
bac- co,bac- co e u o e, o e, bac- co,bac- co e u o e, e u, e u o e, e
bac- co,bac- co e u o e, bac- co,bac- co e u o e, e u, e u o e,

11
u o e, e u o e. Bac- co, bac- co e u o e, bac- co,bac- co
u o e, e u o e. Bac- co, bac- co e u o e, bac- co, bac- co
u o e, e u o e. Bac- co, bac- co e u o e, bac- co, bac- co
o e, e u o e. Bac- co, bac- co e u o e, bac- co, bac- co
16
A capite.
e u o e, bac- co, bac- co e u o e, bac- co, bac- co e u e u.
e u o e, bac- co, bac- co e u o e, bac- co, bac- co e u e u.
e u o e, bac- co, bac- co e u o e, o e, bac- co, bacco e u e u.
e u o e, bac- co, bac- co e u o e, bac- co, bac- co e u e u.
A capite.

This was something that delighted the spectators very much, leaving each one happy with his Bacchus.[175] Therefore, the whole show being finished, and the fatigue of listening and watching having been chased away with very cool wines and sweetmeats, and the night being already well advanced, everyone went away to bed.

The fireworks display was set off a number of days later and was continued till the third day of this month, for one occasion and another. It represented the bold daring of the proud Giants when they tried to seize Heaven from Jupiter and showed also that punishment appropriate for unjust enterprises. Written around the display were these words of Horace: VIS CONSILII EXPERS MOLE RUIT SUA.[176]

We still have to attack a wooden fort, built on the Piazza Maggiore,[177] and when that is over I shall tell all about it. I don't want to hold this letter up too long and, continuing to wait for the fort to be attacked, as I have done up to now, I might delay too long.

I understand that the musical compositions for all these festivities have already been printed. Nor were the people content with printing them; they also mixed up the order of the stanzas, which are not checked, not corrected, and incomplete. This has caused dissatisfaction to the composers. Since, however, the names of these composers are reported there, I am relieved of the trouble of telling them to Your Lordship—to whom, without saying more, I humbly recommend myself. From Florence, the twelfth of August, 1539.

---

[175] That is, with his wine.

[176] "Vis . . . sua" is line 65 of Ode 4 in Horace's Book III: "Force without intelligence always falls of itself." Agostino Lapini, in his *Diario fiorentino . . . dal 252 al 1596,* 124, also describes the fireworks.

[177] Probably the present Piazza della Signoria, which, for most of the period of the Grand Duchy, was called the Piazza del Granduca. Cosimo had not yet introduced this name, but presumably one could no longer speak of the republican Signoria. The term *Piazza Maggiore* avoids the issue.

List of Works Consulted

The abbreviations, *JAMS, MGG,* and *MQ,* used in this list and in the footnotes, refer to *Journal of the American Musicological Society, Die Musik in Geschichte und Gegenwart,* and *The Musical Quarterly,* respectively.

Accone, Frank A. d', "Bernardo Pisano, an Introduction to His Life and Works." *Musica Disciplina,* 17 (1963), 115–35.

———, "Heinrich Isaac in Florence: New and Unpublished Documents." *MQ,* 49 (1963), 464–83.

———, "The Singers of San Giovanni in Florence during the 15th Century." *JAMS,* 14 (1961), 307–58.

Adriani, Giambattista, *Istoria dei suoi tempi.* Venezia, Giunti, 1587. 2 vols.

Alberti, Fra Leandro, *Descrittione de tutta Italia e isole pertinenti ad essa.* Venezia, 1631.

Alciati, Andrea, *Diverse imprese tratte dagli emblemi dell' A.*Lyon, Rovillio, 1551.

———, *Emblematum liber.* Augsburg, 1531.

Alewyn, Richard, *L'Univers du baroque.* Suivi de *Les Fêtes baroques,* par Karl Sälze. Trans. by Danièle Bohler. Genève, Editions Gonthiers, 1954.

Ammirato, Scipione, *Istorie fiorentine di S.A., . . . con l'aggiunte di Scipione Ammirato il giovane.* Firenze, L. Marchini and G. Becherini, 1824–1827. 11 vols.

Ancona, Alessandro d', *Le Origini del teatro in Italia, studj sulle sacre rappresentazioni seguiti da un appendice sulle rappresentazioni del contado toscano.* Firenze, 1877. 2 vols.

———, *Origini del teatro Italiano.* Torino: E. Loescher, 1891. 2 vols.

———, ed., *Sacre rappresentazioni nei secoli XIV, XV, e XVI.* Firenze, 1872. 3 vols.

Angeli, Ubaldo, *Notizie per la storia del teatro a Firenze nel secolo XVI, specialmente circa gli intermedii.* Modena, Namias, 1891.

———, ed., *Personificazione delle città, paesi e fiumi di Toscana festeggianti le nozze di Cosimo Primo ed Eleonora di Toledo, tratta da un raro libretto di Pier Francesco Giambullari e ristampata per cura di U.A.* Prato, Tipografia G. Salvi, 1898.

Aquisgrana, Alfredo Reumont d', *Tavole chronologiche e sincrone della storia fiorentina.* Firenze, Viesseux, 1841.

Archivio mediceo, "Lettere e minute dell'anno 1537 al 1543." Mss. in the Archivio di Stato, Florence.

Aspri, Michele, *Carmen in nuptiis Cosmae et Leonorae . . .* Firenze, In pressum florentiae, 1539.

Baines, Anthony, *Woodwind Instruments and Their History*. New York, W. W. Norton & Company, Inc., 1957.

———, ed., *Musical Instruments Through the Ages.* London, Penguin Books, 1961.

Baja, Anna, *Leonora di Toledo, Duchessa di Firenze e di Siena.* Todi, Foglietti, 1904.

Baldini, Baccio, *Vita di Cosimo Medici, primo Granduca di Toscana.* Firenze, Sermartelli, 1578.

Barbi, A. S., *Un accademico mecenate e poeta* (Giovambattista Strozzi il Giovane). Firenze, Sansoni, 1900.

Baron, Hans, *The Crisis of the Early Italian Renaissance,* rev. ed. Princeton, N.J., Princeton University Press, 1966.

Battisti, Eugenio, *L'Antirinascimento, con un'appendice di manoscritti inediti.* Milano, Feltrinelli, 1962.

Bessaraboff, Nicholas, *Ancient European Musical Instruments.* Boston, Museum of Fine Arts, by the Harvard University Press, 1941.

Besseler, Heinrich, "Dufay." *MGG,* 3, cols. 889–911.

Bo, Carlo, ed., *Lirici del '500.* I Classici italiani. Milano, Garzanti, 1941.

Bonardi, Carlo, *Giambattista Gelli e le sue opere.* Città di Castello, Lapi, 1899.

Booth, Cecily, *Cosimo I, Duke of Florence.* London, Cambridge University Press, 1921.

Borlenghi, Aldo, ed., *Commedie del Cinquecento.* Milano, Rizzoli, 1959. 2 vols.

Boyden, David D., *The History of Violin Playing from its Origins to 1761 and its Relationship to the Violin and Violin Music.* London, Oxford University Press, 1965.

Bridgman, Nanie, *La vie musicale au quattrocento et jusqu'à la naissance du madrigal (1400–1530).* Paris, Gallimard, 1964.

Buck, August, and Bianca Becherini, "Florenz." *MGG,* 4, cols. 367–94.

Burckhardt, Jacob, *The Civilization of the Renaissance in Italy,* trans. by S. G. C. Middlemore. Harper Torchbooks. New York, Harper & Row, Publishers, 1958. 2 vols.

Calamandrei, E. Polidori, *Le Vesti delle donne fiorentine nel Quattrocento.* Firenze, La Voce, 1924.

Cambi, Giovanni, *Istorie di G.C. cittadino fiorentino . . . ,* Fr. Ildefonso di San Luigi, carmelitano, ed. Delizie degli Eruditi Toscani, Vols. 20–23. Firenze, Cambiagi, 1785–1786. 4 vols.

Camerani, Sergio, *Bibliografia medicea*. Biblioteca di Bibliografia italiana, no. 45. Firenze, Olschki, 1964.

Cantini, Giovanni, *Vita di Cosimo I dei Medici*. Firenze, Albinzini, 1805.

Carcereri, Luigi, *Cosimo Primo, Granduca*. Verona, Bettinelli, 1926–1929. 3 vols.

Catullus, *Poésies*, ed. and trans. by Georges Lafaye, 4th ed. Collection Guillaume Budé. Paris, Les Belles Lettres, 1958.

Cellini, Benvenuto, *The Memoirs of Benvenuto Cellini*, trans. by Anne MacDonell. London and New York, J. M. Dent & Sons, Ltd., and E. P. Dutton & Co., Inc., 1942.

———, *Vita*. In *Opere di Baldassare Castiglione, Giovanni della Casa, Benvenuto Cellini*, Carlo Cordie, ed. Milano-Napoli, R. Ricciardi, 1960.

Cianfogni, Pier Nolasco, *Memorie istoriche dell'Ambrosiana Regia Basilica di S. Lorenzo di Firenze*. Firenze, Ciardetti, 1804.

Cini, Giovambattista, *Vita del Serenis. Signor Cosimo de' Medici, primo Gran Duca di Toscana*. Firenze, Giunti, 1611.

Conti, Cosimo, *La Prima reggia di Cosimo I dei Medici nel palazzo già della signoria di Firenze descritta ed illustrata coll'appoggio d'un inventario inedito del 1553 e coll'aggiunta di molti altri documenti*. Firenze, Pellas, 1893.

Contile, Luca, *Ragionamento di L.C. sopra la proprietà delle imprese con le particolari de gli Academici affidati et con le interpretationi e chroniche*. Pavia, 1574.

Coradini, Francesco, "Francesco Corteccia." *Note d'Archivio*, 11 (1934), 199–202.

Corteccia, Francesco, *Libro primo de madriali a cinque et a sei voci di Francesco Corteccia maestro di cappella dello illustrissimo et eccellentissimo Duca Cosimo de Medici Duca secondo di Firenze*. 5 part-books in 4° obl. Venetia, A. Gardane, 1547.

———, *Libro secondo de madriali a quatro voci di Francesco Corteccia maestro di cappella dello illustrissimo et eccellentissimo Duca Cosimo de Medici Duca secondo di Firenze*. 4 part-books in 4° obl. Venetia, A. Gardane, 1547.

Crescimbeni, Giovan Maria, *Dell'istoria della volgar poesia*. Venezia, Baseglio, 1730–1731. 6 vols.

Croce, Benedetto, *Ariosto, Corneille e Shakespeare*. Bari, Laterza, 1929.

Daniello, Bernardino, *La Poetica di B.D., lucchese*. Venezia, Nicolini, 1536.

De Gaetano, Armand, "Giambattista Gelli: A Moralist of the Renaissance." Dissertation, Columbia University, 1954.

Descritione della pompa funerale fatta nelle esequie del Ser.^mo^ *Sig. Cosimo de' Medici, Gran Duca di Toscana. Nell'alma città di Fiorenza il giorno xvii di maggio dell' Anno MDLXXIIII.* Firenze, Giunti, 1574.

Diotallevi, Lamberto, ed., *Teatro italiano del Cinquecento: Catalogo.* Milano, Chiesa, 1953.

Einstein, Alfred, *The Italian Madrigal,* trans. by Alexander H. Krappe, Roger H. Sessions, and Oliver Strunk. Princeton, N.J., Princeton University Press, 1949. 3 vols.

Engel, Hans, *Luca Marenzio.* Firenze, Olschki, 1956.

Essequie del Divino Michelangelo Buonarroti, celebrate in Firenze dall'Accademia de' pittori, scultori et architettori nella chiesa di San Lorenzo il dì 28 giugno MDLXIV. Firenze, Giunti, 1564.

Ferrai, Luigi Alberto, *Cosimo dei Medici e il suo governo (1537–1543).* Bologna, Zanichelli, 1882.

Fusco, Enrico M., *La lirica.* Storia dei generi letterari italiani. Milano, Vallardi, 1950. 2 vols.

Gaddi, J., *De scriptoribus non ecclesiasticis.* Florence, Massi, 1648.

Gauthiez, Pierre, *L'Italie du XVIe siècle. Jean des Bandes noires, 1498–1526.* Paris, Ollendorff, 1901.

———, *Trois Médicis. Cosme l'ancien. Laurent le Magnifique. Cosme Ier.* Paris, Plon, 1933.

Geiger, Benno, *I dipinti ghiribizzosi di Giuseppe Arcimboldi, pittore illusionista del '500.* Firenze, Vallecchi, 1954.

Gelli, Giovambattista, *Opere di G.B.G.,* Agenore Gelli, ed. Firenze, Lemonnier, 1855.

———, *Opere,* Ireneo Sanesi, ed. Classici italiani, Vol. 39. Torino, U.T.E.T., 1952.

Gentile, Michele Lupo, *Studio sulla storiografia fiorentina alla corte di Cosimo I dei Medici.* Pisa, Nistri, 1905.

Ghisi, Federico, *I canti carnascialeschi nelle fonti musicali del xv e xvi secolo.* Firenze, Olschki, 1937.

———, *Feste musicali della Firenze Medicea (1480–1589).* Firenze, Vallecchi, 1939.

Giambullari, Pierfrancesco, *Apparato et feste nelle nozze del Illustrissimo Signor Duca di Firenze, et della Duchessa sua consorte, con le sue Stanze, Madriali, Comedia, et Intermedii, in quelle recitati.* Firenze, Giunti, 1539.

———, *De'l sito, forma e misura dello Inferno di Dante.* Firenze, Neri Bortelati, 1544.

———, *Origine della lingua fiorentina, altrimenti il Gello di Messer P.G., accademico fiorentino.* Firenze, Lorenzo, 1549.

Giovio, Paolo, *Dialogo delle imprese militari et amorose di Monsignor Giovio, Vescovo di Nocera, con un ragionamento di Messer Lodovico Domenichi nel medesimo soggetto.* Lione, Roviglio, 1559.

Gori, Pietro, *Le Feste fiorentine attraverso i secoli. Le Feste per San Giovanni*. Firenze, Bemporad, 1926.

———, *Firenze magnifica. Le Feste fiorentine attraverso i secoli*. Firenze, Bemporad, 1930.

Grout, Donald Jay, *A Short History of Opera*. New York, Columbia University Press, 1947.

Haar, James, ed., *Chanson and Madrigal 1480–1530: Studies in Comparison and Contrast*. Isham Library Papers II. Cambridge, Harvard University Press, 1964.

Hall, Robert A., Jr., *The Italian Questione della Lingua: An Interpretative Essay*. Chapel Hill, The University of North Carolina Press, 1942.

Hare, Christopher, *The Romance of a Medici Warrior, being the true story of Giovanni delle Bande Nere, to which is added the life of his son Cosimo I, Grand Duke of Tuscany: A study in Heredity*. London, Stanley Paul, 1910.

Harrison, Frank, and Joan Rimmer, *European Musical Instruments*. London, Studio Vista, 1964.

Hauser, Arnold, *The Social History of Art*, Vol. II, *Renaissance, Mannerism, Baroque*. London, Routledge and Kegan Paul, Ltd., 1962.

Haydn, Hiram, *The Counter-Renaissance*. New York, Grove Press, 1960.

Haydon, Glen, "The Dedication of Francesco Corteccia's *Hinnario*." *JAMS*, 13 (1960), 112–16.

Helm, Everett, "Secular Vocal Music in Italy (*c.* 1400–1530)," in *Ars Nova and the Renaissance 1300–1540*, Dom Anselm Hughes and Gerald Abraham, eds. Vol. III, *New Oxford History of Music*. London, Oxford University Press, 1960.

Herrick, Marvin T., *Italian Comedy in the Renaissance*. Urbana, The University of Illinois Press, 1960.

Horatius, Flaccus Quintus, *Odes et épodes*, ed. and trans. by François Villeneuve. Collection Guillaume Budé. Paris, Les Belles Lettres, 1956.

Horo, Apollinis, *De scris et sculpturis graeci. . . .* Paris, Kerver, 1551.

Hubbard, Frank, *Three Centuries of Harpsichord Making*. Cambridge, Harvard University Press, 1965.

Jacquot, Jean, "Panorama des fêtes et cérémonies du règne," in *Fêtes et Cérémonies au temps de Charles Quint*, Vol. II, *Les Fêtes de la Renaissance*, Jean Jacquot, ed. Paris, Centre national de la recherche scientifique, 1960.

Jeppesen, Knud, "Costanzo Festa." *MGG*, 4, cols. 90–102.

Kristeller, Paul Oskar, "The Language of Italian Prose," in *Renaissance Thought II: Papers in Humanism and the Arts*. New York, Harper & Row, Publishers, 1965.

Labande-Jeanroy, Thérèse, *La Question de la langue en Italie*. Strasbourg, Istri, 1925.

Landi, Antonio, *Il Commodo; commedia, con i suoi intermedii recitati nelle nozze del illustriss. ed Eccellentiss. S. il S. Duca di Firenze l'anno 1539.* Firenze, Giunti, 1566.

Landucci, Luca, *Diario fiorentino dal 1450 al 1516, continuato da un anonimo fino al 1542,* Iodoco del Badia, ed. Firenze, Sansoni, 1883.

Lapini, Agostino, *Diario fiorentino di A.P. dal 252 al 1596. . . .* Giuseppe Odoardo Corazzini, ed. Firenze, Sansoni, 1900.

Lettioni di Accademici fiorentini sopra Dante. Firenze, 1547.

Lipphardt, Walther, "Liturgische Dramen." *MGG,* 8, cols. 1012–48.

Litta, Pompeo, *Famiglie celebri d'Italia.* Milano, Giusti, 1819–1873. 30 vols.

Livius, Titus, *Ab urbe condita, Liber XXIII,* Aldo Marsili, ed. Firenze, Lemonnier, 1956.

———, *Histoire romaine,* Jean Bayet, ed., trans. by Gaston Baillet. Collection Guillaume Budé. Paris, Les Belles Lettres, 1954. 5 vols.

Lowinsky, Edward E., "A Newly Discovered Sixteenth-Century Motet Manuscript at the Biblioteca Vallicelliana in Rome." *JAMS,* 3 (1950), 173–232.

———, "The Medici Codex. A Document of Music, Art, and Politics in the Renaissance." *Annales Musicologiques,* 5 (1957), 61–178.

Machiavelli, Niccolò, *Opere,* Mario Bonfantini, ed. La Letteratura italiana, storia e testi, Vol. 29. Milano-Napoli, R. Ricciardi, 1954.

McKinley, Ann Watson, "Francesco Corteccia's Music to Latin Texts." Unpublished dissertation, University of Michigan, 1962.

Maffei, Venocchio, *Dal Titolo di Duca di Firenze e Siena a Gran Duca di Firenze; contributi alla storia della politica di Cosimo I dei Medici.* Firenze, Seeber, 1905.

Marconcini, Cartesio, *L'Accademia della Crusca dalle origini alla prima edizione del vocabulario (1612).* Pisa, Valenti, 1910.

Marcuse, Sibyl, *Musical Instruments: A Comprehensive Dictionary.* Garden City, New York, Doubleday & Company, Inc., 1964.

Masi, Bartolomeo, *Ricordanze di B.M., calderaio fiorentino dal 1478 al 1526,* Giuseppe Odoardo Corazzini, ed. Firenze, Sansoni, 1906.

Matasilani, Mario, *La Felicità del Ser*mo *Cosimo de' Medici Granduca di Toscana.* Firenze, Marescotti, 1572.

Mecatti, Giuseppe Mario, *Storia cronologica della città di Firenze, o siano annali della Toscana, che possono servire d'illustrazione e d'aggiunte agli Annali d'Italia del Signor Proposto L.A. Muratori.* Napoli, 1755. 2 parts.

Medici, Cosimo I de', *Lettere, a cura di Giorgio Spini, con prefazione di Antonio Panella.* Firenze, Vallecchi, 1940.

Médicis, Catherine des, *Lettres de Catherine des Médicis, pubilées par Hector de la Ferrière.* Paris, Imprimerie nationale, 1880–1909. 10 vols.

Mellini, Domenico, *Ricordi intorno ai costumi, azioni, e governo del serenissimo Gran Duca Cosimo I scritti di commissione dalla serenissima Maria Cristina di Lorena, ora per la prima volta pubblicati con illustrazioni.* Firenze, Magheri, 1820.

Molmenti, Pompeo, "Una festa in Firenze per le nozze di Cosimo I ed Eleonora di Toledo." *Gazzetta musicale di Milano,* Anno LV, no. 38.

Moreni, Domenico, *Continuazione delle Memorie istoriche dell'Ambrosiana Imperial Basilica di S. Lorenzo di Firenze.* Firenze, Francesco Daddi, 1817.

Musiche fatte nelle nozze dello illustrissimo Duca di Firenze il signor Cosimo de' Medici et della illustrissima consorte sua mad. Leonora da Tolleto. 5 part-books in 8° obl. Venezia, A. Gardane, 1539.

Nagler, A. M., *Theatre Festivals of the Medici,* trans. by George Hickenlooper. New Haven, Yale University Press, 1964.

Nardi, Iacopo, *Istorie della città di Fiorenza.* Lyon, Ancellin, 1582.

Negri, P. Giulio, *Istoria degli scrittori fiorentini.* Ferrara, 1722.

Neri, Filippo de', *Commentari dei fatti civili occorsi dentro la città di Firenze dall'anno 1215 al 1537.* . . . Trieste: Colombo, 1859. 2 vols.

Nestor, Jean, *Histoire des hommes illustres de la maison de Médicis, avec un abbrégé des comtes de Bolongne* [sic] *et d'Auvergne. A la Reine mère du roi.* Paris, Perier, 1564.

Ovidius Naso, Publius, *Les Métamorphoses,* ed. and trans. by Georges Lafaye, 3d ed. Collection Guillaume Budé. Paris, Les Belles Lettres, 1961. 3 vols.

Palazzi, Giovanni Andrea, *I Discorsi sopra l'imprese recitati nell'Accademia d'Urbino.* Bologna, Benacci, 1575.

Panella, Antonio, *Storia di Firenze.* Firenze, Sansoni, 1949.

Perrens, F. T., *La civilisation florentine du XIIIe au XVIe siècle.* Paris, Librairies-Imprimeries Réunies, 1893.

Pieraccini, Gaetano, *La stirpe de' Medici di Cafaggiolo. Saggio di ricerche sulla trasmissione ereditaria dei caratteri biologici.* Firenze, Vallecchi, 1947. 4 vols.

Pirrotta, Nino, "Intermedium." *MGG,* 6, cols. 1310–26.

Poccianti, Michele, *Catalogus scriptorum florentinorum omnis generis*. Florentiae, apud Phillipum Iunctam, 1589.

Poligrafo Gargagni, Unpublished notes for an encyclopedia (eighteenth century). Preserved in the Biblioteca Nazionale Centrale of Florence.

Praetorius, Michael, *Syntagma Musicum. De Organographia*. Parts 1 and 2, trans. by Harold Blumenfeld. Private printing, 1949.

Praz, Mario, *Studies in Seventeenth Century Imagery*. London, Warburg Institute, 1939 and 1947. 2 vols.

Prezziner, Giovanni, *Storia del pubblico studio e delle società scientifiche e letterarie di Firenze*. Firenze, 1810. 2 vols.

Quadrio, Saverio, *Della storia e della ragione d'ogni poesia*. Bologna, Pisarri, 1739.

Rabelais, François, *Oeuvres complètes de Rabelais*, Jacques Boutenger and Lucien Scheler, eds. Paris, Gallimard, 1955.

Reese, Gustave, *Music in the Middle Ages*. New York, W. W. Norton & Company, Inc., 1940.

———, *Music in the Renaissance*. New York, W. W. Norton & Company, Inc., 1954.

Repetti, Emanuele, *Dizionario geografico-fisico-storico della Toscana contenente la descrizione di tutti i luoghi del granducato, ducato di Lucca, Garfagnana e Lunigiana*. Firenze, Mazzoni, 1833–1846. 7 vols.

Rilli, Jacopo, ed., *Notizie letterarie ed istoriche intorno agli uomini illustri dell'Accademia fiorentina*. Firenze, Matini, 1700.

Roth, Cecil, *The Last Florentine Republic, 1527–1530*. London, Methuen & Co., Ltd., 1925.

Rubsamen, Walter H., "The Justiniane or Viniziane of the 15th Century." *Acta Musicologica*, 29 (1957), 172–84.

———, *Literary Sources of Secular Music in Italy* (c. *1500)*. University of California Publications in Music, Vol. I, no. 1. Berkeley, University of California Press, 1943.

Sachs, Curt, *The History of Musical Instruments*. New York, W. W. Norton & Company, Inc., 1940.

———, *Real-Lexikon der Musikinstrumente*, 2d rev. and enlarged ed. New York, Dover Publications, Inc., 1964.

Saltini, Guglielmo Enrico, *Tragedie medicee domestiche (1557–87) . . . , premessavi una introduzione sul governo di Cosimo I*. Firenze, Barbera, 1898.

Salvini, Salvino, *Fasti consulari dell'Accademia fiorentina*. Firenze, nella Stamperia di S.A.R., Tartini and Franchi, 1717.

Sambin, Hughes, *Oeuvre de la diversité des termes dont on use en architecture, reduict en ordre par Maistre H.S., demeurant à Dijon*. Lyon, Jean Durant, 1572.

Sanesi, Emilio, *Dell'Accademia fiorentina nel '500.* Estratto dagli "Atti della Società Colombaria." Firenze, Chiari, 1936.

———, "Maestri d'organo in S. Maria del Fiore (1436–1600)." *Note d'Archivio,* 14 (1937), 171–79.

Sanesi, Ireneo, *La commedia.* Storia dei generi letterari italiani. Milano, Vallardi, 1954. 2 vols.

Schaal, Richard, "Feste und Festspiels." *MGG,* 4, col. 104–28.

Schevill, Ferdinand, *A History of Florence from the Founding of the City through the Renaissance.* New York, Harcourt, Brace, n.d.

———, *The Medici.* New York, Harcourt, Brace, n.d.

Serristori, Averardo, *Legazioni di A.S., ambasciatore di Cosimo I a Carlo Quinto e in corte di Roma* (1537–1568), Giuseppe Canestrini, ed. Firenze, Lemonnier, 1853.

Singleton, Charles S., ed., *Canti carnascialeschi del Rinascimento, a cura di C.S.S.* Bari, Laterza, 1936.

Smoldon, W. L., "Liturgical Drama," in *Early Medieval Music up to 1300,* Dom Anselm Hughes, ed. Vol. II, *New Oxford History of Music.* London, Oxford University Press, 1954.

———, "Liturgical Music-Drama." *Grove's Dictionary of Music and Musicians,* 5th ed. (1954), V, 317–43.

Spingarn, Joel E., *Literary Criticism in the Renaissance,* with Introduction by Bernard Weinberg. Harbinger Books. New York, Harcourt, Brace & World, Inc., 1963.

Spini, Giorgio, *Cosimo I de' Medici e la indipendenza del principato mediceo.* Collana storica, vii. Firenze, Vallecchi, 1945.

Strozzi, Giovambattista, il giovane, *Madrigali di G.B.S. il giovane,* A. S. Barbi, ed. Firenze, Carnesecchi, 1899.

Strozzi, Giovambattista, il vecchio, *Madrigali,* Luigi Sorrento, ed. Biblioteca romanica, nos. 78–79. Strassburg, Heitz, 1909.

———, *Madrigali.* Firenze, Sermartelli, 1593.

Strozzi, Lorenzo di Filippo, *Le vite degli uomini illustri della casa Strozzi. Commentarii di Lorenzo di Filippo Strozzi, ora intieramente pubblicati con un ragionamento di Francesco Zeffi sopra la vita dell'autore,* Pietro Stromboli, ed. Firenze, Landi, 1892.

Surchi, Sergio, "Errore e saggezza nella commedia fiorentina del '500." *Firenze e il mondo, rivista bimestrale di arte, letteratura, e turismo,* I (1948), 52–56.

Sypher, Wylie, *Four Stages of Renaissance Style.* Anchor Books. Garden City, N.Y., Doubleday & Company, Inc., 1955.

Tapié, Victor-L., *Baroque et classicisme.* Paris, Plon, 1957.

Tarantino, N., *La Circe e i Capricci del bottaio di G. B. Gelli*. Napoli, 1917.

Thesaurus musicus continens selectissimas octo, septem, sex, quinque et quatuor vocum Harmonias, tam a veteribus quam recentioribus symphonistis compositas, et ad omnis generis instrumenta musica accomodatas. Tomi primi continentis cantiones octo vocum. 8 part-books in 8° obl. Nürnberg, J. Montanus and U. Neuber, 1564.

Tiraboschi, Girolamo, *Storia della letteratura italiana*. Modena, Società tipografica, 1787–1794. 15 vols.

Toffanin, Giuseppe, *Il Cinquecento*. Storia letteraria d'Italia. Milano, Vallardi, 1960.

Trissino, Giovan Giorgio, *Tutte le opere di G.G.T., gentiluomo valentino, non più raccolte*. Verona, Vallarsi, 1729. 2 vols.

Tutti i trionfi, carri, mascherate, e canti carnascialeschi andati per Firenze dal tempo del Magnifico Lorenzo dei Medici fino all'anno 1559, Neri del Boccia, ed. Firenze, 1750. 2 vols.

Typhotius, Iacopus, and Anselmus de Boodt, *Symbola divina et humana pontificum, imperatorum, regum*. Francoforte, Schonwetterum, 1642.

Uberti, Fazio degli, *Il Dittamondo,* Giuseppe Corsi, ed. Scrittori d'Italia, no. 206. Bari, Laterza, 1952.

Ugolini, Aurelio, *Le opere di Giovambattista Gelli*. Pisa, Mariotti, 1898.

Valacca, Clemente, *La vita e le opere di Pierfrancesco Giambullari. Parte I, 1495–1541*. Bitonte, 1898.

Vallone, Aldo, *Avviamento alla commedia fiorentina del '500*. Asti, Arethusa, 1951.

Varchi, Benedetto, *Sonetti*. Firenze, Torrentino, 1555–1557.

———, *Sonetti spirituali*. Firenze, Giunti, 1573.

———, *Storia fiorentina,* Lelio Arbib, ed. Firenze, 1838–1841. 3 vols.

Vasari, Giorgio, *La vita di Michelangelo nelle redazioni del 1550 e del 1568,* Paola Barocchi, ed. Milano, Ricciardi, 1962. 5 vols.

———, *The Lives of the Painters, Sculptors, and Architects,* A. B. Hinds, trans. Everyman's Library. London and New York, J. M. Dent & Sons, Ltd., and E. P. Dutton & Co., Inc., 1927. 4 vols.

Vaughan, Herbert M., *The Medici Popes*. London, Methuen & Co., Ltd., 1908.

Vergilius Maro, Publius, *Bucoliques,* ed. and trans. by E. de Saint-Denis, 4th ed. Collection Guillaume Budé. Paris, Les Belles Lettres, 1960.

———, *Enéide,* Henri Goelzer and René Durand, eds., trans. by André Bellessort, 9th ed. Collection Guillaume Budé. Paris, Les Belles Lettres, 1959–1960. 2 vols.

———, *Géorgiques,* ed. and trans. by E. de Saint-Denis, 2d ed. Collection Guillaume Budé. Paris, Les Belles Lettres, 1960.

Vogel, Emil, *Bibliothek der Gedruckten Weltlichen Vocalmusik Italiens. Aus den Jahren 1500–1700.* With revisions by Alfred Einstein. Hildesheim, Georg Olms, 1962. 2 vols.

Walker, D. P., ed., *Les Fêtes du Mariage de Ferdinand de Médicis, et de Christine de Lorraine, Florence 1589. I. Musique des intermèdes de "La Pellegrina."* Paris, Editions du Centre National de la Recherche Scientifique, 1963.

Weaver, Robert L., "Sixteenth-Century Instrumentation." *MQ,* 47 (1961), 262–78.

Weinberg, Bernard, *A History of Literary Criticism in the Italian Renaissance.* Chicago, The University of Chicago Press, 1961. 2 vols.

Young, Colonel C. F., *The Medici.* London, John Murray (Publishers), Ltd., 1909. 2 vols.

Index